1ST EDT. 2025-2026

ONSHAPE FUNDAMENTALS WORKBOOK

INSTRUCTOR

ED CHARLWOOD
JAKE O SUGDEN
JOSHUA MANLEY

CADclass

Onshape Fundamentals Workbook Edt.1 2025-2026

Authors: Jake O Sugden, Joshua Manley, & Ed Charlwood

Edition & Publication Details
1st Edition (2025–26)

ISBNs:
Instructor Version: 979-8-9927988-1-4
Student Version: 979-8-9927988-2-1

Publisher: CADclass
Written by: Jake O Sugden, Joshua Manley & Ed Charlwood
Edited by: Jake O Sugden & Ed Charlwood

Source materials include Saturn V Rocket, Wikimedia Commons, Public Domain.

Contact: For inquiries about bulk sales, licensing, translations, or other collaborations, email us at Create@CADclass.org.

About the Authors

Jake O Sugden is the co-founder and CTO of CADclass, a platform dedicated to empowering future engineers and designers. As the co-author of several best-selling CAD books and an Autodesk Learning Partner, Jake brings a wealth of expertise in mechanical engineering and a lifelong passion for making. His work goes beyond writing and editing tutorials—he also produces and edits instructional videos and oversees the thriving CADclass YouTube channel. A daily user of CAD, Jake is a hands-on expert who blends creativity with precision, inspiring others to excel in the world of engineering and design.

Joshua Manley is the cofounder and CEO of CADclass, co-author of several best-selling CAD books, and an Autodesk Learning Partner. As a CNC/CAD professor and published scientist, he is dedicated to empowering makers, engineers, and educators to transform their ideas into reality.

With experience as the former education director of a leading maker space, Joshua has taught thousands of students, educators, and administrators across the globe. His TED-Ed talk on bicycle physics has millions of views.

Ed Charlwood is a best-selling author, award-winning educator, and expert in CAD curriculum development. He holds a Bachelor's in Engineering & Product Design and a Master's in Education from Cambridge University.

With 20 years of teaching experience and a passion for empowering students, Ed has developed STEM curricula for 10,000+ students worldwide. His teaching approach has earned him prestigious accolades, including being a Google Certified Innovator, Apple Distinguished Educator, and Autodesk Academic Partner.

He also serves as a Fellow of the Royal Society, which recognizes people who make a "substantial contribution to the improvement of natural knowledge, including mathematics, engineering science, and medical science."

Table of Contents

How To Use This Book

Welcome to the browser-based, parametric world of Onshape! Get ready to explore powerful tools and tackle creative challenges as you build transformational design skills.

This workbook is your companion to hands-on learning. Learning the fundamentals takes around 12 hours—but true mastery is a lifelong journey.

Your path begins here. Let's design something amazing.

To keep track of your progress, you should check these boxes.

When you see this **Q?**.................................. write your answer on it.

Changes the view left/right or up/down

Want to follow along with these projects with an online video course? Then check out the Onshape Fundamentals Course designed to accompany this workbook!

If you're a student learning the basics or an instructor teaching a class, this course walks you through the entire book, step by step!

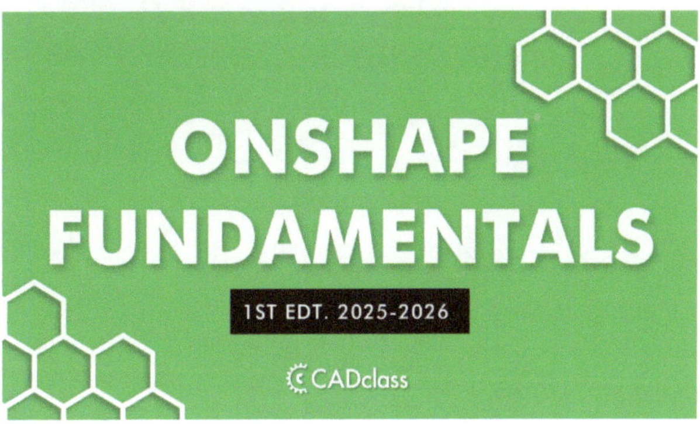

If you'd prefer to read on a computer or tablet, visit ***CADclass.org/pages/books*** to download a digital copy of this book—and others in the series.

If you'd like a printed version, you can purchase a physical copy on **Amazon**. If you enjoy the book, we'd love it if you left a review, it really helps!

<< Now this page is complete, check this off, to keep track of progress.

How To Use This Book

Welcome to the fantastic world of Onshape! We are delighted that you are empowering your students with this powerful tool.

- The student workbook is designed to accompany a taught Onshape course, while this Instructor workbook is designed to help you teach Onshape yourself.

- You will need to sign up and create Onshape Educators account beforehand: ***t.ly/anw2y***

All the pages with this gray background, like this one, are for instructors and self-learners. They provide answers, links, QR codes for further reading, and valuable background knowledge to add depth and richness.

The student workbook is divided into colored sections representing tools, techniques, and program functionality. Learners should use the checkboxes to keep track of progress, answer questions, and write longer answers on dashed lines or in boxes. The more they write, the better they'll get.

There are many open-ended challenges. These help expand students' knowledge and reinforce learning. There is specific vocabulary used in CAD, and students should develop fluency in using it. Students can also add definitions to the glossary at the back as they go along.

This book is carefully sequenced in a logical, interleaved way. We suggest you and your students follow along to build knowledge, skills, and understanding.

You may find that some students grasp the fundamentals quickly, in this case we encourage you to send them additional resources at:

learn.onshape.com

Most importantly, have fun, learn, encourage exploration... and enjoy!

This page is complete, so you can check this off >>>

What is CAD?

CAD, which stands for Computer-Aided Design, offers a unique blend of creativity, problem-solving, and technical skills. By using CAD software, students can bring their ideas to life, designing everything from simple shapes to complex 3D models. In the broadest sense, CAD is any tool that helps a designer... design, on a computer.

Q? What can you create with other design software?

Minecraft	Make a 3D world
Excel	
Garageband	
PowerPoint	

Before CAD, design was a manual, time-consuming process. Designers used drawing boards and physical tools to create blueprints, which were prone to errors and difficult to modify. Prototyping involved building physical models, making iterations expensive and slow. Collaboration was limited by the need to share physical drawings, and visualization relied on 2D sketches or scale models.

Types of CAD

- 2D (Autocad)
- 3D (Tinkercad)
- Parametric (Onshape)
- Textiles and clothing (Clo3d.com)
- Forms, surfaces and characters (Blender.org)

Q? What other examples can you think of? ....

What is CAD?

CAD stands for:

C:

A: Aided

D:

Q? What is another word for "aided"?

Today, CAD is ubiquitous across industries: Architects use it to design buildings and urban landscapes, Engineers use it to create mechanical parts and electrical systems, Product Designers to conceptualize and prototype consumer goods... Film and Animation, Fashion, Medicine... the list is endless. While the software they use differs, the principles are the same: using a computer to help you create something. CAD is a tool of empowerment. It combines art, math, and technology. And, as you will soon see, it requires critical thinking and creative problem-solving.

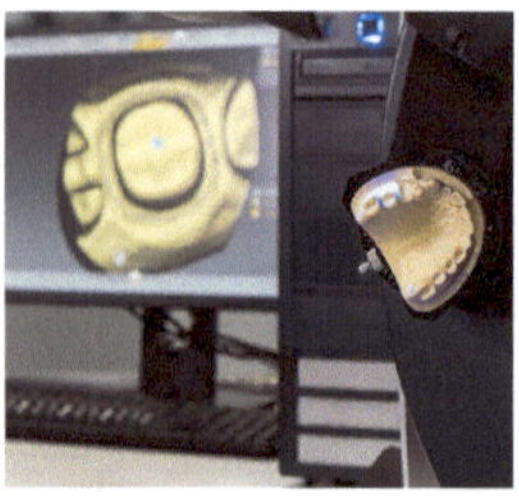

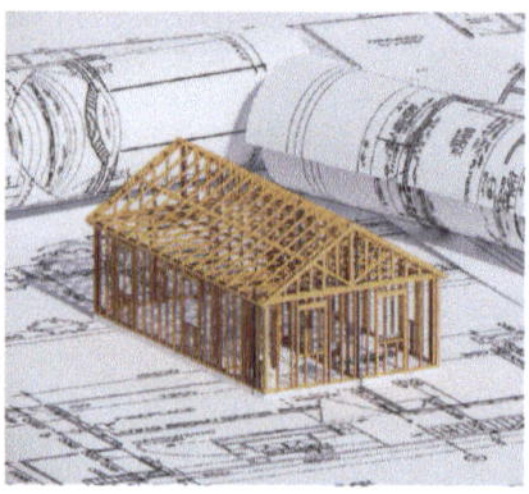

The first 747 "jumbo jet" flown in 1969 was designed using 75,000 paper drawings of 4.5 million parts, 136 miles of electrical wiring, 5 landing gear legs, 4 hydraulic systems, and 10 million labor hours.

CAD revolutionized the design process. Designs are now created digitally, allowing for easy modifications and precise measurements. Virtual prototyping enables rapid testing and iteration without physical production. Collaboration is enhanced through digital file sharing and simultaneous work on designs. 3D visualization provides photo-realistic representations, while integrated simulation tools allow for comprehensive analysis before manufacturing. CAD also facilitates integration with other technologies like 3D printing and CNC machining, enabling mass customization, and reducing material waste. These advancements have made design faster, more accurate, and more innovative.

What is Onshape?

Onshape is a browser-based Computer-Aided Design (CAD) software that lets you create 3D models and collaborate in real-time. Think of it like Google Docs instead of Microsoft Word—or like using Netflix instead of popping in a DVD. No installs, no updates, just open your browser and start building when inspiration strikes.

Onshape models can be 3D printed, laser cut, CNC milled, or shown to your friends and colleagues for feedback on designs.

Unlike other CAD software, it can be used on almost any device, including smartphones, tablets, and computers.

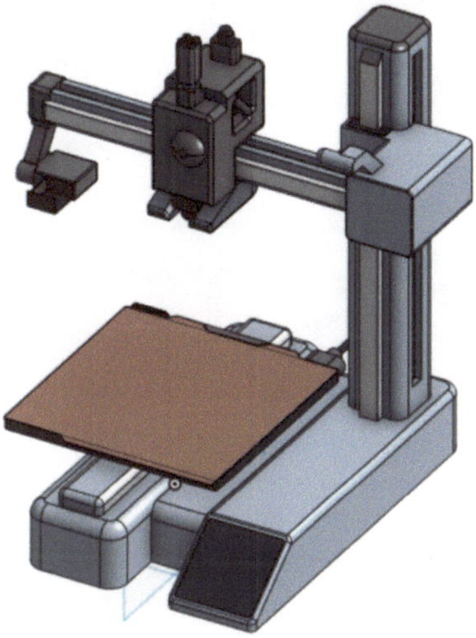

t.ly/O58zM: Bambu A1 by Andrew Schreiber via the Public Library

According to ***Engineering.com***, it's the #1 fastest growing CAD software.

Why Learn CAD?

t.ly/vFg1k: Headphones by Bala Radharamana via the Public Library

Designers and Engineers are human superheroes with unique skills to improve the world. They created everything you see, hear, touch, and feel—from the shoes on your feet to the phone in your hand, and even the bridges, rockets, and robots that shape the future.

CAD (Computer-Aided Design) is like having a superpower that lets you bring your imagination into the real world. With it, you can build solutions to real problems, invent products no one has seen before, and turn wild ideas into detailed 3D models.

Onshape is your digital toolkit, cloud-powered, real-time, and used by professionals across industries. So, let's dive in and master the fundamentals of Onshape together. Because once you learn the tools, there's no limit to what you can create.

Why Learn CAD?

Reasons to Teach CAD

- CAD skills are in high demand across various industries (engineering, architecture, product design, etc.)
- Onshape is widely used in professional settings, giving students relevant experience
- Integrates multiple disciplines: design, engineering, mathematics, and technology
- Provides practical application of theoretical concepts
- Allows students to bring their ideas to life in a digital space
- Challenges students to think critically about design and functionality
- Teaches iterative problem-solving through design revisions and
- Prepares students for a digitally-driven future

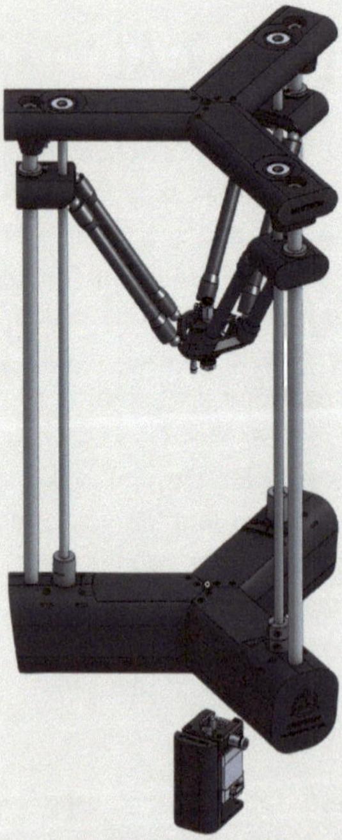

Reasons to Learn CAD

- Opens doors to careers in engineering, architecture, industrial design, and more
- CAD skills are transferable across various fields and software platforms
- Onshape specifically offers a comprehensive toolset (3D modeling, simulation, sheet-metal)
- Facilitates prototyping and product development
- Enhances ability to visualize and manipulate 3D objects
- Develops a better understanding of geometry and spatial relationships
- Links directly to modern manufacturing techniques like 3D printing and CNC machining
- Onshape includes simulation tools, promoting analytical thinking about design performance
- Learn to optimize designs based on functional requirements

Now you have read this page, check this off >>>

Get an Account

If you are not in education and want a free account:

SIGN UP NOW

1. Go to: ***Onshape.com***

2. Click Sign Up Now. Enter your details.

3. Go to Step 5 below.

If you are a Student or an Educator:

Create a Student Account

1.Go to ***Onshape.com/en/education/sign-up***

2. Enter your details.

3. Confirm if you are a student or teacher and what grade you are in teach.

4. Enter your school details and agree to the terms and conditions.

5. Find the verification email (it might be in your junk) and click the button.

ACTIVATE YOUR ACCOUNT

6. Set your password

Your account is activated!

But there are still a few more steps until you are done.....

Getting Set Up

7. When prompted, set your default units to Millimeters then press **Next** (you will be able to change units and we will soon do this in a project.)

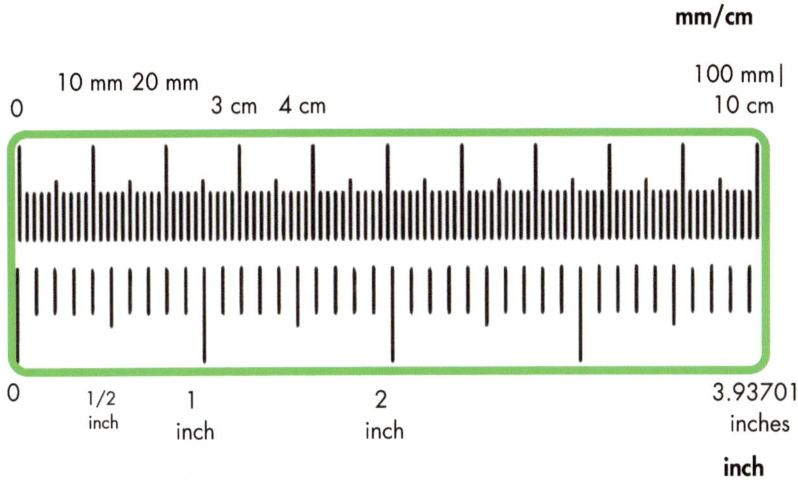

8. Then review the mouse controls, and if you have used a different CAD program before you can use those settings.

These are the default Onshape settings:

- **Zoom in|out**: Roll the scroll wheel [1]
- **Pan**: Press & Hold scroll wheel + Move mouse [1]
- **Select**: Left click [2]
- **Orbit:** Hold & Drag + Right button [3]
- **Context menu**: Right click [3]

9. Check your profile name is as you'd like it.

10. If you pass the browser check, press **Done** and, you will land on the **Documents page**.

No mouse? If you don't have a mouse, a trackpad will still work, but you will need to work out the combinations of clicks, pinches and swipes, as every trackpad is different.

Documents Page

The home page in Onshape is called the **Documents Page.**

You can always get to it by pressing the Onshape Logo in the top left corner of the screen.

This group take you to Action Items, App Store, Learning Centre, Help and Account settings.

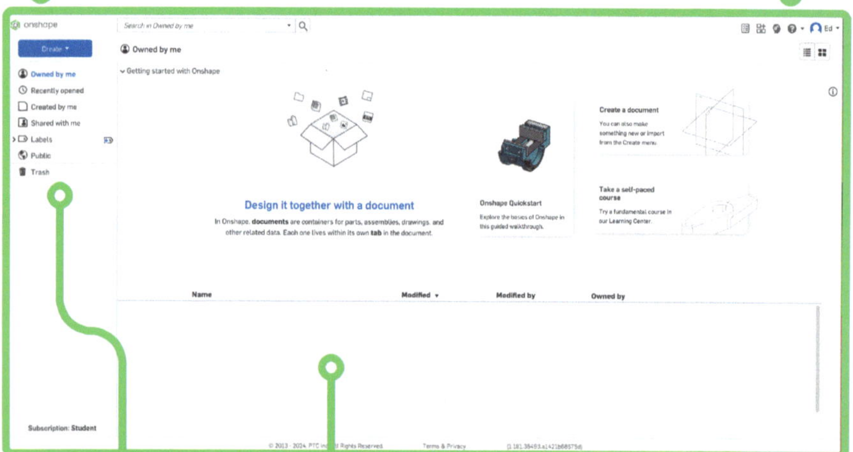

This is where all your folders and documents will appear.

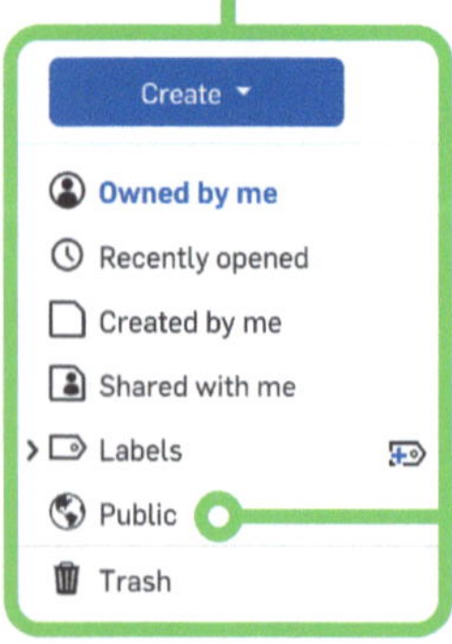

These buttons help you filter and file your documents.

This button is for the **Public library**.

Note: Documents in a Free account are Public by default.

Education Account documents are private, but can be made public if required.

Public Library & Docs

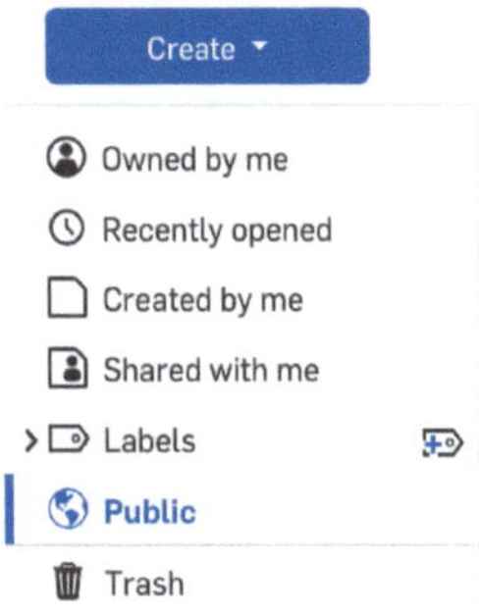

Click on the Public icon. This will show you a full list of all publicly available files that other Onshape users have created.

The ones shown are official Onshape files that you can open and explore!

To see the most Liked files, click on "Likes" in the right column which organizes the list into the most liked projects.

The *PERRINN LMP1*, by *Nico Perrin*, is Onshape's most popular project, at the time of writing, had been copied 13022 times, linked to 283 times, and liked 6399 times!

The public library is a great place to showcase your work and to see what others make with the power of CAD!

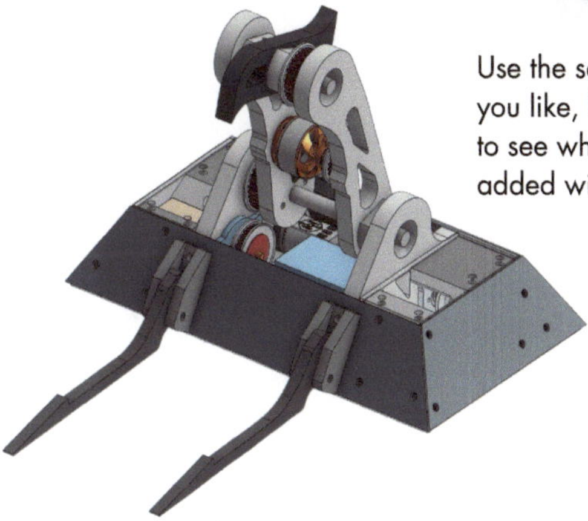

Use the search bar to look for something you like, like "Ice Cream" or "Battlebot" to see what amazing projects have been added with that name.

Hammer Saw Bot by *Nathan Collins* via the Public Library.

Change the view from list view to grid view with these button in the top right.

Sort the public documents by clicking the sort buttons.

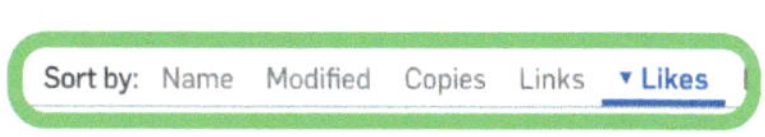

Public Library & Docs

Because this document is public, when you open it, it is View Only.

Even someone without an Onshape account can open a link to view a document in the public library!

You can make a copy for yourself by pressing the button and selecting a folder to move it into (Owned by me is the default).

Make a copy, then press the Onshape Logo in the top left corner of the screen to go back to the **Documents Page.**

If you want to change your username (as it appears in the Public Library), adjust mouse controls, switch units, or update other preferences, just click the profile icon (the head-and-shoulders symbol) next to your name in the top-right corner of the screen.

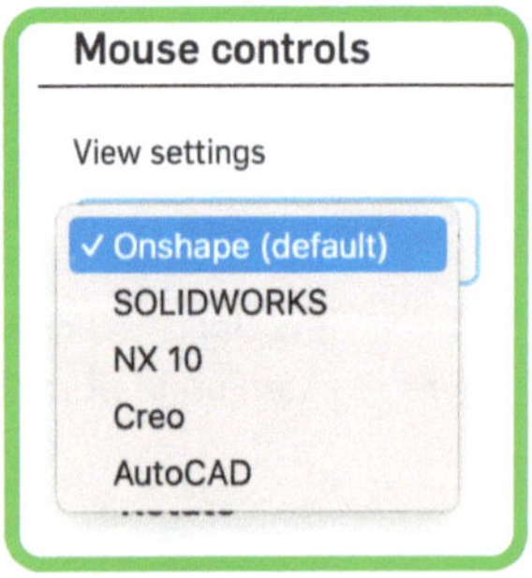

Click on your **Name** in the top left corner, **My Account** then look through **Profile** (name setting), and **Preferences** (units and mouse settings).

Press **Save** after each change, then **Return to document** when ready.

If you have experience with other CAD programs and are more comfortable with their Mouse Controls then feel free to change the default to match your muscle memory. If you are new to CAD then keep the default as Onshape.

Files & Folders / UI

From the **Documents Page** click the **Create** button in the top left, select **Folder** and call it "CADclass.org" and press Create.

Remember: If you need to get back to the **Documents Page** press the Onshape logo in the top left or the three horizontal bars next to it and click Close Document.

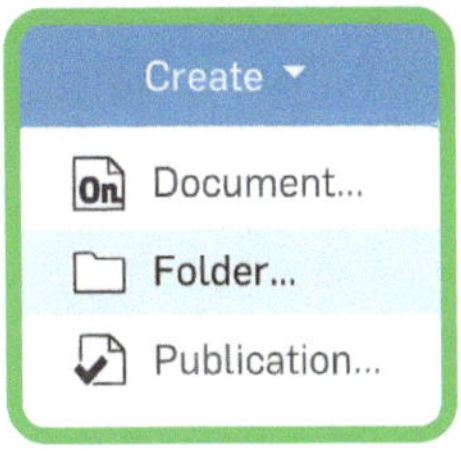

Click the new folder in the folders list to open it, then click the blue **Create** button again but this time press **Document**.

This will create a new Onshape document inside the folder.

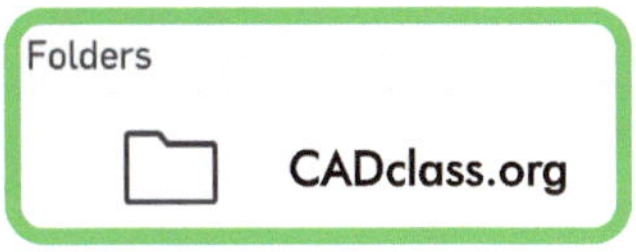

Call it "CADclass UI" and the user interface will change to the **Part Studio** interface.

Your screen will look like this!

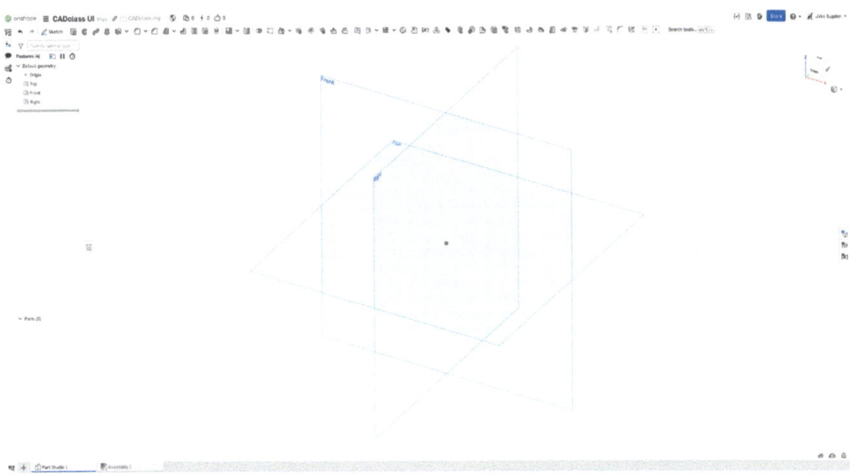

Parts Studio / UI

At the very top of the page, you'll find the Document Toolbar. Just below that is the Dynamic Toolbar, which changes based on what you're working on—it could show the Feature, Sketch, Assembly, or Drawing tools depending on your current task.

As a general rule, the tools are organized by how often they're used: the most commonly used tools are on the left, and the more specialized ones appear toward the right.

The Feature Toolbar is the default toolbar:

The 3 default planes (Top, Front, Right)

Some tools have a dropdown to show additional options.

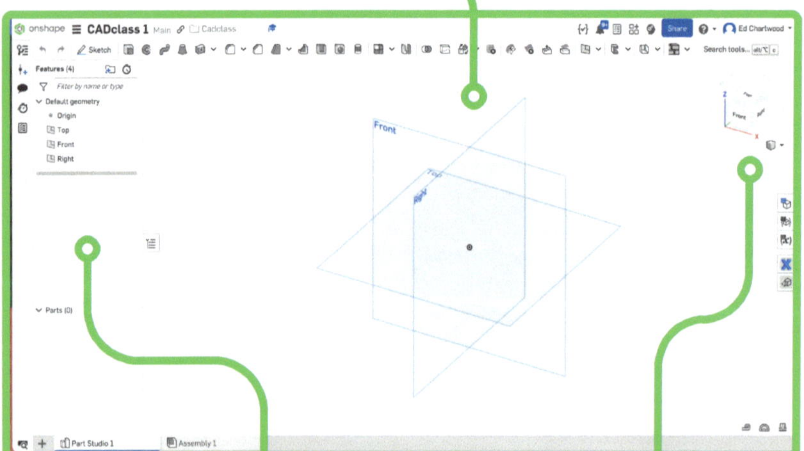

The Feature List and Parts List

The View Cube and other view options

Note that some tools may disappear if your window isn't maximized.

View Cube

The View Cube is a navigation tool that helps you control the orientation of your model. You can click and drag the cube itself to rotate your view, and the model's planes will move with it. Alternatively, you can right-click and hold anywhere in the workspace to freely rotate the view—watch how the View Cube moves along with you.

You can also click the arrows surrounding the cube to rotate your model in 90-degree increments, making it easier to switch perspectives quickly.

The View Cube has clickable faces and corners (called vertices).

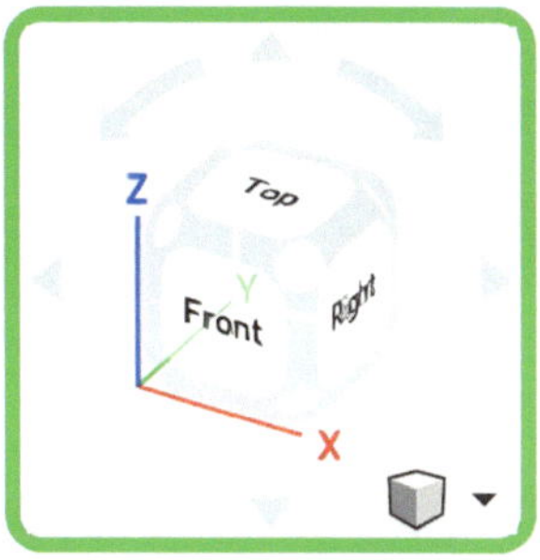

Clicking on a face snaps the view to that side (like Top, Front, or Right), while clicking on a vertex gives you a smooth 3D angle. It's a simple but essential tool for navigating your workspace efficiently.

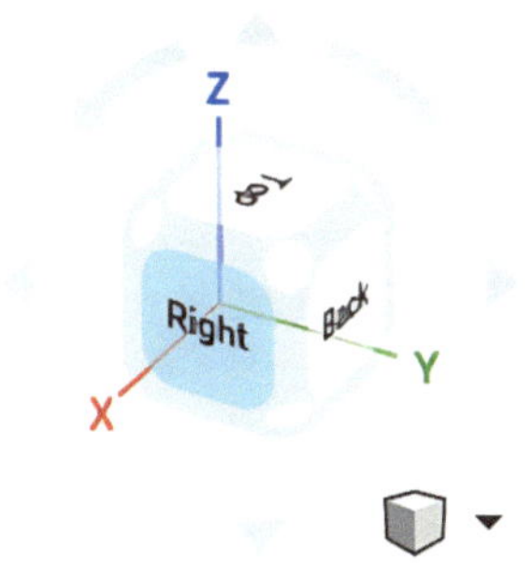

Click the Right **face**.

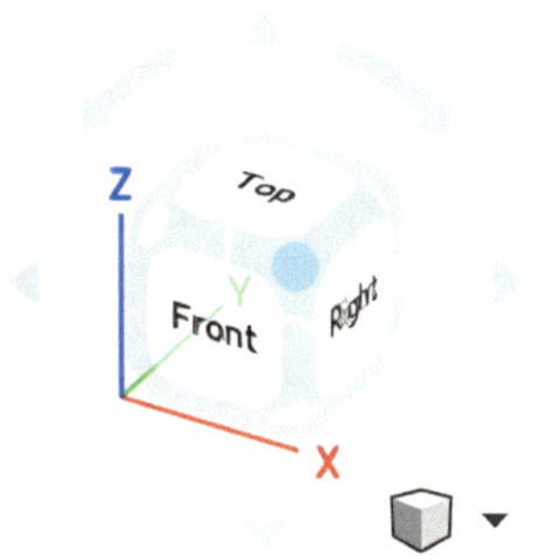

Click the Top / Front/Right **vertex**.

Q: Add up the number of faces and vertices a cube has and write it here.

Mouse Control

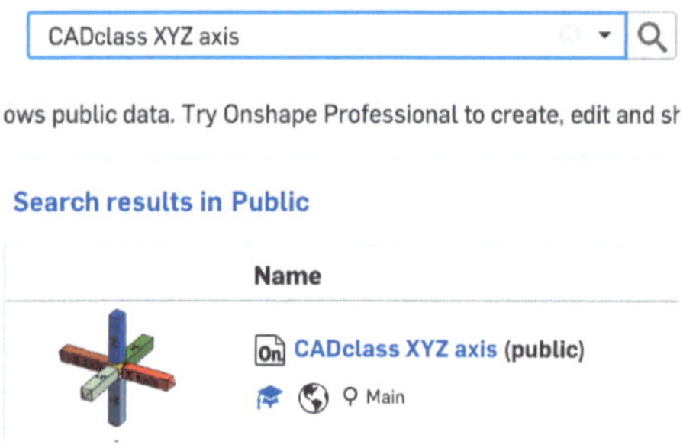

Head to the Public Library and search for "CADclass XYZ axis".

Click on the name in blue which will open it.

This file showcases the 6 positive and negative axes and Origin in the workspace.

Now practice the Onshape mouse controls:

Zoom in | out: Roll the scroll wheel [1]
Pan: Press & Hold Scroll Wheel + Drag [1]
Select: Left click [2]
Orbit: Press + Hold Right button & Drag [3]
Context Menu: Right click [3]

Q: What color are the eyes on the smiley on the back of the Z axis. Red, Green or Purple ?

Q: What is the answer to the sum on the underside of the -X axis?

Q: What color are the faces on the octagon on the chamfer point of the -Z axis: Pink or Orange?

Solutions

Mastering a 3-button mouse is essential for developing true proficiency in CAD. It gives you the ability to navigate quickly, access commands efficiently, and control your designs with precision.

In Onshape, each button has a purpose: the left button is used for selecting, the scroll wheel zooms in and out and also acts as a middle button for panning, and right-clicking opens up contextual menus for fast actions. Learning to use all three buttons fluidly makes your workflow smoother, faster, and much more intuitive.

Taking the time to practice and build muscle memory with proper mouse techniques will pay off quickly. Not only will it boost your speed and accuracy, but it will also make even complex projects feel more manageable. In short, mastering your mouse is one of the simplest ways to level up your design game.

Q: What color are the smiley face's eyes on the back of the Z axis. Red, Green or Purple ?
A: Purple

P

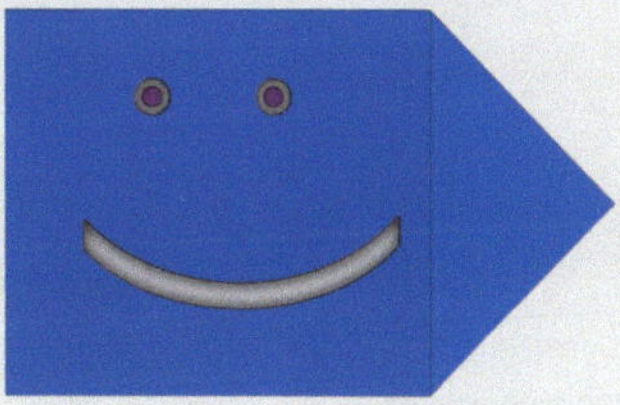

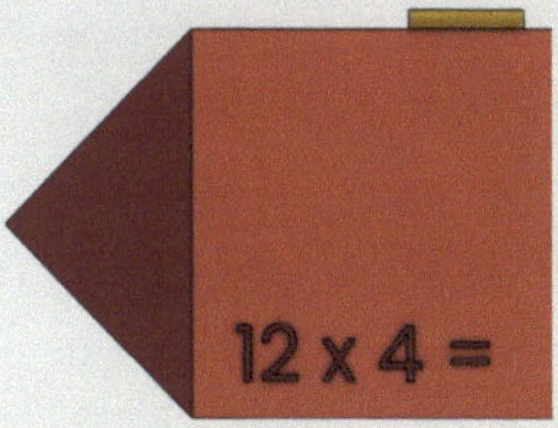

Q: What is the answer to the sum on the underside of the -X axis?
A: 48

48

Q: What color are the faces on the octagon on the chamfer point of the -Z axis: Pink or Orange?
A: Orange

O

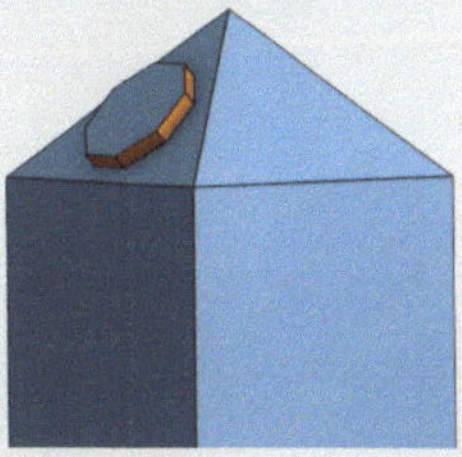

Planes, Axes & Origin

In Onshape, you begin by sketching in two dimensions (2D) to create designs that will be transformed into three-dimensional (3D) models.

In geometry, 3D space is defined by a Cartesian coordinate system, where three values—X, Y, and Z—are used to specify the position of a point.

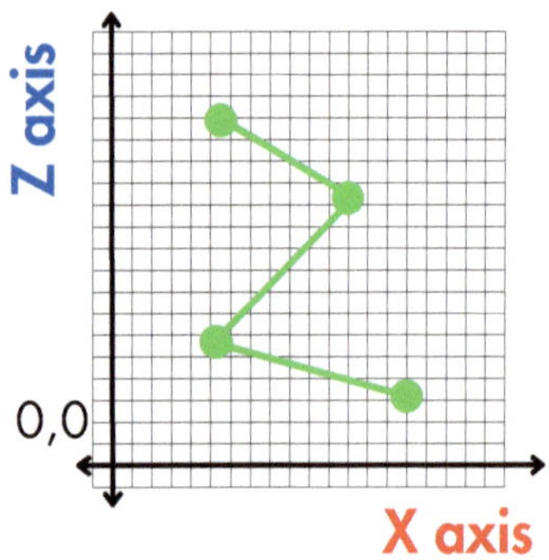

This system allows for precise placement and manipulation of objects in three directions: width, height, and depth.

Understanding this coordinate system is fundamental to working effectively in any 3D CAD environment.

The 3 blue squares are the default "planes:" Top, Front and Right.

The **Y axis** is the 'new' axis if you have only used 2D CAD.

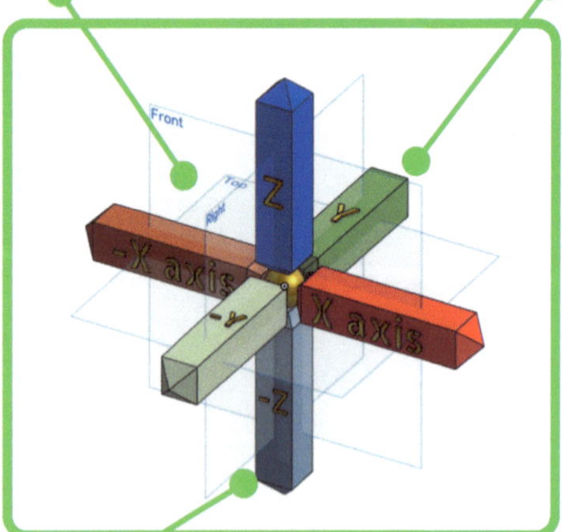

The golden orb in the design is the "**Origin**" or coordinate 0,0,0.

Z axis coordinates are positive (+) above the Top plane and negative (–) below it.

Active Engagement

U.I. (User Interface)
Mastering Onshape's UI is crucial because it directly impacts design efficiency and creativity. UI mastery matters because it reduces time spent hunting for commands, keyboard shortcuts speed up repetitive tasks, and quick navigation means more time for actual design. You can try:

- A UI scavenger hunt: give students features to find (timed)
- Try "speed modeling" using only shortcuts
- Celebrate finding multiple ways to access the same command, and
- Encourage sharing "productivity tips" with classmates

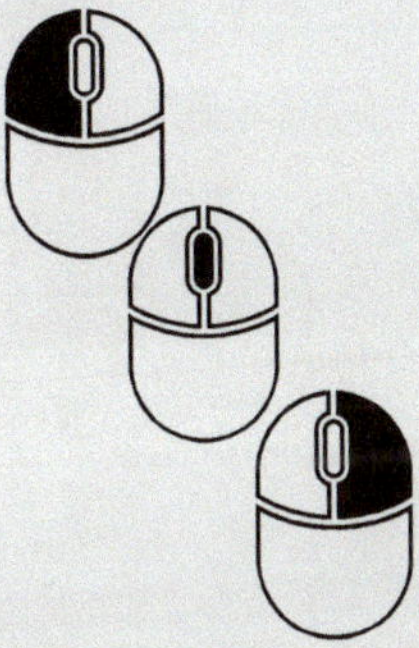

Mouse
We strongly encourage everyone to use a 3-button mouse (with a clickable scroll wheel).

Encourage students to test and experiment with mouse controls, change the default settings, and get comfortable with right and left-clicking. Touchscreens are so ubiquitous that some students rarely use a mouse. Since you will click, orbit, pan, and zoom more than any other activity, it is worth slowing down to practice.

Planes and axes
Use pieces of paper to demonstrate sketch planes and offset planes. Each piece of paper represents a sketch in Onshape. Talk about what happens if you start a new sketch on a new piece of paper but want to make an edit to the Original design.

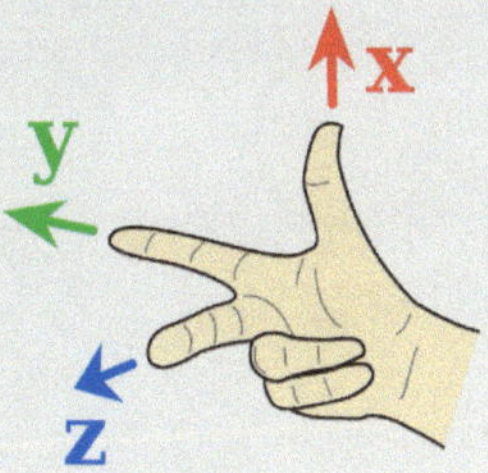

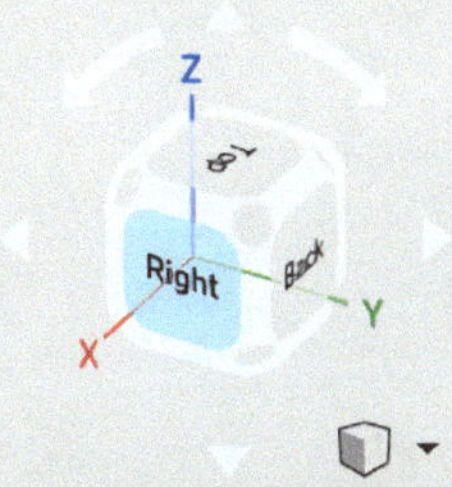

View Cube
Mastering the View Cube matters! Quick orientation saves time and improves spatial understanding. Encourage students to click on all the edges, faces, and corners and encourage them to use these terms when discussing their 3D designs with you.

True or False?

Q: Documents in a Free Onshape account are Public by default?

Q: Education Account documents are private, but can be made public if required?

Q: If you need to get back to the Documents Page press the Head logo in the top right>

Q: Onshape uses a 3-Axis coordinate system: X, Y, and Z?

Q: Rolling the scroll wheel up and down pans left to right?

Solutions

Q: Documents in a Free Onshape account are Public by default?

A: Yes, that is correct... so be careful!

Q: Education Account documents are private, but can be made public if required?

A: Yes, that is correct. Share using the Share button and set your permissions.

Q: If you need to get back to the Documents Page press the Head logo in the top right?

A: No, press the Onshape Logo in the top left.

Q: Onshape uses a 3-Axis coordinate system: X, Y, and Z?

A: Yes, that is correct.

Q: Rolling the scroll wheel up and down pans left to right?

A: No, incorrect. That zooms in / out.

Number The UI Features

1 View Cube

2 Part Studio Tab

3 Toolbar

4 Planes

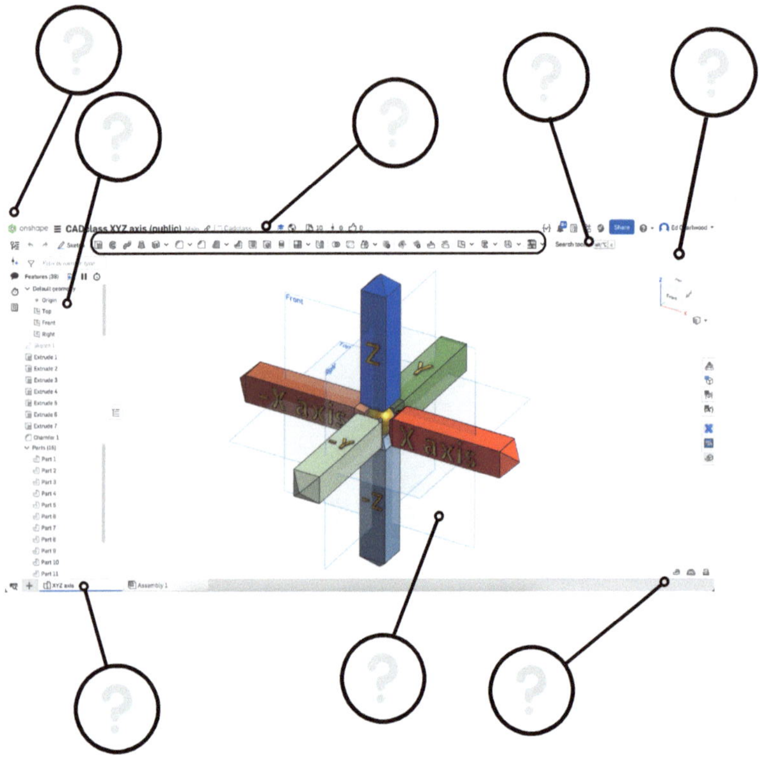

5 Dashboard

6 Search

7 Feature List

8 Measure

Solutions

1 View Cube

2 Part Studio Tab

3 Toolbar

4 Planes

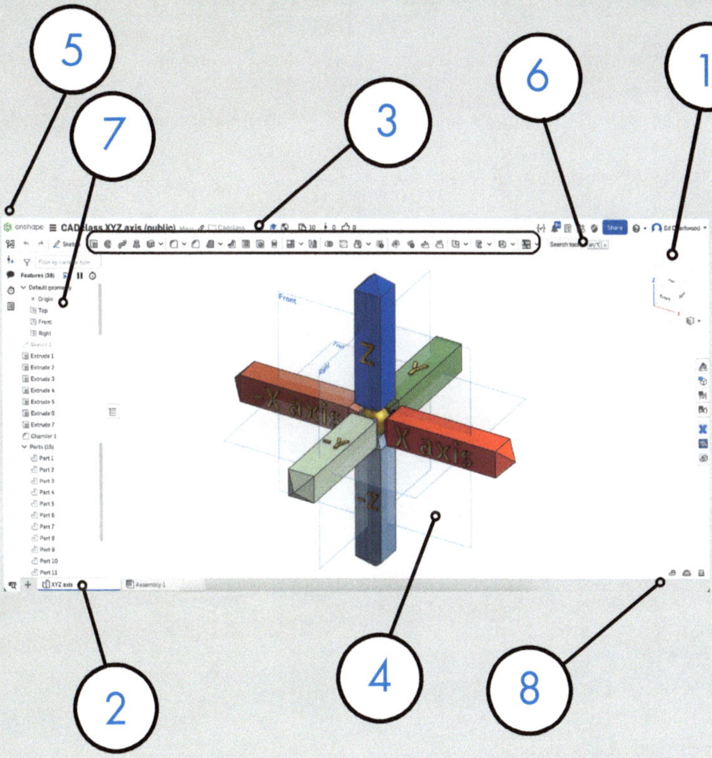

5 Dashboard

6 Search

7 Feature List

8 Measure

Success Metric

The one thing you must remember when teaching CAD is this: **Your success goes up in proportion to the amount of fun your students have.**

The sooner they have fun, the better. The more fun they have, the more likely it is that they master the fundamentals and continue to learn and enjoy it on their own.

What makes a CAD lesson effective and fun?

1 - Doing is fun. Watching someone do is okay. Passive listening is boring.

2 - The context is genuinely exciting (think rockets, classic toys, and games).

3 - The instructions are clear but leave room for creativity and problem-solving.

4 - The model introduces new concepts and functionality, but not too many.

5 - Aim for "just right" difficulty. Too easy is boring. Too hard is overwhelming.

6 - Model objects everyone can relate to (please, not another pulley!)

7 - Students are encouraged to move at their own pace. Students working quickly should work ahead and students falling behind may need your help.

8 - Additional experimentation and play are encouraged.

Fun does not mean easy. Challenges at the right difficulty inspire students to push their current CAD knowledge, providing enough "aha moments" to stimulate their problem-solving brains.

Our thesis is this: Fun should be your metric.

TTF (Time to Fun)

Here at CADclass, we use a metric called TTF (Time to Fun). We aim to introduce the best, most entertaining part of the lesson as quickly as possible. If we can make it on a 3D printer while they're in the lesson to bring it to life, we do. If we can show a picture instead of describing with words, we do.

As you plan your lessons and reflect on previous ones, always keep the metric **TTF** in mind.

Our Pedagogy

This chapter in the Onshape *Fundamentals Workbook* is designed to teach 3D modeling concepts to beginners. The goal is to build foundational knowledge and practical skills through a simple, engaging project everyone is familiar with. By focusing on intentional practice and play, students will develop the mindset of a CAD designer and can take these basic building blocks as far as their imagination goes.

Here's a deconstruction of the teaching methods used:

The Classic Donut in the section ahead is a tangible, relatable object. It provides a clear goal, making the abstract concepts of 3D modeling concrete. It's easy to visualize, reducing cognitive load and freeing up space to complete other taxing tasks.

Our step-by-step approach reduces the complex process of creating a 3D model into manageable, sequential steps. This scaffolding approach helps students build confidence as they progress, reducing the risk of overwhelming beginners with too much information. The images are carefully selected to dual-code the instructions and are accompanied by icons and visual cues which help students quickly identify key actions or important notes.

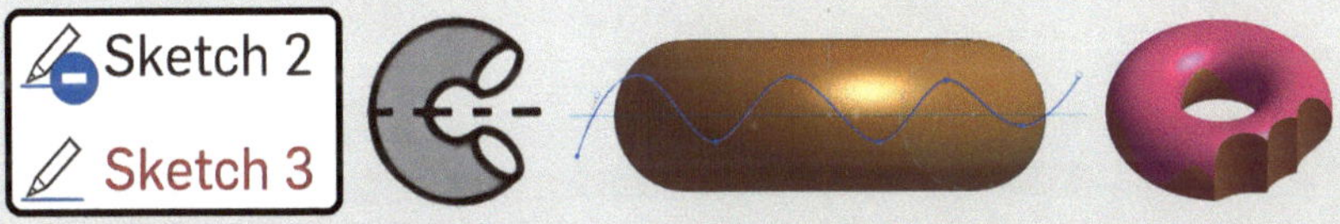

There are many technical terms and tools (like Revolve, Extrude, and Spline) within the context of creating the Classic Donut. This helps students understand not just what these tools do, but when and why they would use them in a real modeling scenario.

The instructions encourage students to experiment with the software, such as adjusting spline curves and changing colors. This hands-on approach promotes active learning and allows students to see immediate results of their actions.

The Classic Donut project strategically introduces new skills and concepts, starting with basic operations like sketching and revolving, then progressing to more advanced techniques like splitting faces and applying Physical Materials. This progression helps build a foundation of fundamental workflows and will be used throughout the book. For now, these steps are written in detail. However, the level of detail (the scaffolding) is gradually removed throughout this book.

After the project, key concepts and vocabulary are reinforced. This helps solidify learning and encourages students to reflect.

Our Pedagogy

The chapter mentions additional resources, like **CADclass.org**, for more detailed walkthroughs, encouraging students to seek more information and continue their learning journey.

The Classic Donut combines these pedagogical elements to introduce complex 3D modeling concepts in an accessible, engaging manner. It provides a balance of guided instruction and opportunities for exploration, catering to different learning preferences and skill levels. This approach teaches the technical skills needed for 3D modeling and fosters creativity and problem-solving, crucial design and engineering skills.

Sources:

Tangible, relatable object approach:

- Situated Learning Theory (Lave & Wenger, 1991)
- Constructivism (Piaget, 1936; Vygotsky, 1978)

Scaffolding and sequential steps:

- Zone of Proximal Development (Vygotsky, 1978)
- Cognitive Load Theory (Sweller, 1988)

Dual-coding with visual cues:

- Dual Coding Theory (Paivio, 1971)
- Multimedia Learning Theory (Mayer, 2001)

Contextual introduction of technical terms:

- Contextual Learning Theory (Hull, 1993)

Hands-on experimentation:

- Experiential Learning Theory (Kolb, 1984)
- Active Learning (Bonwell & Eison, 1991)

Progressive skill introduction:

- Spiral Curriculum (Bruner, 1960)

Review section for reinforcement:

- Spaced Repetition (Ebbinghaus, 1885)

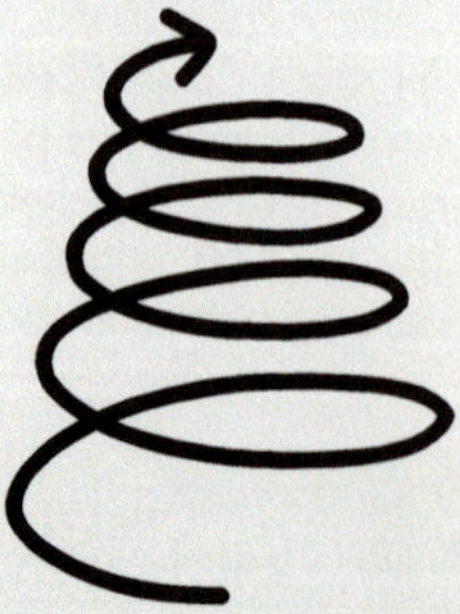

Encouraging further learning:

- Self-Directed Learning (Knowles, 1975)

Other ideas:
Bring in donuts / 3D print a sliced donut
Bring in a bagel & bread knife and slice

Our Pedagogy

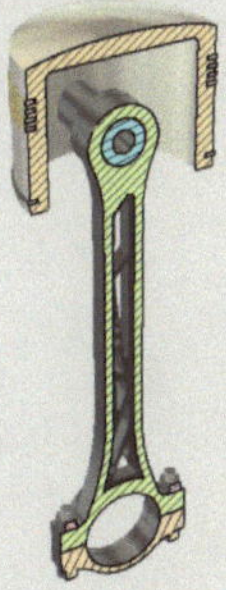

As your students complete the donut project, you've established the perfect foundation for CAD instruction. This engaging first exercise does more than just teach sketching, revolving, and split body functions—it creates an immediate connection between technical skills and tangible objects students already understand.

Consider taking a moment to show cross-sectioned examples that reveal internal structures, reinforcing how these same visualization principles apply across engineering disciplines from automotive components to building systems: ***YouTube.com/c/cutinhalf***

The beauty of these food-based models lies in their ability to transform abstract CAD operations into approachable learning experiences. Many students who might feel intimidated by technical terminology will eagerly engage with familiar objects like donuts. This is an excellent opportunity to encourage exploration—have students manipulate their models, using different cross-sectional profles to create new 3D shapes.

You could even bring in actual donuts to class - slicing them to show the circular profile or as rewards for completion, reinforcing the connection between digital design and physical objects while creating a memorable learning experience.

The upcoming lollipop challenge provides a perfect progression in technical complexity while maintaining student engagement. This project introduces critical new concepts—reading a technical drawing, multiple features in new sequence, and more appearance applications but in a different, yet familiar context.

Also, you won't believe the famous designer in the Chupa Chup story: **t.ly/Inp-H**

As you transition between these projects, we encourage you to highlight the iterative nature of design work these exercises demonstrate. Consider having a brief discussion about how real-world engineers use cross-sectional analysis to understand everything from material composition to structural integrity. If time permits, actual lollipops can serve as both motivation and tangible reference objects—perhaps even as rewards for successfully completing the donut exercise. This progression from donut to lollipop isn't just about increasing technical skill; it's about building students' confidence through achievable challenges with visible results.

Active Engagement

The Classic Donut tutorial is the perfect introduction to 3D CAD for beginners. This approachable project builds confidence through immediate success while interleaving fundamental CAD concepts and workflows that will serve students well throughout their design journey.

A donut is a relatable item, so students immediately intuitively understand what they're creating, reducing the intimidation factor and increasing engagement.

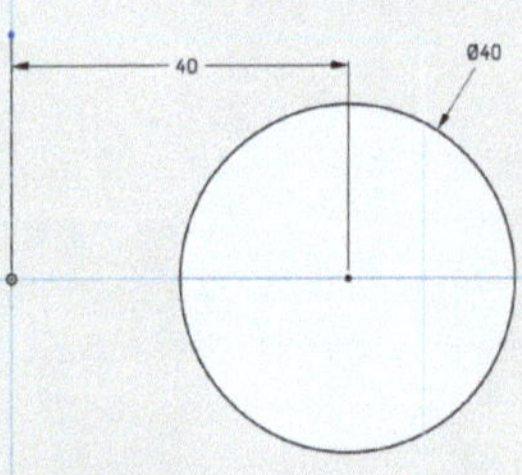

Natural Learning Progression:

- Begins with basic 2D sketching
- Introduces constraints and dimensions
- Transforms 2D into 3D through the Revolve tool
- Explores modification techniques (splitting and "bites")
- Adds visual appeal with custom appearances

Core Skills Taught:

- Origin-based reference geometry
- Sketch constraints and dimensioning
- Feature creation workflow
- Extrude (cut) operations
- Material appearances

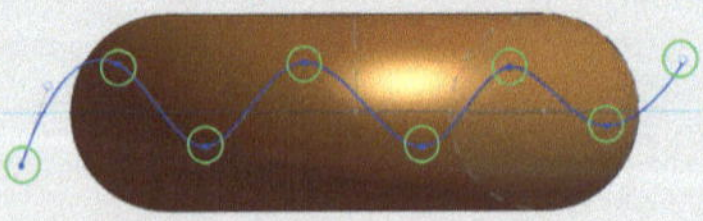

A donut provides quick wins (torus creation) while building complexity (splitting, customization) for sustained engagement, and students are able to keep in mind "what a good one looks like."

Creativity Within Structure:

- Students follow clear steps but can personalize through custom spline curves, placement choices, and appearance options.

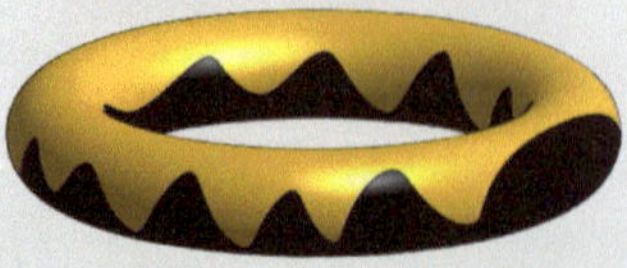

Project #1
Sketch
Revolve
Splines
Split Face

Split Face
Extrude Cut
Appearance

where makers are made.

Estimated Time: 1 hr
Onshape Fundamentals
Workbook

Classic Donut

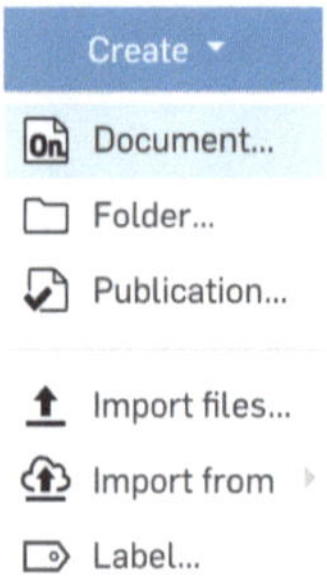

From the Dashboard create a new Document called "Classic Donut" in the CADclass.org Folder.

Navigate to the 3 horizontal lines near the top left corner and click them, then open Workspace Units.

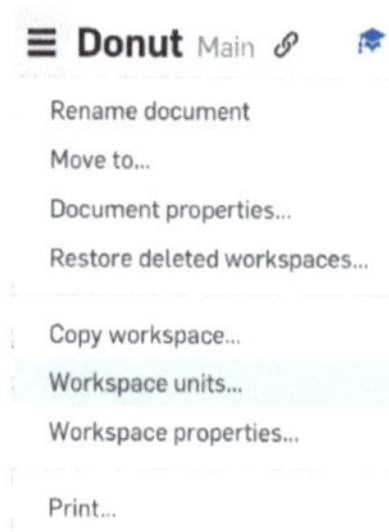

Q? Is your Length default unit set to mm?

If not, change it to mm via the dropdown arrows then confirm by pressing the green checkmark ✅.

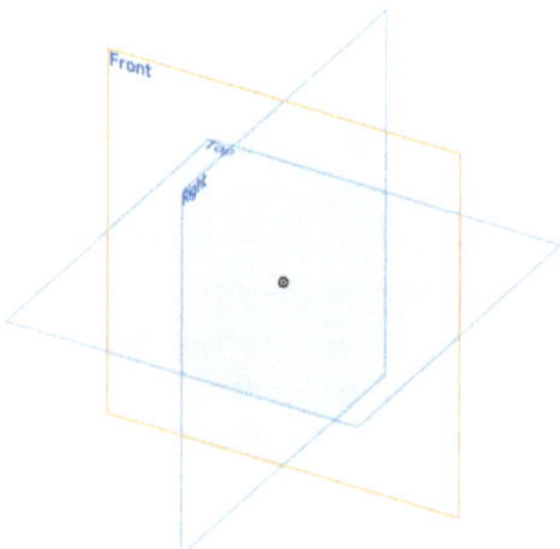

Start your first Sketch by clicking the Sketch tool ✎ Sketch in the top left corner then apply the sketch to the Front Face by clicking it.

You have just transitioned from the 3D to the 2D Toolbar!

Notice that Sketch 1 appears on the Front Plane. Change the view by (1) clicking the Front face on the View Cube or (2) press [N] on your keyboard, for Normal view.

Q? What changed about the toolbar across the top?

....

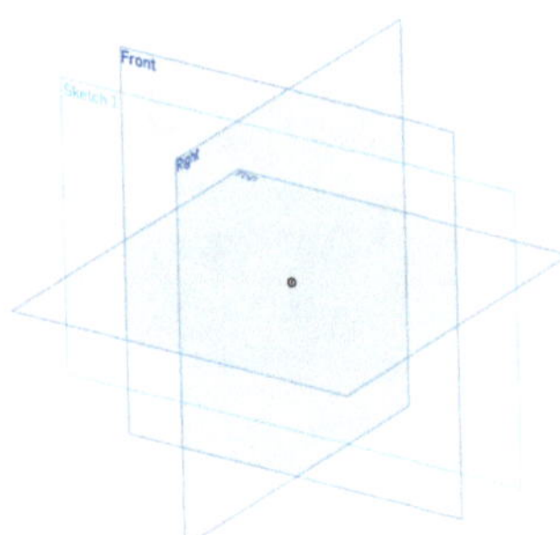

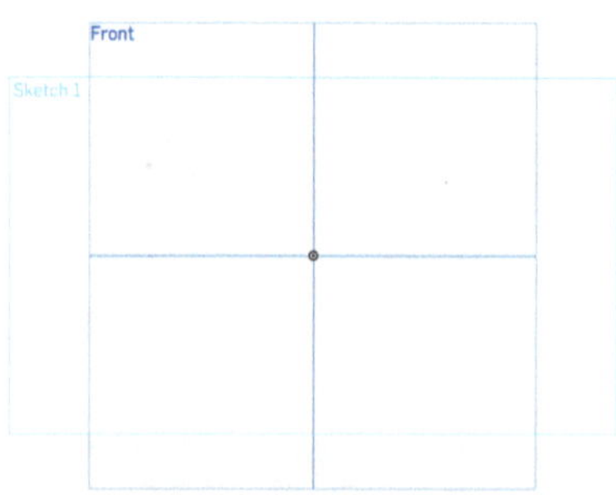

In engineering and CAD, Normal view refers to a direction perpendicular to a surface or plane, or a head-on view of a plane.

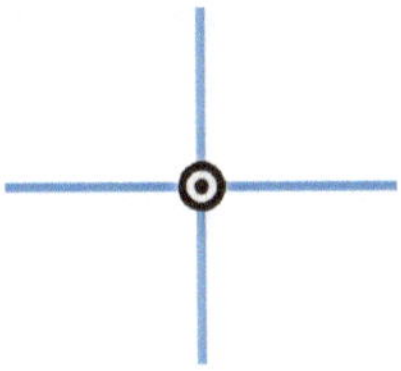

Now you are in the 2D Sketching environment on the Front Plane; notice the vertical Z-Axis, the horizontal X-Axis and the black circle at the center.

This circle is the Origin and is the only fixed point in the Onshape universe. Most of your sketches will reference it.

Press [C] for Circle, click to the right of the Origin near the X-axis, move your cursor up, and click again to define the circle's diameter, then Esc to deselect the Circle tool. Don't worry exactly how big it is, for now.

Press [L] for Line, click the Origin, move your cursor vertically upwards and click again. Press Esc to deselect the line tool.

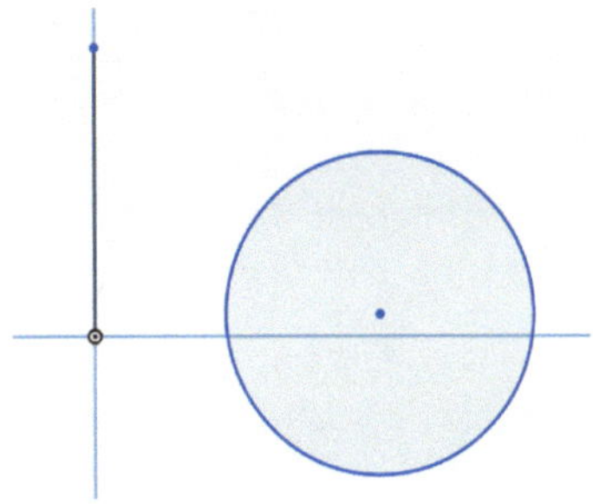

To make the Donut shape, you will rotate this circle about a vertical axis. Because the vertical line is assisting you in making the donut shape, you can turn it into a Construction line. Click the line and press [Q]. It should now be dashed.

Construction geometry are lines, points, and planes used to make parts, but aren't strictly part of the final design.

Q? What happens if you do not press Esc after using a sketch tool?

....

To horizontally align the circle's center with the Origin, you will use a Constraint, a tool used to limit the movement and scale of geometry without dimensions.

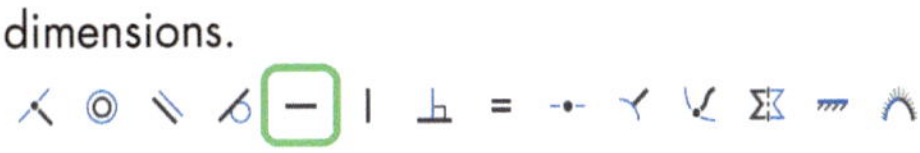

Navigate to Horizontal constraint or press [H], and select the Origin and the circle's center, or vice versa. Press Esc to deselect the tool.

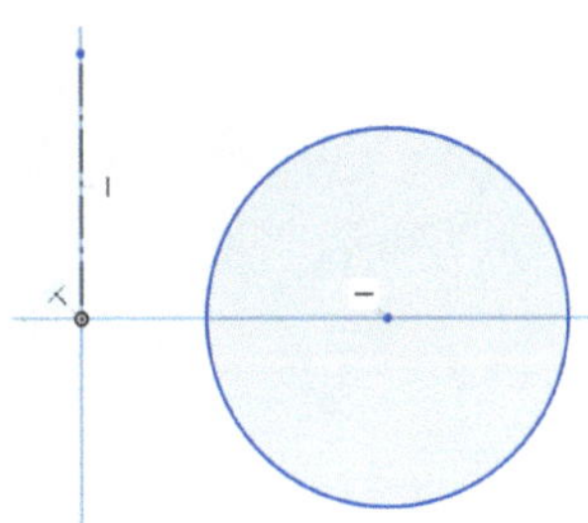

Show constraints

Q? What happens if you click the Show Constraints checkbox in the Sketch 1 dialogue box?

....

Some tools may be hidden in a sub-menu depending on the width of your screen. If you can't find a tool, you can use the Search Tools box in the top right.

Try to search for "horizontal".

Search tools... alt/⌥ c

Type [D] for Dimension, click on the Origin, then the circle's center, move your cursor up, click, type 40, and press Enter.

This has defined the location of the circle's center, but not the circle's size.

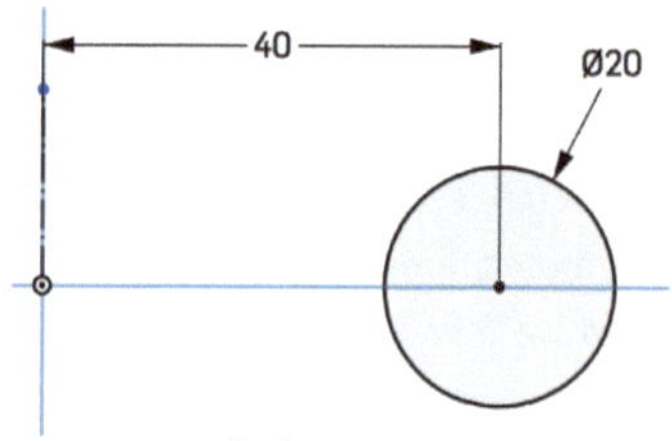

Click the circle's circumference, move your cursor away, click again, type 20, and press Enter.

Q? What happens if you double-click on the 40 mm dimension?

....

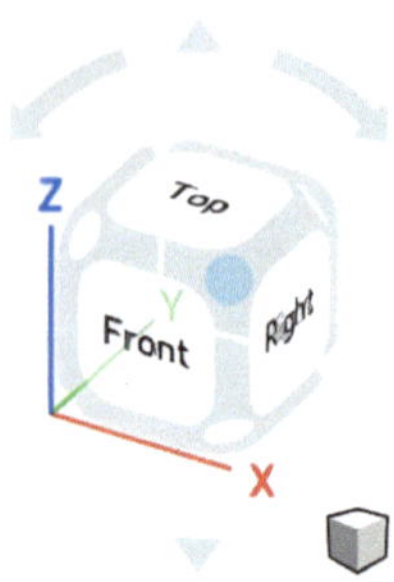

Notice that circle was blue but is now black; this is because it is now fully defined and unmovable, as its location and size is fully known.

Click Finish Sketch ✅ in the Sketch 1 Dialogue Box and click the corner as shown on the View Cube [Shift + 7] to get an isometric view of your sketch. When transitioning from a 2D Sketch to the 3D Workspace, always have a 3 dimensional view.

Navigate to and click Revolve in the toolbar. The blue box "Faces and sketch regions to revolve" prompts you to click the circle. Click the circle.

Faces and sketch regions to revolve
Face of Sketch 1 ×

Revolve axis

Notice that Revolve Axis is highlighted red. Click it to highlight it in blue, then Click the vertical Construction line. Now you have a Torus, the mathematical name for a Donut! Press the green checkmark in the Revolve Dialogue Box ✅.

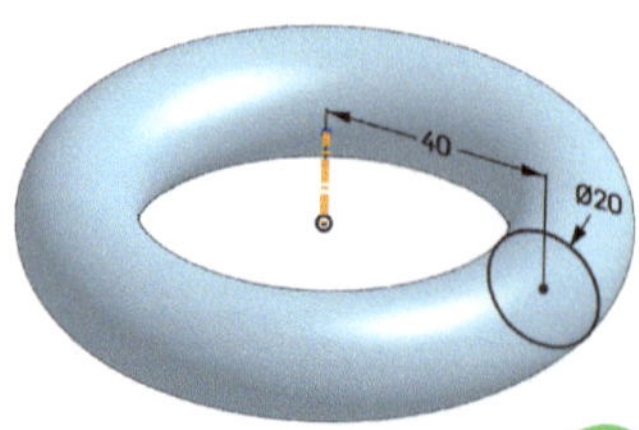

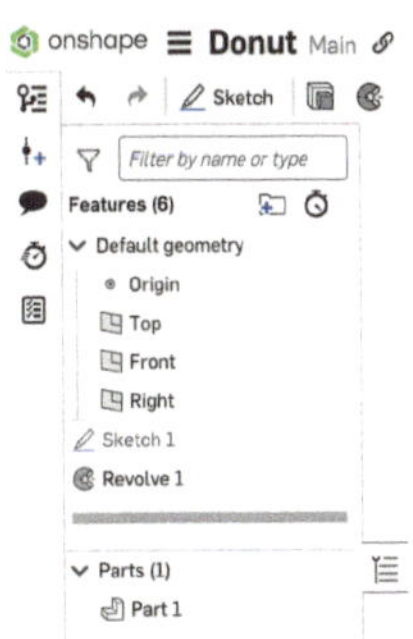

You have just made your first revolved 3D object! In Onshape, this is called a Part.

Look on the left-hand side of the page. You will see the Feature List with Sketch 1 and Revolve 1, and below the line, in the Parts List, Part 1 (your Torus / Donut).

Q? How many options appear if you right-click Part 1?

....

Whoops! The Donut looks very skinny; a Classic "Cartoonish" Donut should be much bigger. Let's go back into the first sketch and edit the diameter of the circle.

There are two main ways to go back into the 2D Sketch workspace:

1. Right click Sketch 1 in the Feature List and click Edit
2. Double-click Sketch 1

The first method gives you more options, but the second is faster.

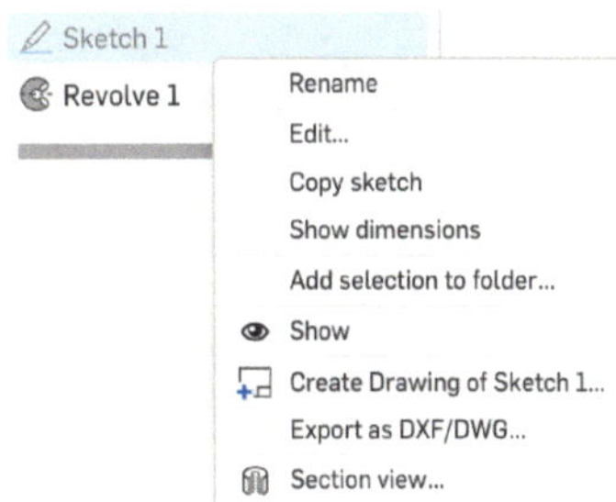

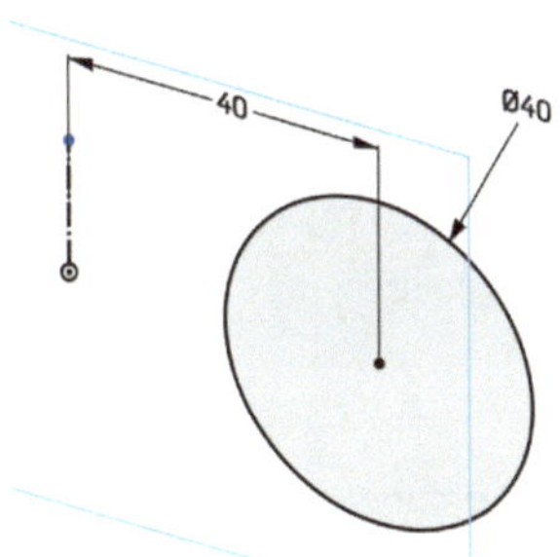

In the 2D workspace, double-click on the circle's diameter dimension, type 40, and press Enter.

In CAD, the symbol for a value being a diameter **Ø** is a circle with a slash through it.

Confirm the sketch by clicking the green checkmark ✅ in the Sketch Dialogue Box.

This change in the Sketch will then update the Part.

The default appearance and material in Onshape is a light blue. To edit it, right-click on Part 1 in the Parts List and select Edit Appearance. Select a light brown color from the Palette and press the green checkmark ✅.

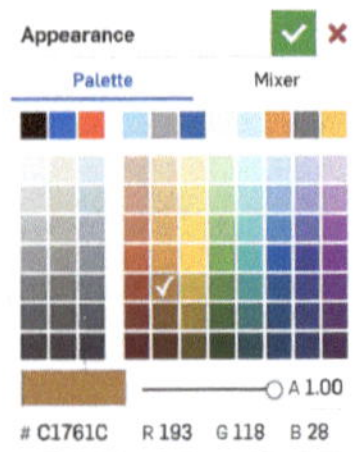

You can also change the transparency of the part and enter specific Hex values or RGB codes here by typing in numbers. The Hex code for **Onshape green** is **#64BB58**.

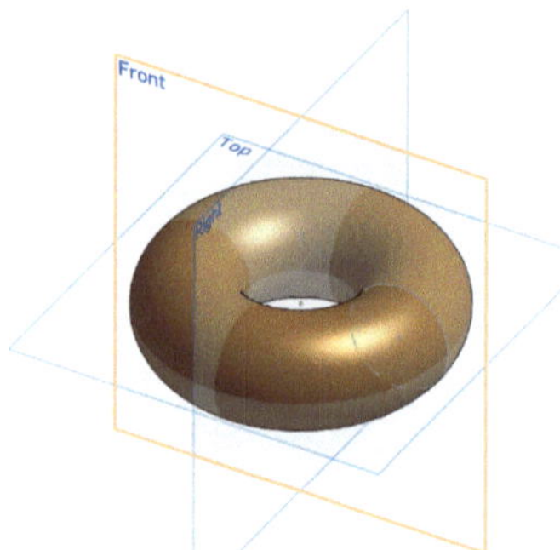

Create a new Sketch on the Front Plane.

Press [N] to set the view to be head-on.

In CAD and engineering, N which stands for Normal, is another word for a perpendicular view of a plane.

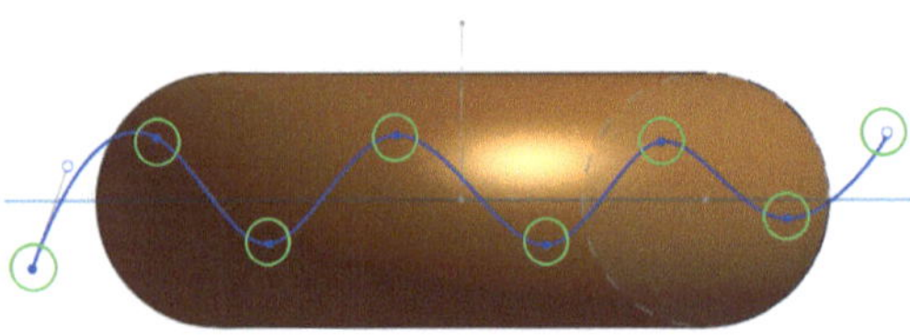

Navigate to Spline, click above and below the X-axis 6 times (so the first and last points are outside the donut), double click the last point or press Esc to finish the spline.

Q? What happens when you click, hold, and drag the blue dots on the spline?

....

Splines are not dimensionally driven. Instead, they can be better described as organic or artistic shapes. Navigate to the Constraints, select Fix [Shift + J], and click the Spline, then ✅. Your Spline should turn black.

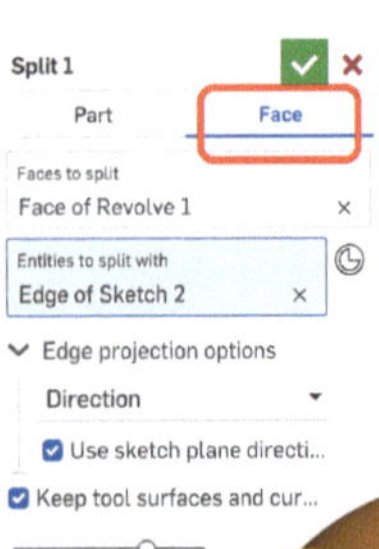

To divide the Donut into two with a curvy edge, select the Split tool. Change the type from Part to Face in the dialog box, then select the Donut Part as the Faces to Split.

Click the Entities to Split With in red, select the spline, and click ✅.

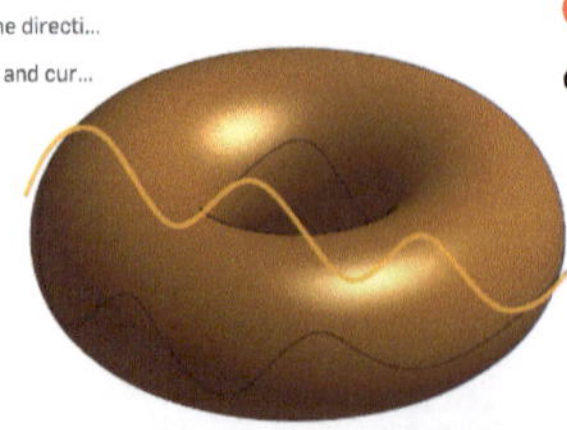

Q? What happens when you click the eye icon next to Part 1 in the Parts List?

....

To take a bite out of the donut, place a new Sketch on the Top Plane and get a normal top-down view [N].

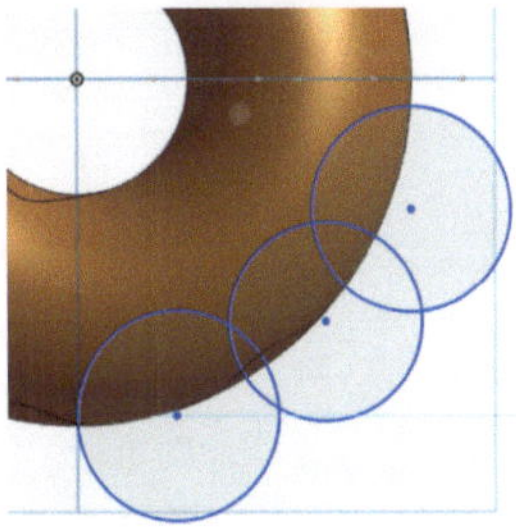

Type [C] for Circle and draw 3 circles near the outer edge of the donut, where the circle's centers are outside the Donut's volume and the circles overlap. Press Escape to deselect the circle tool.

Press Ctrl / Cmd and select each circle so they are highlighted in yellow. Navigate to the Constraints toolbar and select the Equal tool. Click ✅ in Sketch 3 dialogue box.

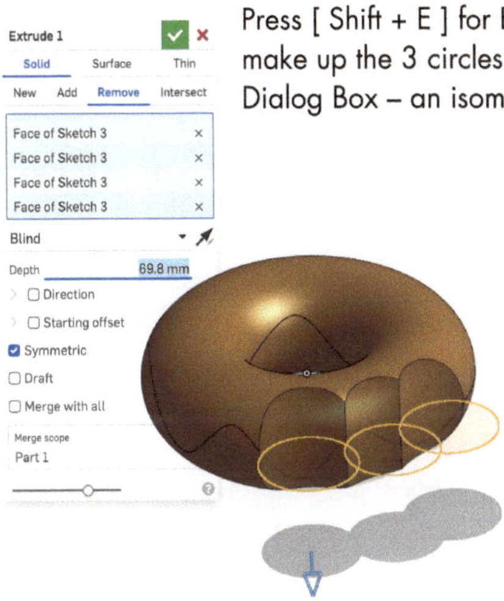

Press [Shift + E] for Extrude and select all 5 profiles that make up the 3 circles. Notice the 5 Faces Selected in the Dialog Box – an isometric view is best to see this.

Change the Extrude type from New to Remove and select the Symmetric checkbox, then click and drag the arrow downwards through the Donut in both directions. Click ✅.

Q? What happens if the direction is not set to Symmetric?

....

To make the top half of the Donut look like dripping colorful icing, you need to add an appearance to the top face. Unfortunately, there is no premade Pink Icing color in the Onshape Appearance Panel...so let's make a custom one!

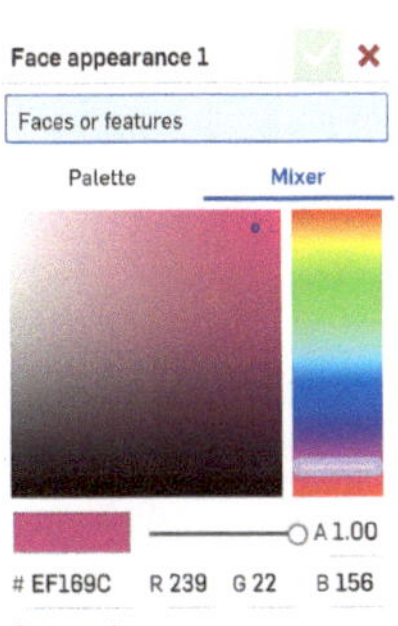

Press the Appearance Panel icon in the menu on the right middle of the page. Click the Add face appearance button in the top right corner of the pop out box. Then explore the Mixer tab to find your perfect pink.

Click the top face of the donut to apply it. ✅

Q? What happens when you type 255 into all RGB number boxes?

....

To give the effect of dripping icing, select the Thicken tool, select the icing surface of the Donut, and set the Thickness 1 as 2.0 mm.

Then select the Fillet tool [Shift + F], select the top icing surface, set the radius to 1.75 mm.

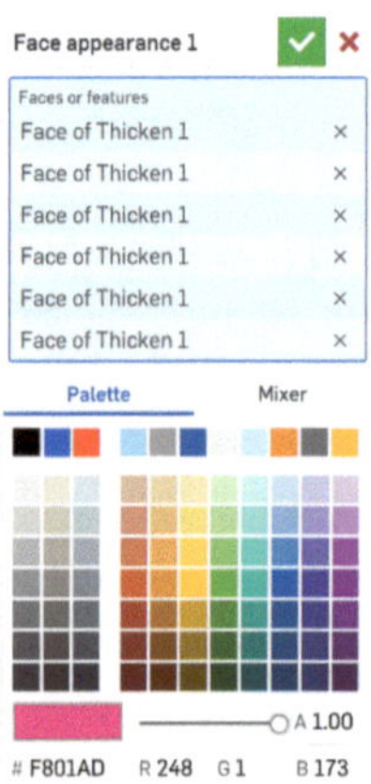

Orbit to the underside of the donut to view the edge faces of the icing that still need to be colored pink.

In the Appearance Panel, double-click the pink color rectangle to open its dialog box, then select those edge faces.

Click the Appearance Panel again to close it.

To remove the black lines click the cube under the View Cube, Shaded with Edges, and change to Shaded without edges.

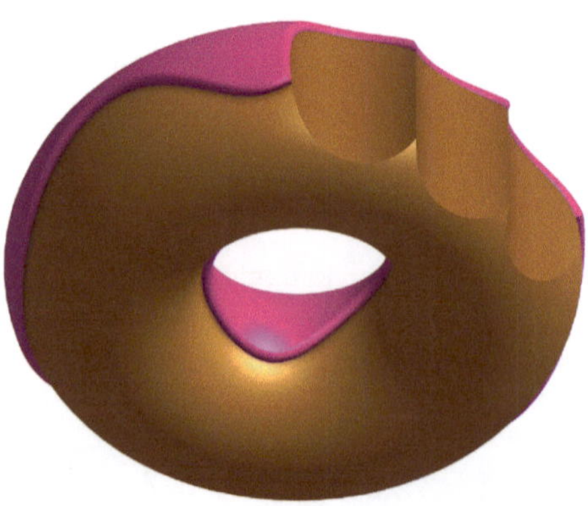

Navigate to the Feature List on the left side of your screen, click the Origin, hold down Shift, select the Right Plane, right click, and select Hide.

Congratulations, you are finished!

Onshape autosaves, so there is no need to search for the save button!

Rendering with AI

Rendering is the process of creating a realistic image based on the 3D objects you have created. When you render, you can apply materials to surfaces, change the lighting, and add background scenes to make the design look like a photograph.

A huge advantage of Onshape is that it works in a browser, but this also limits its rendering capabilities because most browsers aren't optimized for the intense GPU and CPU usage that professional rendering requires.

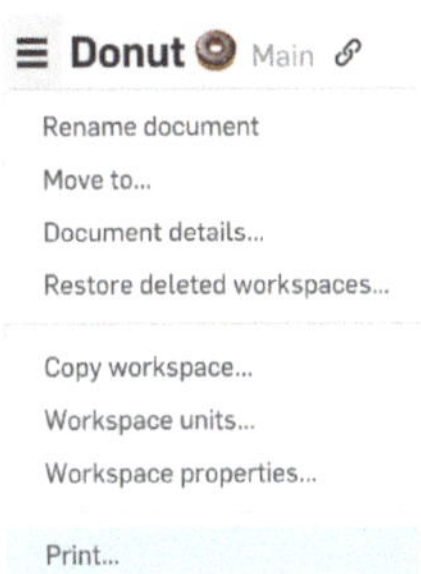

But no fear! New AI tools make this easy.

Click the 3-line menu, and select Print, choose your image size, set the orientation to landscape, adjust the Donuts scale and position on your screen, and click Download (not Print).

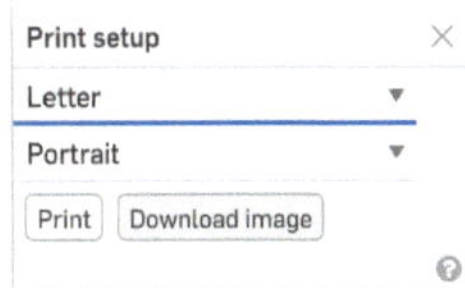

Head to an AI image generator and try some prompts. We love NewArc.ai (not affiliated with CADclass) because it is free for education and balances very creative outputs with very easy to use input tools.

Reinforce & Stretch

Reinforce & Stretch pages are designed to deepen your understanding of CAD tools by encouraging you to explore beyond the main project. It's easy to learn tools in isolation, but true mastery comes from seeing how they affect an entire model. These exercises show how tweaking a single feature can change your project, sometimes in helpful ways, sometimes not, so you can better understand each tool's full impact.

Every Reinforce & Stretch page will offer several things to edit in your model. To preserve your polished project, navigate to the bottom left corner of your screen, right click Part Studio 1, and select Duplicate.

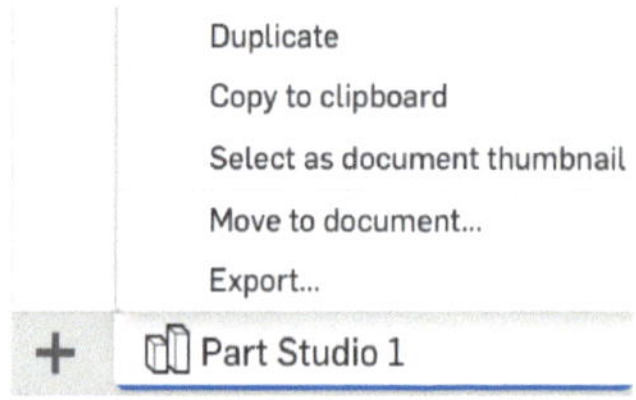

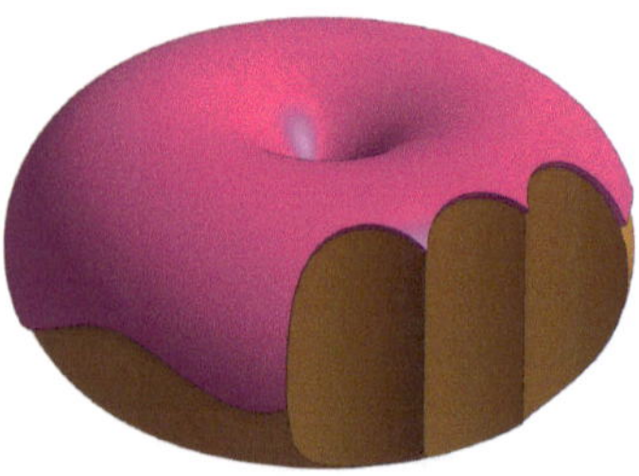

Return to Sketch 1 and edit the dimensions of the circle's diameter and the Origin to circle center distance.

Set the diameter to 60 mm and the Origin to circle center to 35 mm. Confirm the Sketch and see how it changes the final project.

Q? Are you able to rename Features in the Feature List? What would be a better alternative name for Sketch 1?

Try to make the curves on the splines used to Split the Donut more 'extreme.' Hint: you may need to delete the Fix constraint.

Change the appearance of the icing to make a custom flavor like matcha or lemon drizzle.

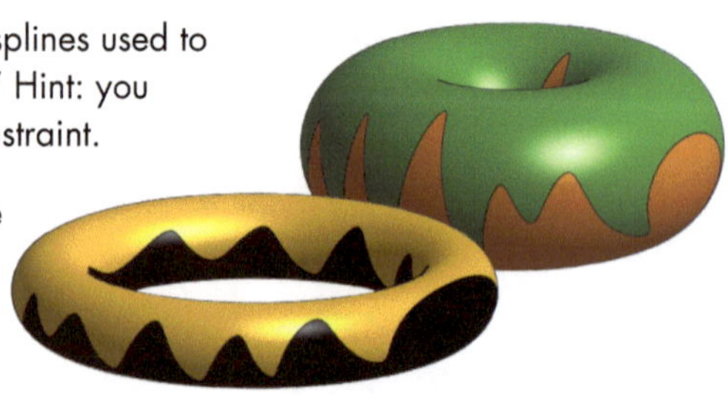

Q? Can you alter the transparency of a part when editing appearances?

Q? Which new terms can you fill out in the Glossary?

Rubric

Criteria	Excellent (4)	Good (3)	Fair (2)	Needs help (1)
UI Navigation	Confidently navigates the UI, utilizing all major tools and features	Can navigate most of the UI and use common tools	Navigates basic UI elements but struggles with some features	Has difficulty navigating the interface
Sketch tools	Can create and edit all required sketch entities	Can create and edit most sketch entities	Can create the minimum sketch entities	Has difficulty creating simple sketch entities
Solid tools	Can create and edit all required 3D donut	Can create and edit most of the 3D donut	Can create the 3D donut	Has difficulty creating the 3D donut
Dimensions and constraints	Can apply and edit a range of dimensions and constraints	Can apply and edit some dimensions and constraints	Can apply limited range of dimensions and constraints	Has difficulty applying any dimensions and/or constraints
Appearances	Can apply and modify a range of appropriate appearances to faces	Can apply a range of appearances to faces	Can apply an appearance to a face	Has difficulty applying an appearance
Problem solving	Can ask insightful questions and solve issues independently and creatively	Asks for help and tries to solve issues	Tries to solve problems but often gets stuck	Is often stuck and cannot get un-stuck

Tool Review: Revolve

Revolve is used to create 3D shapes by rotating a 2D sketch profile around an axis. The profile becomes the cross-section of the 3D object, and the axis determines the direction and extent of the rotation.

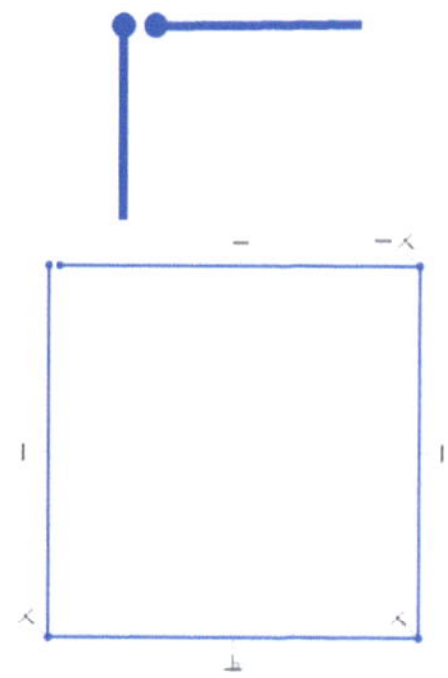

To turn 2D profiles into 3D objects, the profile must be enclosed. Enclosed profiles turn light gray. A common problem is a sketch profile that looks enclosed but isn't.

Shown here is an unenclosed rectangle. Can you spot where it is disconnected? In this case it's the top left corner where there are two blue dots. If the face of the shape has not turned gray, it is not fully enclosed.

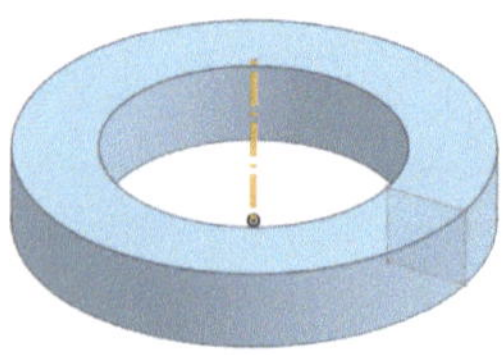

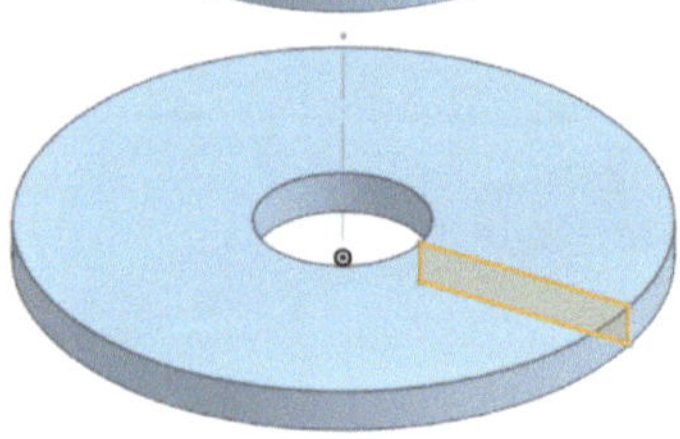

The Axis that you rotate your profile around can be the X, Y, or Z Axis, or another line in your sketch.

You can even revolve about another round object that shares the same Axis you would like your profile to be revolved about. Simply select the inner or outer cylindrical face of the other Part as the Axis.

Not all Revolve features need to cover a full 360 degrees, you can revolve a partial angle to create arcs, segments, or open profiles.

Simply change the Type from Full to One Direction to define a specific angle of rotation.

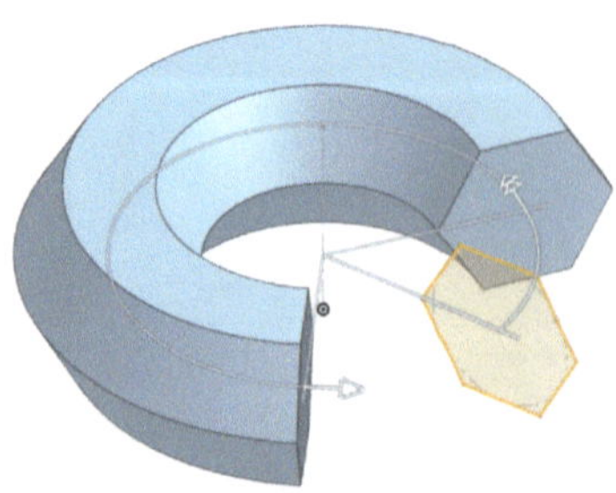

For more complex geometry, you can also select Two Directions to revolve different angles on either side of the profile, or Symmetric to revolve equally in both directions from the original sketch. These options give you greater flexibility when shaping detailed or asymmetrical parts.

Tool Practice: Revolve

Tool Practice Pages aim to test you on specific tools used in the previous project so you can fully understand the uses of each tool.

Because Onshape is a Public Library platform, there are several mini challenges in each file, one in each tab at the bottom of the screen.

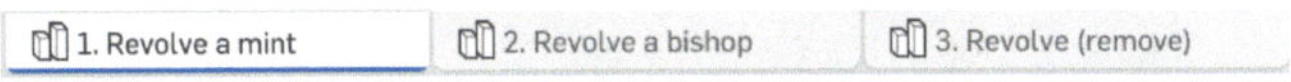

Copy the link into your browser or scan the QR code and make a copy. Work your way along the tabs at the bottom to practice the Revolving tool.

t.ly/fLbD6

...or go to the Public Library, and search for "CADclass revolve" and open the file made by the user ***CADclass***. Select Make a Copy to Edit.

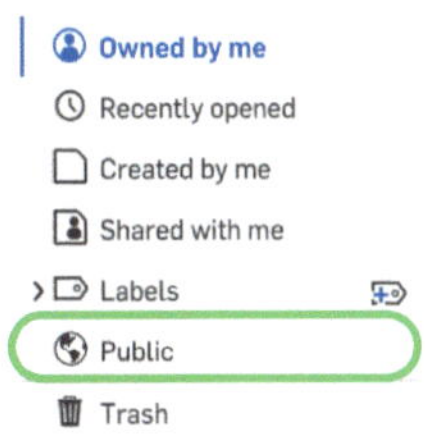

Tool Practice #1:

Create a mint with a hole by revolving a square profile about a vertical Construction line as the axis. This practice is similar to the donut project and allows you to experiment with other tools in the Dialog Box.

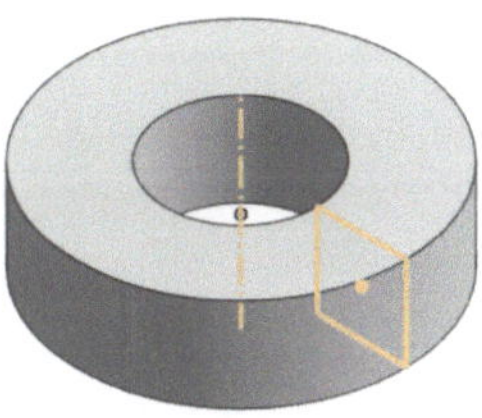

Tool Practice #2:

Create a Bishop for Chess by revolving multiple profiles about an edge on the profile which makes a solid revolved part with no hole or cavity in the middle.

Tool Practice #3:

Create a trophy by creating a cylinder, then revolving a profile about a central axis but setting the style to Remove instead of Add. This is known as subtractive design instead of additive design.

Tool Review: Dimensions

Dimensions are used for 2 main purposes, setting the exact sizes of individual parts and defining the placement and spacing of geometry. While dimensions are essential, there are some potential pitfalls. Applying too many dimensions can lead to sketches that are visually busy and hard to read, but also almost impossible to edit effectively.

To make any dimension you need to click the line or arc, move your cursor away, click again, type the value, and press Enter.

The idea of moving your cursor away from your sketch is to keep all dimensions more organized. Easily readable sketches with clearly organized dimensions are best practice.

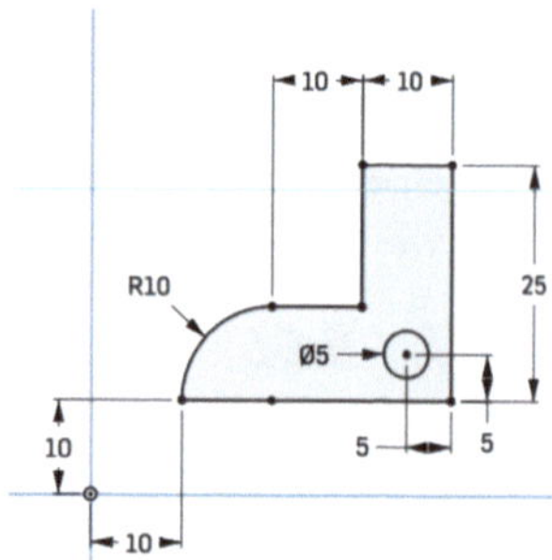

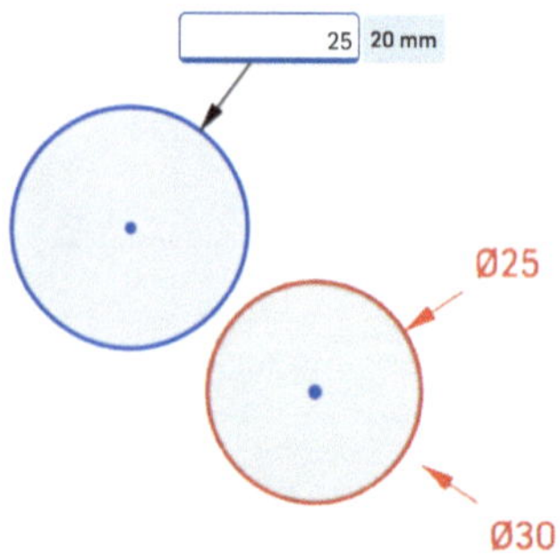

If you need to change the value of a dimension double-click it, type in the correct value, and press Enter. If you need to delete a dimension, click it, and press Delete.

If you add too many or conflicting dimensions you will see the numbers turn RED - this means your sketch is over constrained and you have a problem you need to address.

If you have set your Units to mm, but need to add in a value in inches, or vice verse, you can type "in" or "mm" after your value, and Onshape will make the unit conversion for you, but will display it as the default document units.

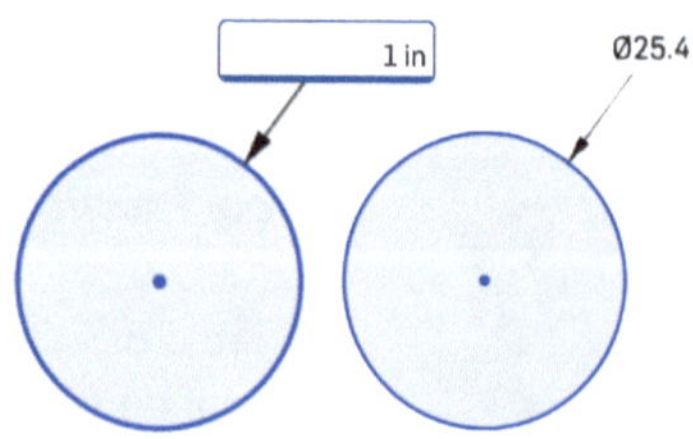

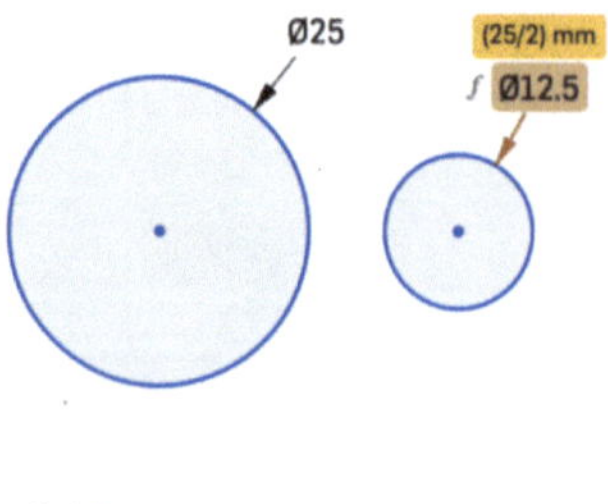

You can add mathematical equations into your dimension. Easy math like doubling or halving the current value by adding *2 or /2 can save you a ton of time.

You can add dimensions "on-the-go" as you are sketching by typing in a number and pressing "Enter" immediately after placing a sketch entity.

Tool Practice: Dimensions

After Sketching comes Dimensioning. This means adding sizes, angles, and distances to all the sketch features. There are several ways to add dimensions.

Most involve using the dimension tool, which you can access by the dimension icon or by using the keyboard shortcut [D].

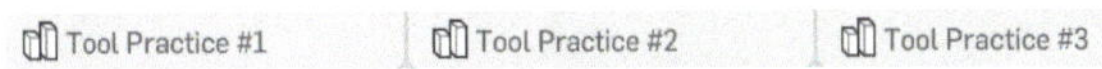

Once the Dimension tool is activated, you can select sketch features to add sizes.

t.ly/X-e2d

Copy the link into your browser, scan the QR code, or search the Public Library for "CADclass dimension". Select Make a Copy to Edit.

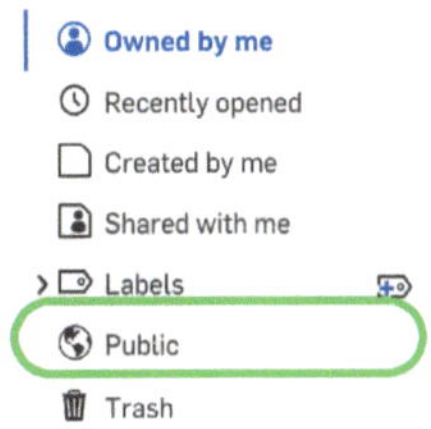

Tool Practice #1:

In the first tab, you will practice the three ways to dimension two points: horizontally, vertically, or between the shortest distance.

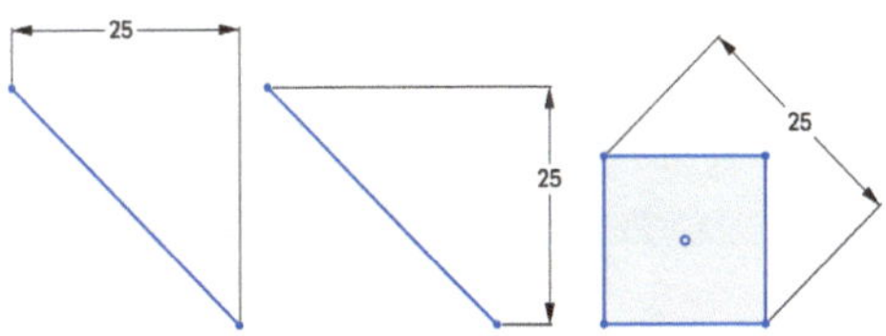

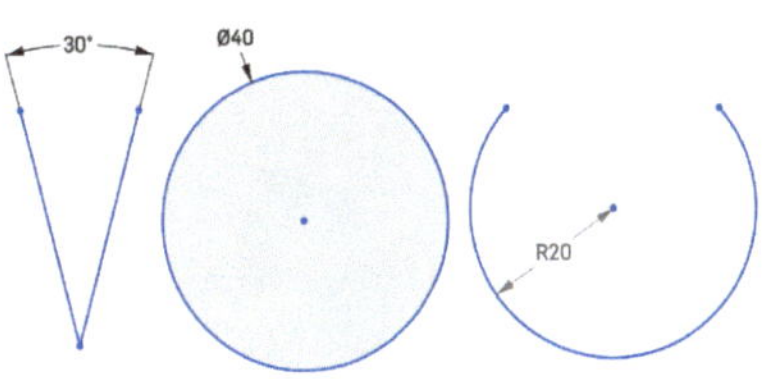

Tool Practice #2:

Here you will dimension other types of Sketch Geometry like angles between lines, circle's diameters, and arc's radii.

Tool Practice #3:

Try to sketch the letter E and add dimensions to it. Try to make all the dimensions as fractions of the height of the profile (e.g. 15/5). Try to over-constrain it, then fix it.

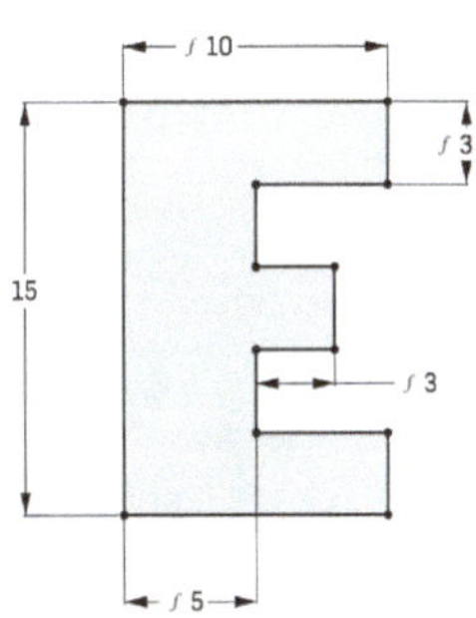

True or False?

Q: You can only Revolve profiles about the X, Y, and Z axes?

Q: Construction Geometry assists in making a sketch such as mirror lines and axis of revolutions?

Q: The Split tool can divide a Part into two Parts?

Q: You finish a Spline by pressing the Esc key?

Q: The first 3D object created is called Part 1?

Solutions

Q: You can only Revolve profiles about the X, Y, and Z axes?

A: False, you can revolve about any lines in a sketch regardless of length or location.

Q: Construction Geometry assists in making a sketch such as mirror lines and axis of revolutions?

A: True. Construction Geometry is technically part of a sketch but is used to help you to make more.

Q: The Split tool can divide a Part into two Parts?

A: True. The Split tool cuts a Part in half, and also divide its Face.

Q: You finish a Spline by pressing the Esc key?

A: True

Q: The first 3D object created is called Part 1?

A: Correct. "Andy" or "Dave" would've been confusing.

Review

Dimension	D
Construction	?
Space	?
?	De-select
?	Shift + E
Line	?
	?
	?

Solutions

Dimension	D
Construction	Q
Space	Clear selection
Escape	De-select
Extrude	Shift + E
Line	L
	Confirm
	Revolve

Challenge

Challenge pages in this book are designed to deepen your understanding of 3D design by guiding you through the process of reverse engineering real-life objects and translating a 2D drawing into a 3D model—one of the most valuable skill sets in CAD.

On the next page, you'll find an engineering drawing: a technical diagram of a part or assembly used by engineers and machinists to manufacture components with precise tolerances. These drawings commonly display multiple views: Front, Right, and Top, each labeled with dimensions and tolerances to ensure parts are built accurately.

The objects you'll recreate in Challenge pages use tools you've just practiced, such as Revolve and Extrude (Remove), to model practical, real-world parts from these technical references.

Your first challenge is to model a famous multicolor Lollipop to go along with your Classic Donut. Once you've finished both projects, reward yourself with some real sweets to celebrate the end of the chapter.

Lollipops are some of the most iconic candies in the world, instantly recognizable by their bold swirl design and playful shape. This project challenges you to recreate its classic form: a spherical candy with a flat ring mounted on a simple cylindrical stick, while focusing on symmetry, curvature, and proportion to bring the shape to life.

This challenge utilizes not only the same tools as the Classic Donut project, but also the same methodology. Before you make this project try to think about the steps first and how each step gets you closer to the final delicious product!

- Make the profile of the Lollipop on the Front Plane
- Add Dimensions and Constraints to fully define it
- Revolve it about a central axis
- Sketch a 5-point Spline that cuts through the candy on the same Front Plane
- Use the Split tool to separate it into two halves.
- Color to the stick white, and the top and bottom face of the candy your ideal Lollipop flavor's colors!

Constraints to Add:

- Coincidently constrain the arc's center to the vertical line
- Make the top and bottom horizontal lines on the candy to be equal
- Fix the Spline before Splitting

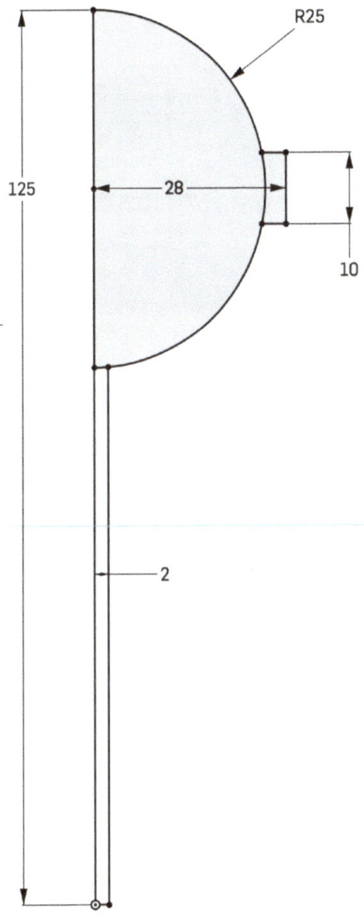

Active Engagement

In this project, your students will explore the process of making a ring that can clip a toy building brick onto it. This project facilitates the repetition of the 2D to 3D workflow (Sketch to Extrude) to create the ring's basic shape and then again by sketching on a face, not a plane as before.

There are many opportunities to add dimensions and constraints to sketches to personalize the design, and also a technical design challenge to ensure the Extruded posts (male) have a tight fit with the plastic holes (female) on the bricks. The 3D design is appropriate to 3D print quickly.

Most students love building bricks, making this lesson relatable and expandable. Play, build, print, and have fun!

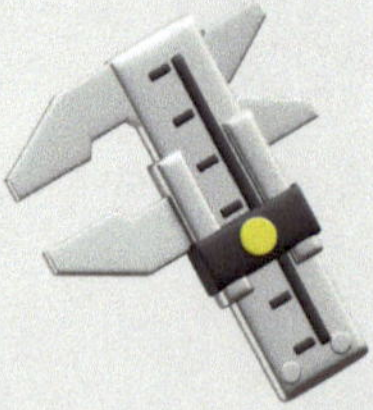

3D print a brick ring before the lesson and then use digital Callipers to take key measurements. You can also have a 3D printer making the ring (if you have one) to build intrigue as students arrive.

How to Use Your Digital Calipers: 7 Tips from Make: **t.ly/YCGwx**

3D printable ring sizer from Printables **t.ly/DVTIB**

Invest in some ring sizers: **t.ly/foI7E** or print your own. This is a great opportunity to discuss anthropometrics and size standardization.

You can also buy some toy bricks for "fit testing" and general adornment.

If you only have a single 3D printer it will be important to verify the design is correct before printing the entire design.

You can use your Slicer software to "cut" the design to isolate key features that you can print quickly to check dimensional accuracy, for example, the ring diameter and the fit of the brick to the posts.

BRICK RING
Onshape Fundamentals Workbook

brick ring.

Project #2
Sketch
Extrude
Sketch
Extrude Cut

Taper Extrude
Fillet
STL Export

where makers are made.

Estimated Time: 1 hr
Onshape Fundamentals
Workbook

Brick Ring

From the Dashboard page, press the blue Create button and select Document. Call it "CADclass Brick Ring" and place it in the CADclass.org folder, then press Create and your document will open.

Click the three horizontal lines (The Document Menu) near the top left corner and select Workspace Units. Verify the Length Default Units are in mm, then press the green checkmark.

Q? Can you add a description of the document in any of the other options in The Documents Menu?

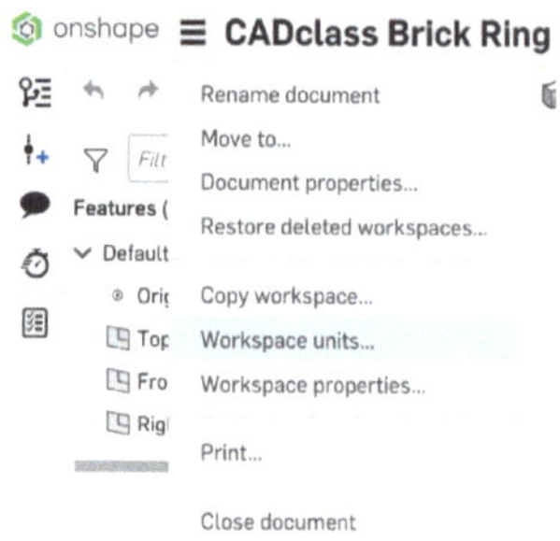

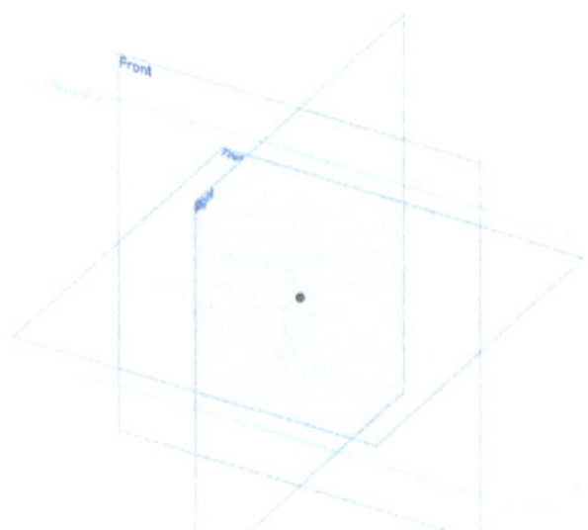

Start a new Sketch by clicking Sketch in the toolbar and selecting the Top Plane. Press [N] to change to a Normal View of the plane.

Verify you selected the correct plane by checking the View Cube reads Top.

Press [C] for the Circle tool, click on the Origin so it turns orange, move your cursor away, and click again to establish the circle.

Since you don't need to make more circles, press Esc to deselect the Circle tool.

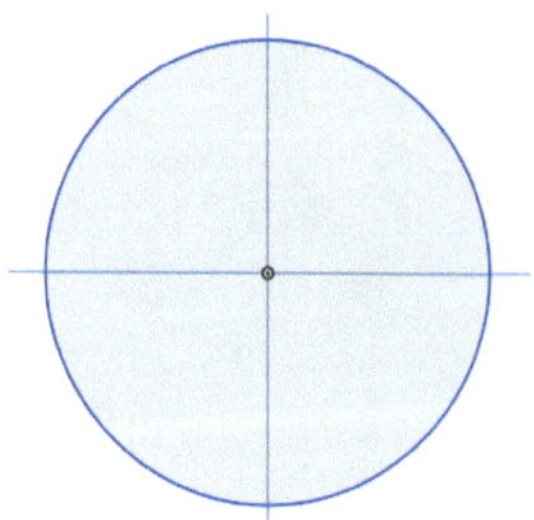

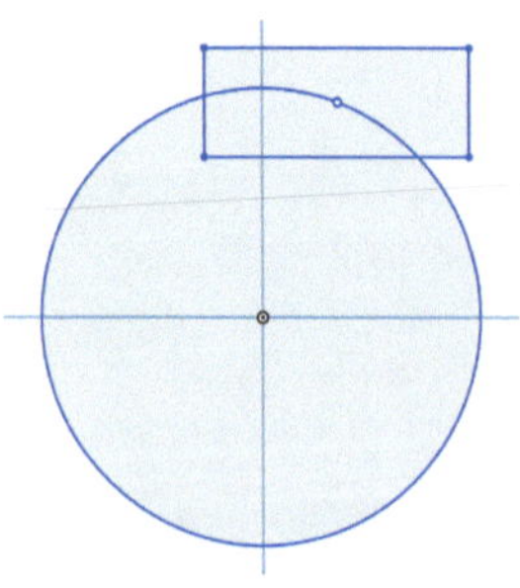

Look along the Sketch toolbar, and use the dropdown arrows to see additional sketch tools.

Open the dropdown for Rectangle.

Select Center Point Rectangle or type [R], move your cursor to the top of the circle till it turns orange, click, move your cursor up and to the right, click again, and press Esc to deselect the Center Point Rectangle tool.

You want the center of the rectangle to be directly above the Origin. This is done with Constraints, a set of tools that limits the movement and scale of 2D geometry so you don't need as many dimensions.

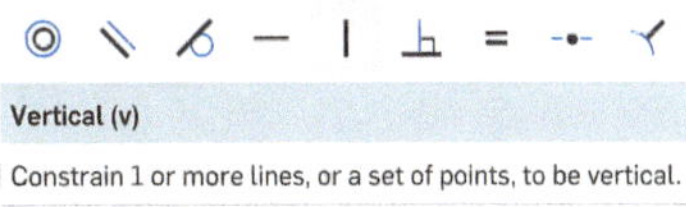

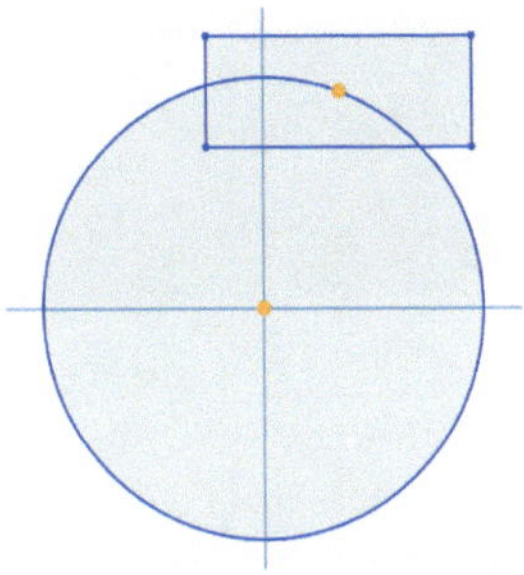

Select the Vertical constraint tool [V]. Click on the circle's center followed by the rectangle's center, or vice versa. Press Esc to deselect this tool.

Q? Click, drag, and move the rectangle's center. What did the constraint do?

....

Select the Coincident constraint tool [i] which moves two sketch entities in the same place. Co = two, Incident = one location, so two elements that share the same location.

Select the rectangle's bottom right point, and the circle's perimeter, and then press Esc to deselect the tool.

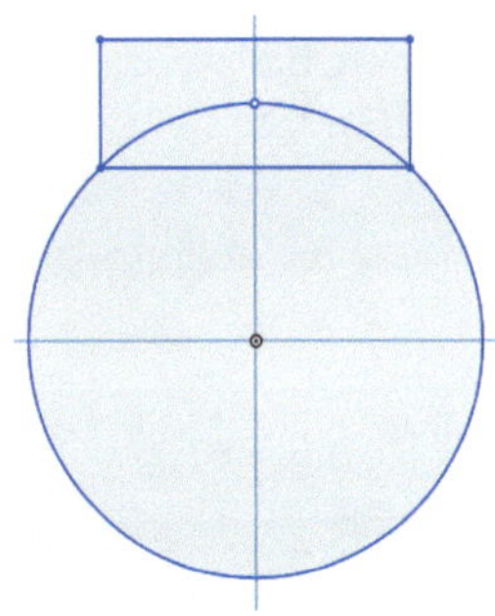

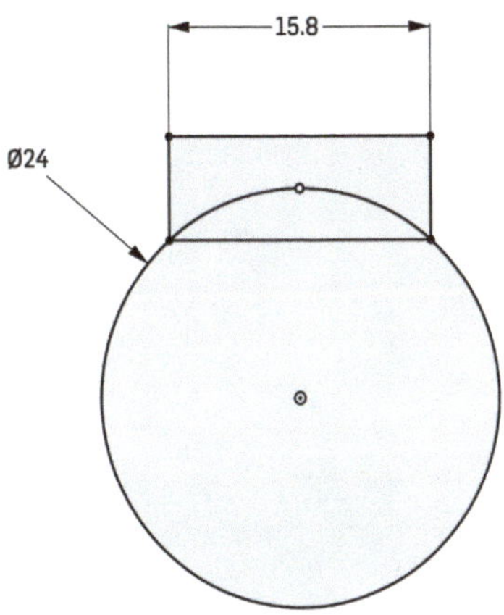

Type [D] to open the Dimension tool, click on the circle's perimeter, move your cursor away, click again, type 24, and press Enter.

Click on the rectangle's top horizontal edge, move your cursor up, click again, type 15.8, and press Enter.

Notice how the circle and rectangle turned black meaning they are fully defined. This indicates the size and location of all sketch elements are known.

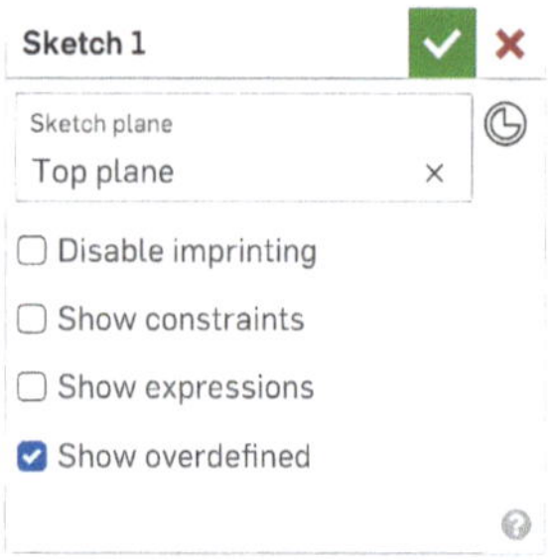

This sketch is complete, so click the green checkmark in the top right corner of the Sketch dialogue box to confirm it. In this book we will denote this step with this icon ✅.

Q? Can you move on to the next step if you don't finish the Sketch?

....

Click the cube under the View Cube and select on the word Isometric or type [Shift + 7] to get a 3D view of your Sketch. This is good practice after finishing every sketch.

To transition from a 2D sketch to a 3D part, select the Extrude tool [Shift + E], select on the 3 profiles that make up your sketch, type 8 mm in the Depth box in the Dialog Box.

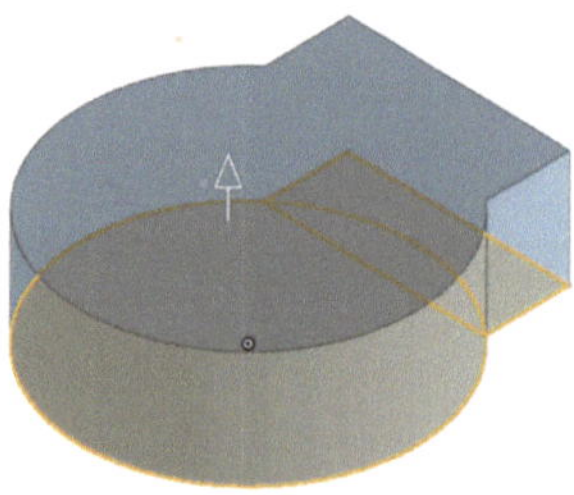

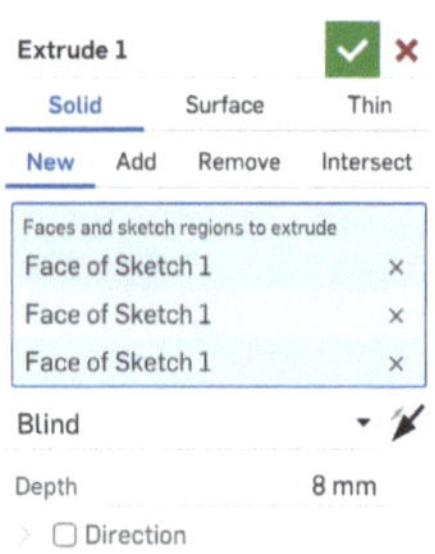

Notice there are other checkbox options in the Extrude Dialogue Box.

Try checking and unchecking some of the boxes and opening some of the pulldown menus to see the other functionalities within the Extrude tool.

Finish this tool by clicking the green checkmark ✅.

In Onshape, you can start sketching 2D geometry on the 3 Origin Planes (Front, Right, and Top) or any flat face.

Select the Sketch tool, and click on the Part's top face (not a default sketch plane). Change to a top-down Normal view [N].

Press [C] for the Circle tool, click on the Origin, move your cursor away, click once to place it then type 20, and press Enter. ✅

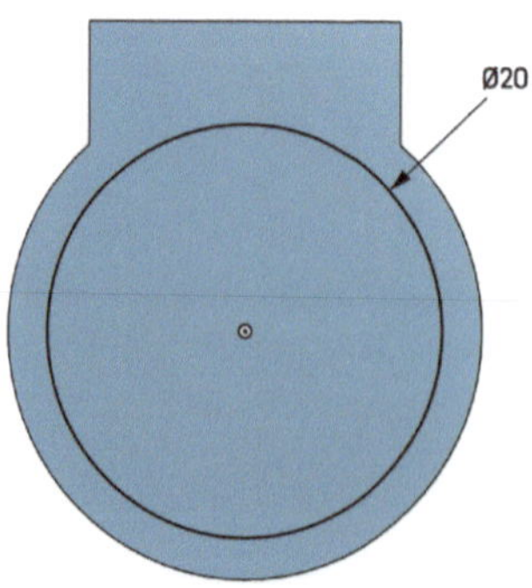

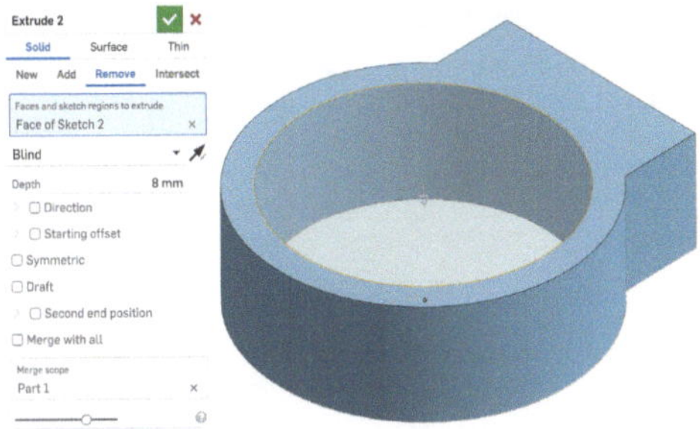

Press [Shift + 7] to get an Isometric view, press [Shift + E] for Extrude, and click the circle's inner area.

Set the Depth to 8 mm and change the Extrude type from Add to Remove to make the ring's hole. Click Confirm Extrude ✅

Q? What other types of Extrude operations are there in the top line of the dialogue box?

....

Click and hold your right mouse button and move your mouse to orbit to the flat back face of the ring. You can also click and drag the View Cube to orbit, but the mouse is a faster operation.

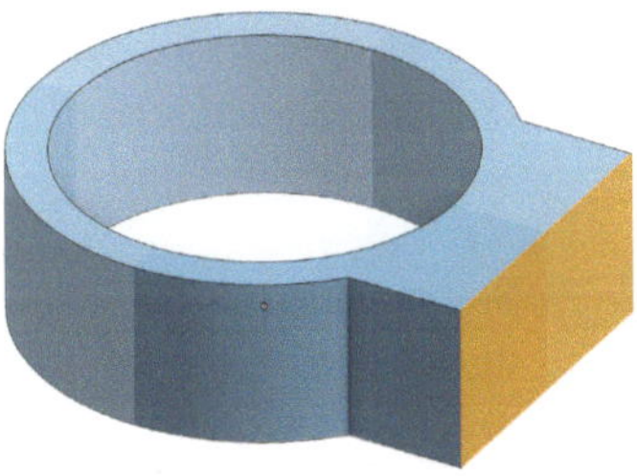

Select the Sketch tool, select the back flat face of the Ring, and press [N].

Verify you selected the correct face by checking that the View Cube reads Back.

Type [C] for the Circle tool, and sketch two circles on the flat face.

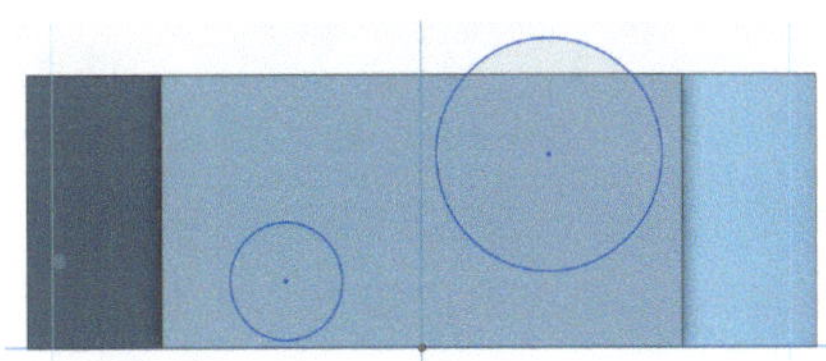

Select the Horizontal constraint tool [H] and click both circle's centers.

Select the Equal constraint tool [E] and click both circles' perimeter to make them the same diameter.

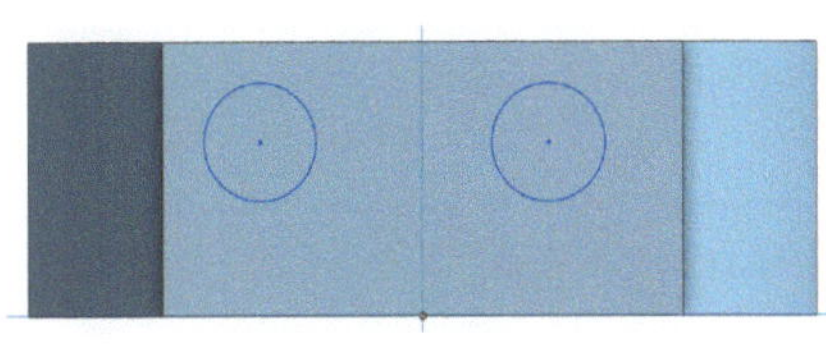

☑ Show constraints

Press Show Constraints in the Sketch Dialogue Box and notice the new constraint icons on the two circles.

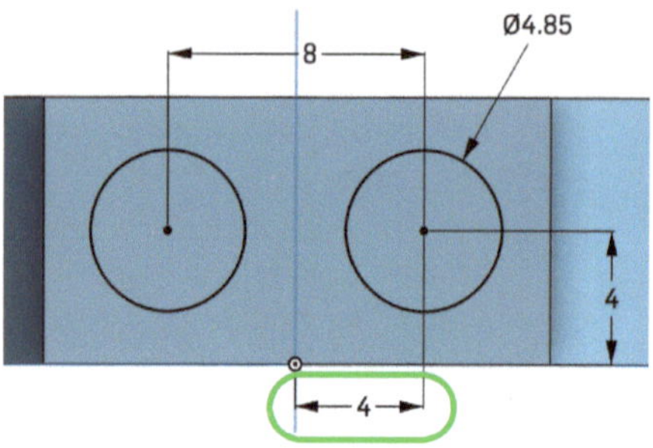

Press [D] for Dimension and add all of the following dimensions. Click Confirm Sketch ✓.

As you're applying the circled dimension, notice what happens as you move your cursor around between two diagonal points.

Navigate to View Cube and select the Top, Back, Right corner for the correct view.

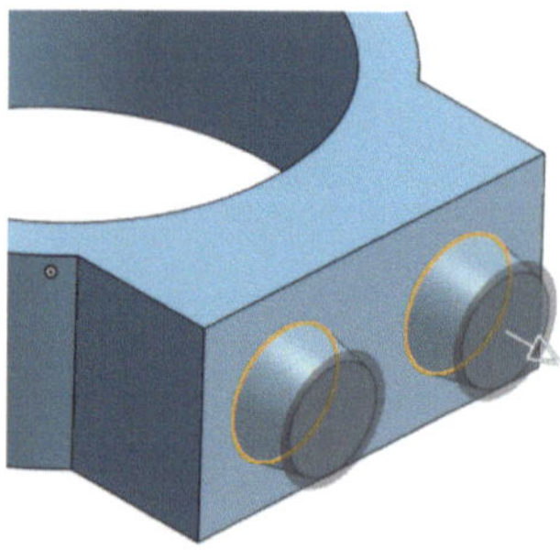

Press [Shift + E] for Extrude, select the 2 circles, set the Depth to 2.25 mm, the Draft to 2 degrees, and then change the direction with this button ↻ then click to confirm Extrude. ✓

This draft angle will allow your plastic mini figure to grab onto the 3d printed Brick Ring.

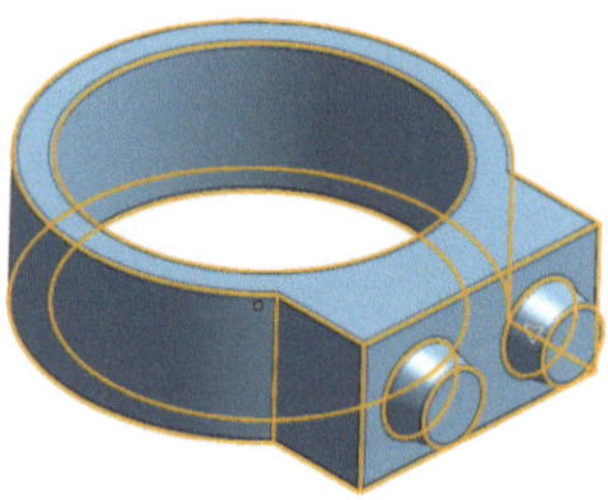

Press [Shift + F] for Fillet, highlight the entire model, set the radius to 0.25 mm.

Q? What happens if you type "0.03 in" into the units box?

....

Fillets (pronounced Fill - et) round over sharp corners in your design by adding a radius.

Click ✓ to Confirm the Fillet.

Right-click on the part and select Edit Appearance for Part 1 near the bottom of the list. Pick a color you like from the Palette or the Mixer and Confirm Appearance ✓.

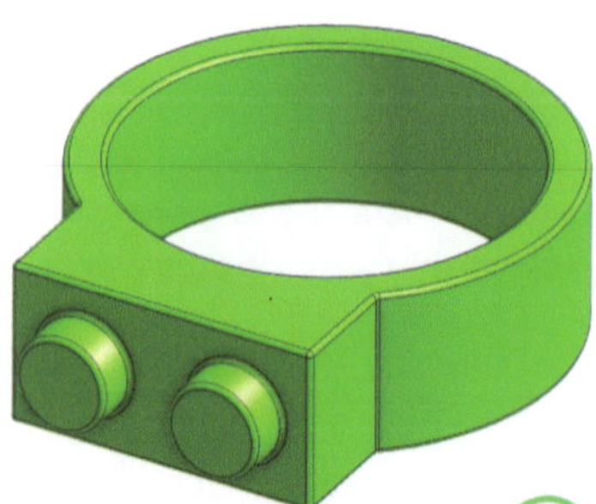

Done! Onshape autosaves so you can return to the dashboard. onshape

3D Printing

3D Printing (a form of Additive Manufacturing) is a process where a three-dimensional object is created by adding layer upon layer of material. This is done using a computer-controlled machine that can print objects from a digital design file.

The most common type is called Fused Filament Fabrication (FFF), where a plastic filament is melted, extruded, and built up 1 layer at a time.

This technology is more commonly called FDM (Fused Deposition Modeling), but that term is trademarked and less technically accurate.

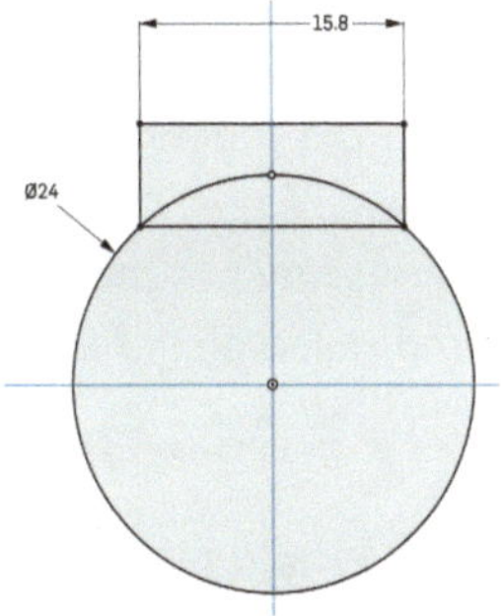

A 2D sketch...

...becomes a 3D design...

...which can be **exported** and then 3D printed!

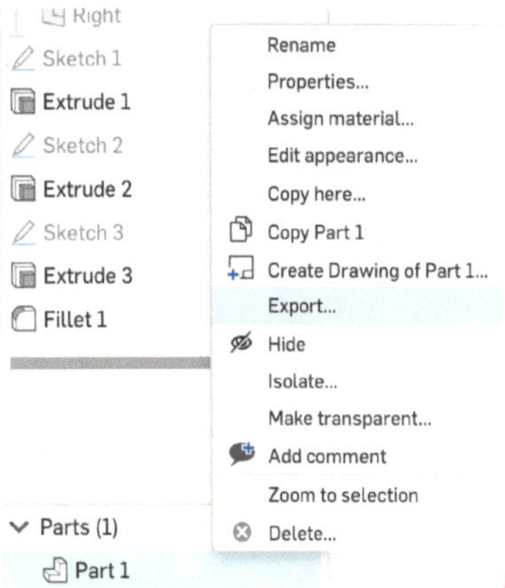

To save your project as a 3D printable STL file, right-click on Part 1 in the Parts List on the left-hand side, Export, set the Format to STL, and press Export.

Import this file into your slicer software of choice (PrusaSlicer, Bambu Studio and Cura are all popular options) and print it without support material.

Slicers turn .STL files into a 3D printer readable format called Gcode.

Q? Can you export to SoildWorks, a very popular CAD program used in professional engineering firms, from the export menu?

Circle the answer: YES NO

Teacher Notes

CAD and CAM unite design and manufacturing, allowing you to translate ideas in your head to ideas on a computer and ideas on the computer to an automated machine that makes real-world stuff.

CAD is the program that aids the Engineer, Architect, or Designer responsible for creating 3D drawings of imagined ideas. Since you're working through this book, that's you and your students!

CAM (Computer-Aided Manufacturing) is a set of instructions that tells the machines what to do based on 2D or 3D objects. In 3D printing, for example, your machine must know how much material to extrude, how fast the hot end moves, how much plastic the inside of your model has, and many other things. Like coding, these machines require precise step-by-step instructions to work. Fortunately, CAM software simplifies most of these instructions, allowing you to focus on the desired outcome instead of how to write each instruction (line of G-code).

You will know if you have ever used Word or Google Docs (a type of CAD) that getting CAM (an inkjet printer) to make it can be problematic. Things can get tricky when you want to use a particular type of paper or change a default setting.

Some 3D printing design guidelines:

- Avoid overhangs and wide bridges.
- Don't make the walls too thin.
- Maximize the flat area on the print-bed - reorient if necessary.
- Add fillets and chamfers to sharp edges if you can.
- Avoid sharp and narrow points.

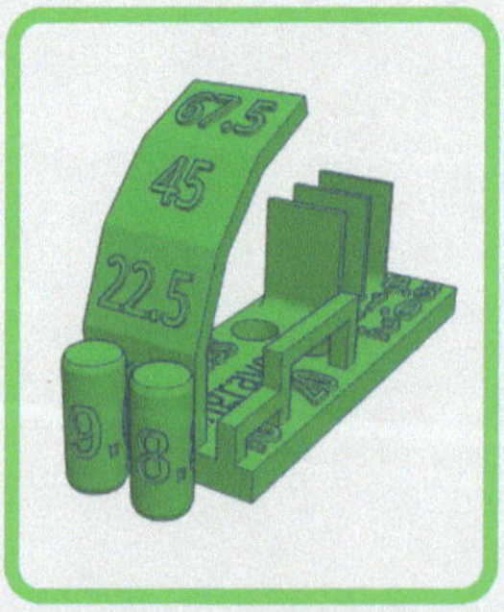

Get to know your printer - find out what it can and cannot do using a design like "FFF Print Rules Block" by Sam Booth **t.ly/Yv3XU**

Teacher Notes

3D printing, like paper printing, is seemingly simple. However, there are many steps to get your machine set up properly and many things that can go wrong! Here's a basic 3D printing workflow overview:

You can do many things when designing to give yourself the best chance of success. Here are some useful links:

From our friends at Printlab:
Designing for 3D Printing
t.ly/R-MYe

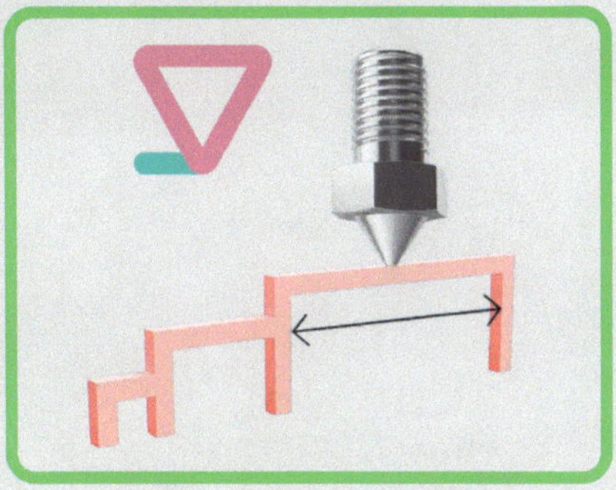

PrusaSlicer: Slice with style!
The Beginner's Guide
t.ly/haZ7v

Bambu Studio: Setup to
success 3D printing guide
t.ly/kzEkA

Reinforce & Stretch

Reinforce & Stretch pages help you explore how each CAD tool affects your whole model.

To preserve your polished project, navigate to the bottom left corner of your screen, right click Part Studio 1, and select Duplicate.

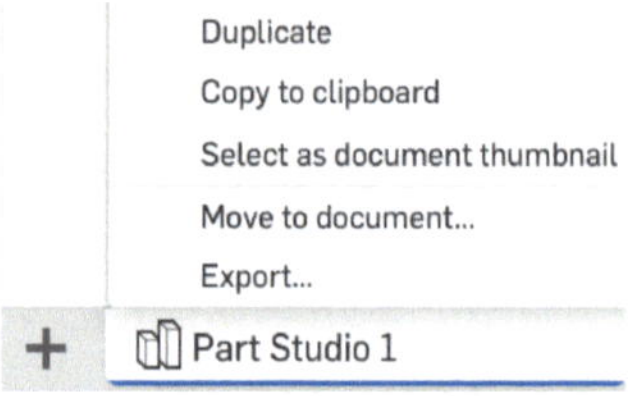

Return to Sketch 1 and edit the outer diameter to 35 mm.

Edit the circle in the second sketch so the wall thickness of the ring matches the Brick Ring project's wall thickness. You might need to use the Measure tool to find some values.

Q? What happens if the circle in the second Sketch is a Construction circle?

....

The Brick Ring project had just two tapered pips to hold onto a plastic miniature figure, but others require a 2 x 4 grid.

Create a larger platform for the 8 pips that share the same spacing as the Brick Ring project.

Color the Brick Ring so it matches a figure that would fit on it.

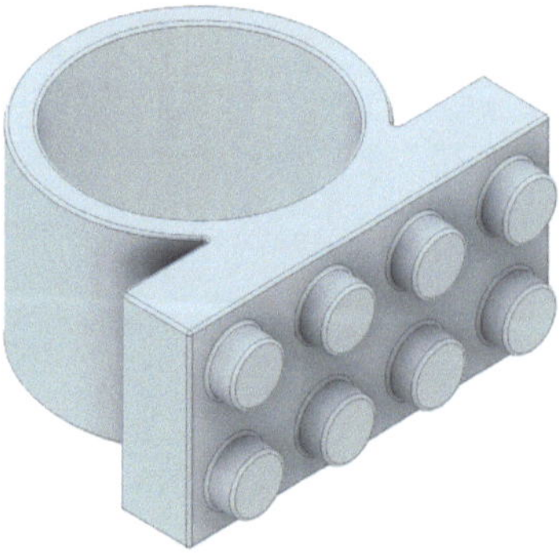

Q? What happens if the Draft is not changed to Opposite Direction?

....

Q? Which new terms can you fill out in the glossary in the back of the book?

Rubric

Criteria	Excellent (4)	Good (3)	Fair (2)	Needs help (1)
UI Navigation	Navigate the UI, utilizing all major tools and features	Navigate most of the UI and use common tools	Navigate basic UI elements but struggle with some features	Has difficulty navigating the interface
Sketch Tools	Create sketches on faces and planes	Sketch on faces and planes but sometimes has trouble	Only sketch on faces or planes	Has difficulty sketching on faces and planes
Solid Tools	Create and edit all ring Extrusions	Create and edit most ring Extrusions	Create and edit some of the ring Extrusions	Has difficulty creating and editing the ring Extrusions
Dimensions and Constraints	Apply and edit a range of dimensions and constraints	Apply and edit some dimensions and constraints	Apply a limited range of dimensions and constraints	Has difficulty applying any dimensions and/or constraints
3D Printing	Export a 3D printable .STL file	Export a 3D printable .STL file with some difficulty	Export a 3D printable .STL file with some help	Is unable to export a 3D printable file
Process	Explain how to create the ring using the technical CAD terms above	Mostly explain how to create the ring	Explain how to create parts of the ring	Has difficulty explaining how to create the ring

Tool Review: Extrude

Extrude creates 3D objects from enclosed 2D Sketch profiles. It works by extending a 2D shape and adding (or removing) depth. You can specify the direction and exact depth of the Extrusion, or use other parameters like "Up to face"

When you start to Extrude a profile, notice the arrow. This is a way to Extrude without needing to add strict dimensions.

This type of CADing' is more freeform and is often used when the final design isn't completed.

The Draft checkbox in the dialogue box allows you to set a draft angle, like in the picture.

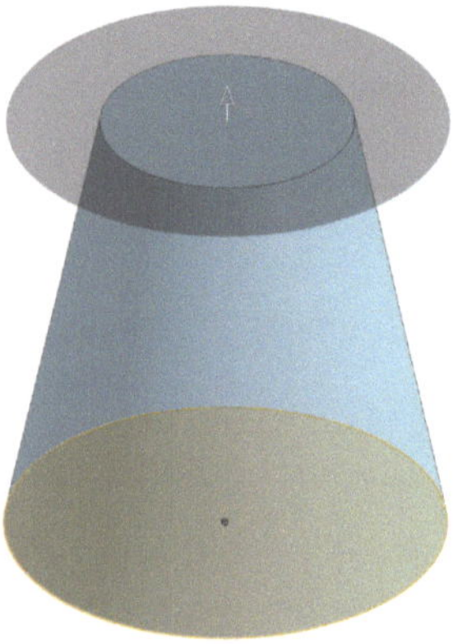

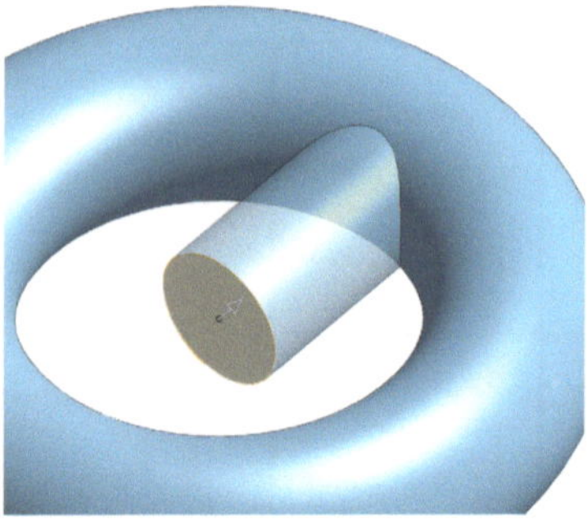

You can set the starting and ending point of your extrusion using Starting Offset and Second End Position in the Extrude dialog box.

You can also cut through an entire model with Blind with a value greater than the depth of the model, or stop when it hits another part of the design using Up to Next as seen in the figure.

When extruding one profile into another, you can set what the overlapping volume will do.

New will create a new volume inside the existing volume, Add will join new material to the existing part, Remove will remove the Extruded volume from the existing one, and Intersect will only keep the overlapping volume.

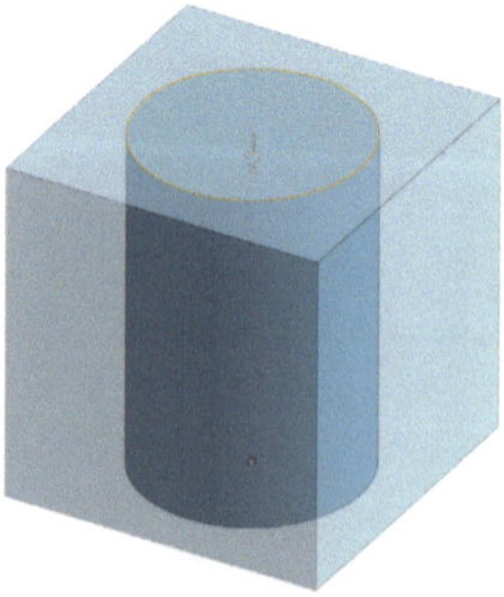

Finally, at the top of the Dialogue Box, you can set the extrusion as Solid, Surface, or Thin. Solid produces a solid part, Surface extrudes just a profile with no thickness, and thin adds a thickness to a profile like a tube.

Tool Practice: Extrude

Because Onshape is a Public Library platform, there are several mini challenges in each file, one in each tab at the bottom of the screen.

Copy the link into your browser or scan the QR code and make a copy. Work your way along the tabs at the bottom to practice the Extrude tool.

t.ly/8ylzG

...or go to the Public Library, and search for "CADclass Extrude" and open the file made by the user *CADclass*. Select Make a Copy to Edit.

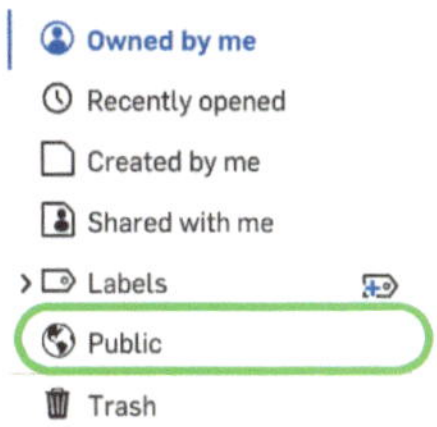

Tool Practice #1 & 2

Extrude a profile from a Blind Distance, and Extrude a profile symmetrically to the same distance.

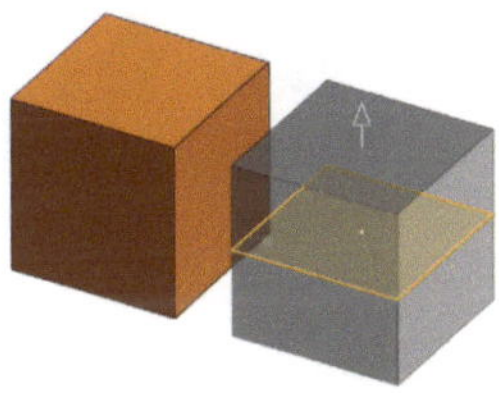

Tool Practice #3

Extrude Remove a series of profiles from a Part on different faces.

Tool Practice #4

Extrude a profile upwards with an inward draft angle of 25 degrees.

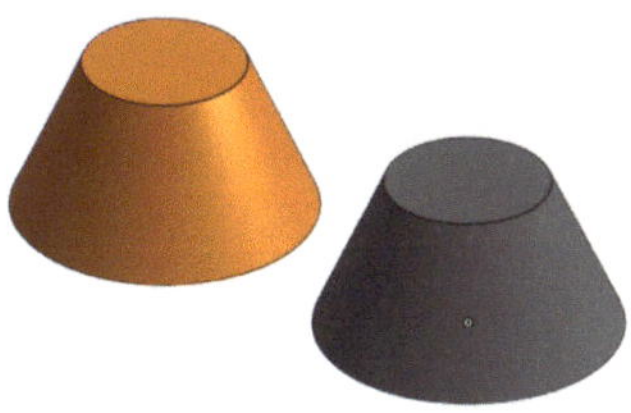

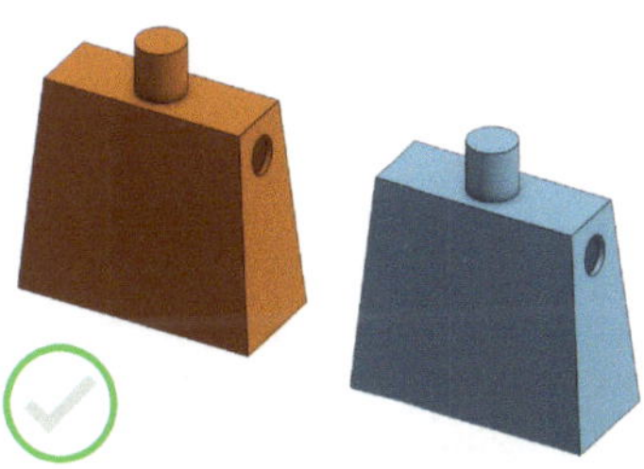

Tool Practice #5

Extrude Remove and Add a series of mirrored profiles from a Part.

Tool Review: Fillet

Fillets create rounded transitions between edges on 3D objects, adding a radius to sharp corners, enhancing aesthetics and functionality. You can specify the radius or use options like "Conic" or "Variable Fillet."

You can apply Fillets, pronounced Fill-et, not Fill-ey, to edges, faces or entire bodies.

If you design a cylinder and want rounded edges, you can select both edges, or the cylindrical face.

Model a 25 mm cube, type [Shift + F] for Fillet, click any edge, type 4 and this will add a 4 mm Fillet to that edge. What if you want more? Simply click on more edges to fillet more.

Want a larger Fillet? Click and drag the arrow away.

Standard Fillets apply a constant radius to an edge, but you can also apply a Variable Fillet, which changes in radius along the length of an edge.

Open the Fillet tool, select an edge, check Variable Fillet, click the black dots at the end of the edges to add the Start and End radii, and set the Fillet values.

Want your fillet to stop suddenly? Check Partial Fillet and adjust where the Fillet ends.

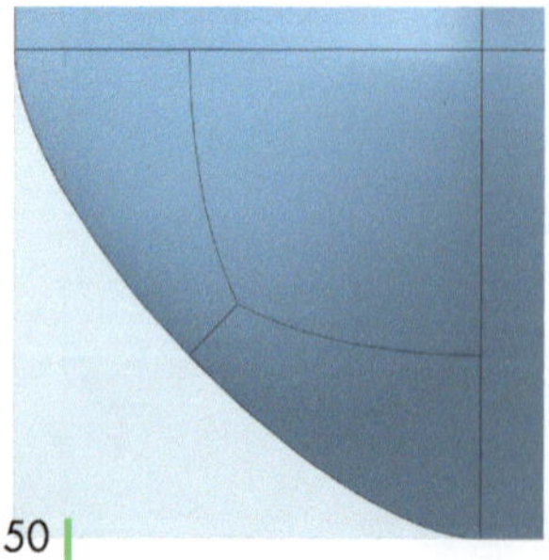

As a default, the Fillet tool will apply a perfect radius to any edges, but what if you want a conical fillet that has a more mathematical curve?

Well that is doable in Onshape, simply change the Control to Conic, and adjust the Rho to a value between 0.1 and 1.0 to get an adjustable filleted edge.

Tool Practice: Fillet

Try the mini challenges below to test your skills and improve your understand of the Fillet tool.

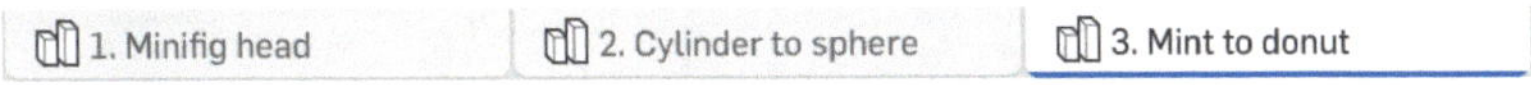

Copy the link into your browser or scan the QR code and make a copy. Work your way along the tabs at the bottom to practice the Fillet tool.

t.ly/4oxW7

...or go to the Public Library, and search for "CADclass Fillet" and open the file made by the user ***CADclass***.

Select Make a Copy to Edit.

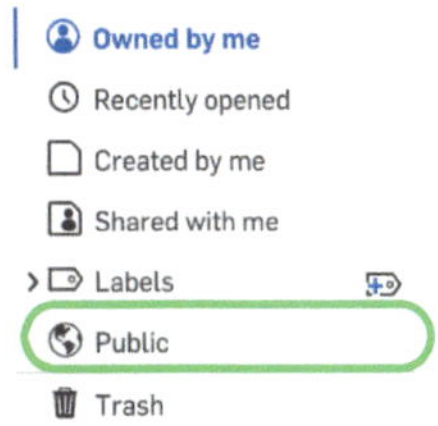

Tool Practice #1

Add a series of internal and external Fillets to the Part of different sizes to make a miniature figure head shape.

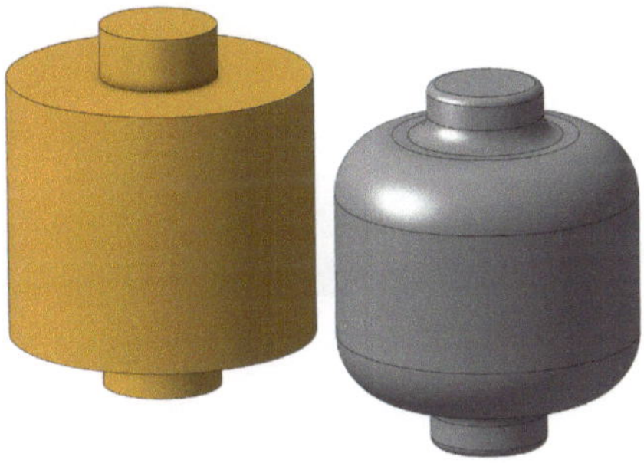

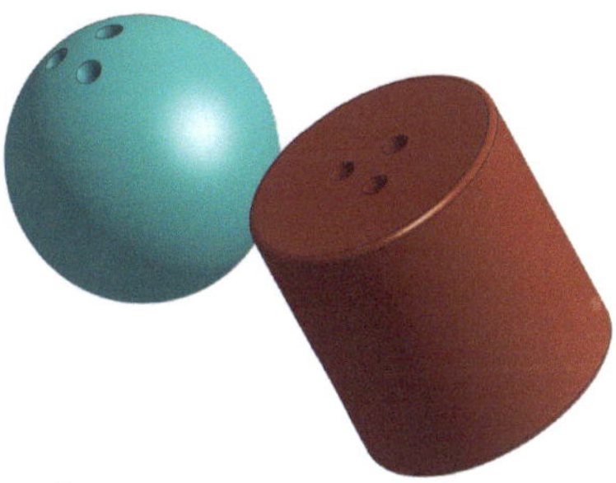

Tool Practice #2

Increase the size of the Fillets of the red cylinder until it forms a sphere and turns into a bowling bowl.

Tool Practice #3

Apply Fillets to the annular disk until it forms a torus (the mathematical name for a donut).

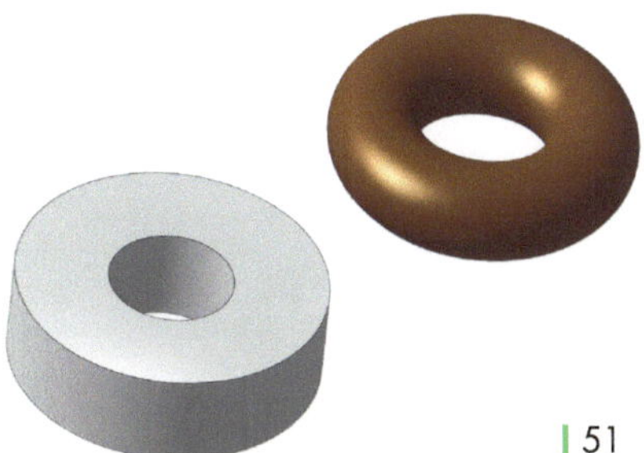

True or False?

Q: An undefined Sketch has all BLACK lines?

Q: You can click on parts of the View Cube to change the view?

Q: A fillet applies a 45 degree angle to an edge?

Q: The icon to Confirm a Feature (e.g. a Sketch) is a Red House?

Q: Draft angles can only go in one direction?

Solutions

Q: An undefined Sketch has all BLACK lines?

A: Undefined Sketch features are **BLUE** lines. **BLACK** lines are fully defined.

Q: You can click on parts of the View Cube to change the view?

A: True.

Q: A fillet applies a 45 degree angle to an edge?

A: False. A fillet applies a radius to and edge. A chamfer applies an angle.

Q: The icon to Confirm a Feature (e.g. a Sketch) is a Red House?

A: No. It's a green checkbox like this ✅

Q: Draft angles can only go in one direction?

A: False. The direction can be reversed.

Review

Dimension	D
onshape	?
✓	?
?	De-select
?	Circle
Extrude	?
	?
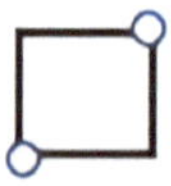	?

Solutions

Dimension	D
onshape	Back to the Dashboard
	Confirm
Esc key	De-select
C	Circle
Extrude	Shift + E
	Sketch
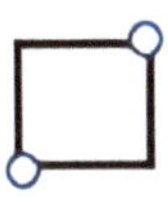	Corner Rectangle

Challenge

Your next challenge is turning a 2D Drawing into a 3D Model to design your own custom keycap! As mechanical keyboards have surged in popularity featuring custom switches, braided cables, and color-matched keys, making custom keycaps is a slowly rising addition to this hobby.

Using the tools you learned in the Brick Ring project: Extrude Add, Extrude Remove, and Extrude with Draft Angle, you'll model a keycap with: four drafted side faces, a circular cutout on top for a finger press, and a cross-shaped cutout on the bottom to mount to a keyboard switch. This mini project challenges you to combine design intent, form, and function, just like in real-world CAD work.

Some CAD power users work so efficiently that they've built their own custom mini-keyboards, called macro-pads.

These devices are programmed to activate specific tools at the press of a key, saving time by eliminating the need to hunt through menus. Check out this awesome example by u/luisdaed, who designed an entire macro-pad that can be fully 3D printed!

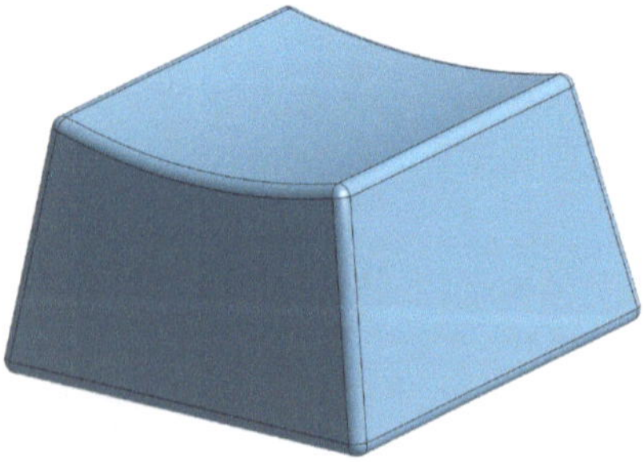

As you will soon find out, in CAD, there are always many ways to make a part. Below is a rough set of instructions to help you make this part.

Once successful, we recommend trying to find other ways to make this custom keycap.

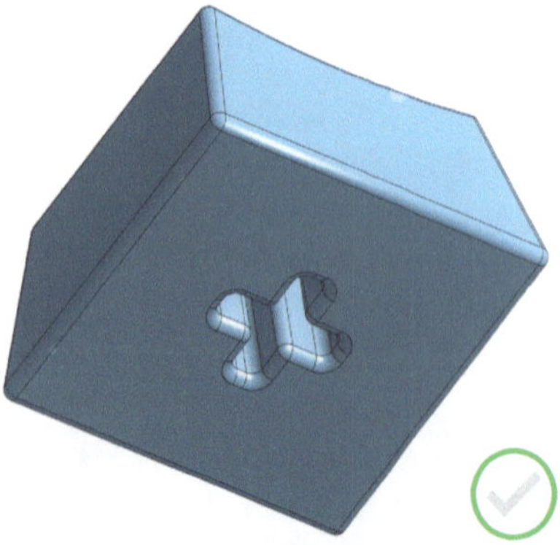

- Sketch a Center Point Rectangle on the Top Plane
- Extrude upwards with a Draft
- Sketch a large circle on the Front Plane that touches the top two corners
- Symmetrically Extrude Remove
- Sketch the cross and Extrude Remove
- Add a 0.5 mm Fillet to the entire Part

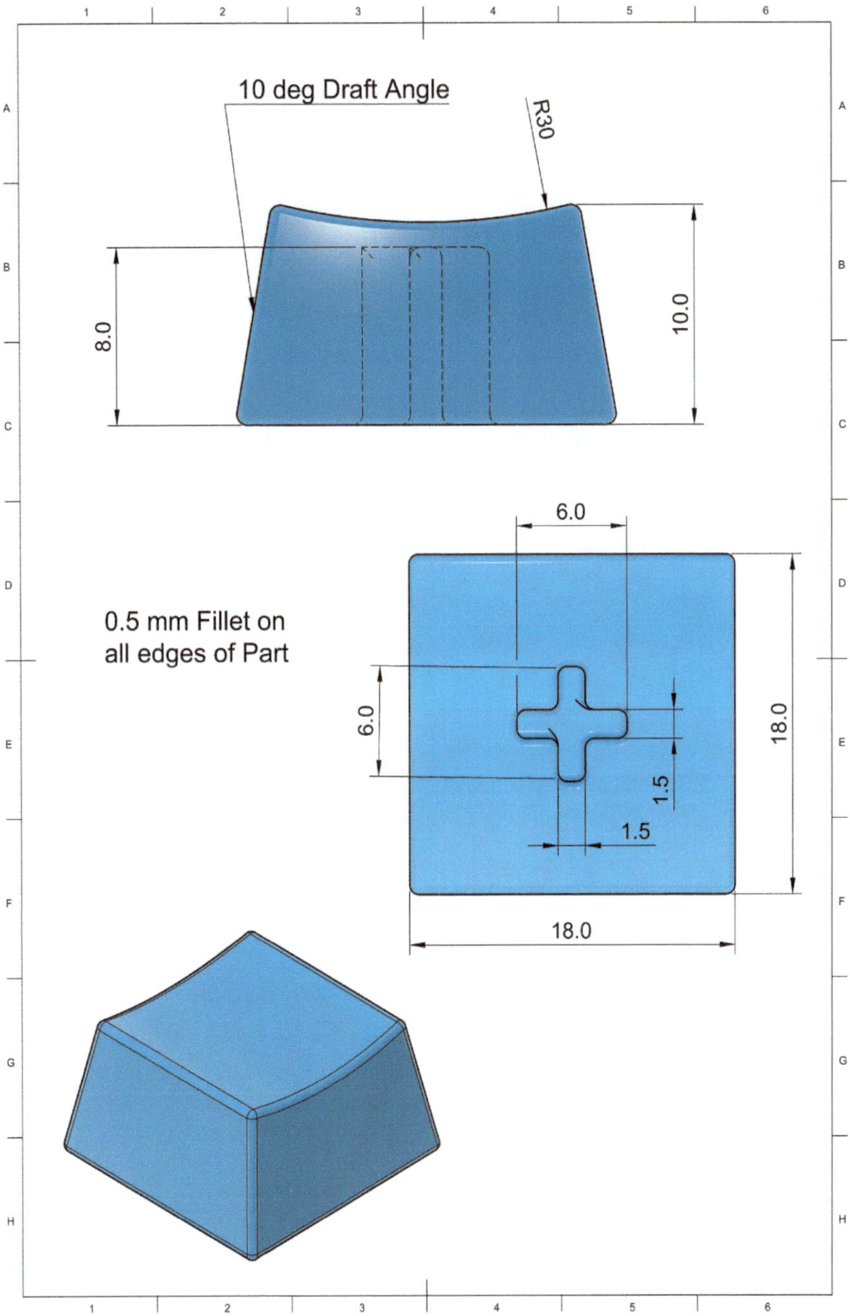
10 deg Draft Angle
R30
8.0
10.0
6.0
0.5 mm Fillet on
all edges of Part
6.0
18.0
1.5
1.5
18.0

Active Engagement

The chapter uses highly engaging and relatable subject matter that connects with students' daily digital experiences while teaching fundamental CAD skills.

The progression from simple shapes to a recognizable character makes learning accessible and rewarding.

The methodology follows a clear "scaffold and release" approach. It begins with guided instruction through specific steps and gradually moves toward independent practice and creative exploration. The workbook's principle of "CAD Vomit" (sketch first, constrain later) teaches students a practical workflow while reducing their initial cognitive load, allowing them to focus on creativity before technical precision.

Here are some practical ways instructors could enhance this activity:

Start with a physical warm-up exercise where students draw emojis on paper and identify basic geometric shapes within them. This helps students understand how complex designs can be broken down into simple components before moving to CAD.

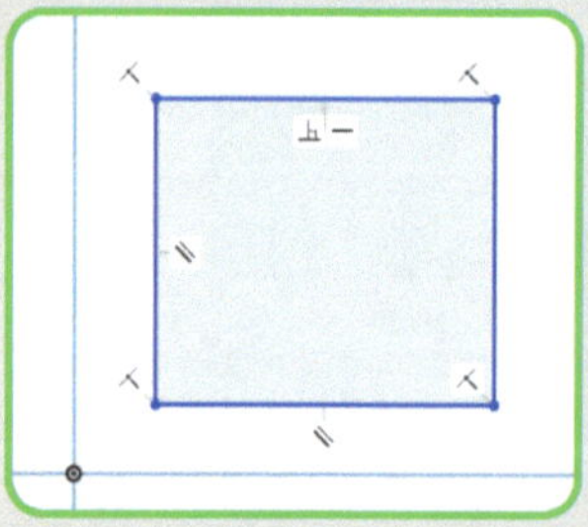

Create a "constraint scavenger hunt" where students work in pairs - one student creates a simple sketch, and their partner identifies and labels all the constraints used. This reinforces understanding of different constraint types in an interactive way.

Extend the learning by challenging students to 2D emoji variations using Emoji Kitchen **emojikitchen.dev** which requires them to manipulate existing constraints and dimensions.

Emoji Kitchen
emojikitchen.dev

This reinforces the value of parametric design while keeping engagement high.

EMOJI FACE
Onshape Fundamentals Workbook

emoji face.

Project #3
New Sketch
Coincident
Tangent
Midpoint

Horizontal
Mirror
DXF Export

where makers are made.

Estimated Time: 1 hr
Onshape Fundamentals
Workbook

Emoji Face

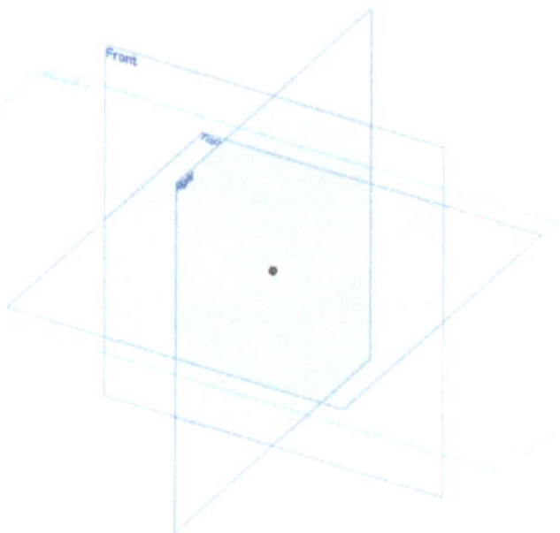

From the Dashboard page, Create a new Document called "CADclass Emoji Face" and place it in the CADclass.org folder.

Start a Sketch on the Top Plane and get a top-down view.

Expand the Sketch tools with the down arrows and notice the different tools that are available when sketching.

The most commonly used tools are towards the left of the toolbar (Line, Rectangle, Circle, etc) and many have their own shortcut key (e.g. [C] for the Circle tool) to the right of the tool.

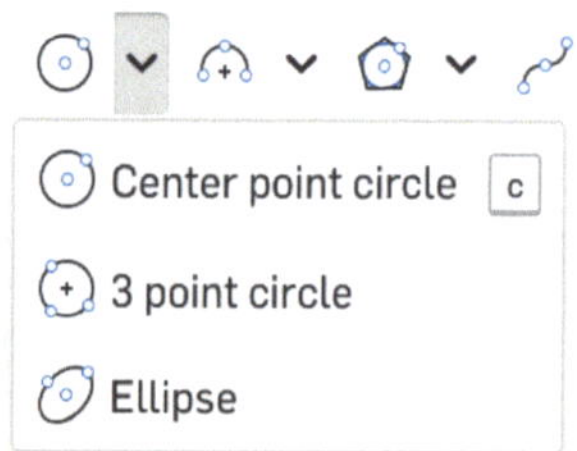

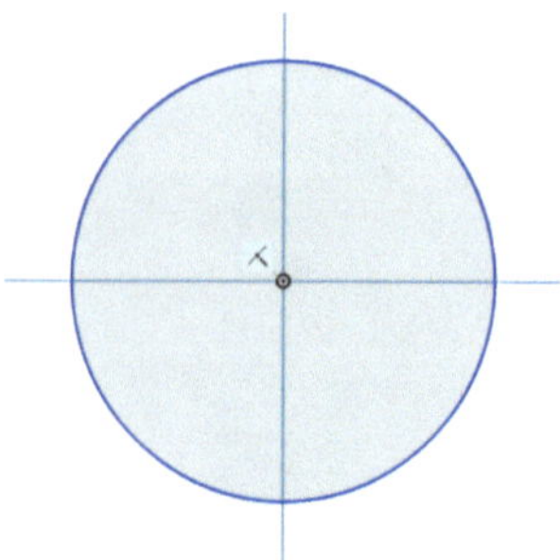

Select the Circle tool, click on the Origin, move your cursor away to make a lager circle that fills up your screen.

When you start a circle at the Origin, its location is Defined but its size/diameter is unknown, meaning the entire circle is still Undefined.

In this project, you will keep your sketch elements undefined and blue so they can be manually moved to change the shape and expression of the Emoji.

Q? What is the shortcut key for a Line?

Write it here [ ]

Q? What is the shortcut key for a Corner Rectangle?

Write it here [ ]

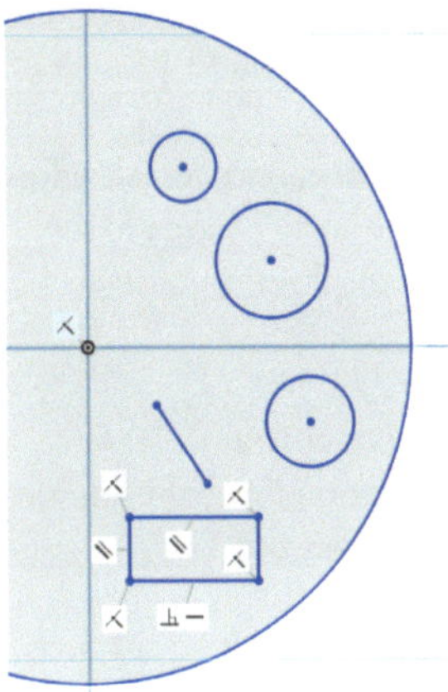

When sketching, it is a good principle to add your geometries first and fast, then add constraints, and lastly dimensions.

Inside the larger circle, draw 3 more circles, a corner rectangle, and an angled line.

Select the Concentric constraint tool and click on the top 2 circle's perimeters to place one inside the other to make the Emoji's eye. Co meaning two and Centric meaning center, this tool makes round geometries share the same center.

Select the Vertical constraint tool and click on the angled line.

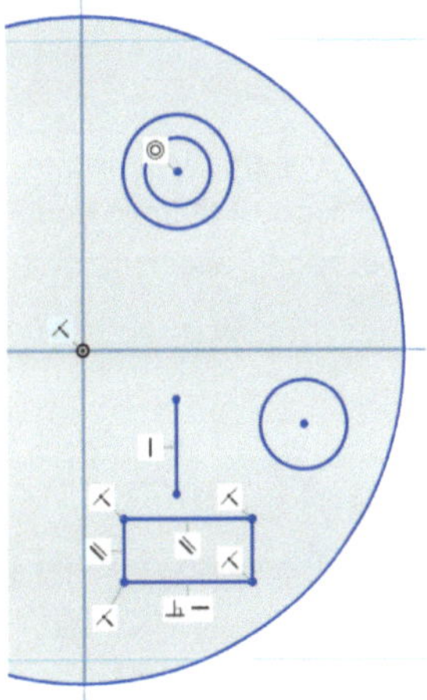

Q? What does the keyboard shortcut Ctrl + Z / Command + Z do?

....

Select the Coincident constraint tool and click the rectangles left vertical edge and the Origin. Co meaning two and incident meaning one location, this tool sets two geometries to the same location. In this example, if you extend the line it would intersect the Origin.

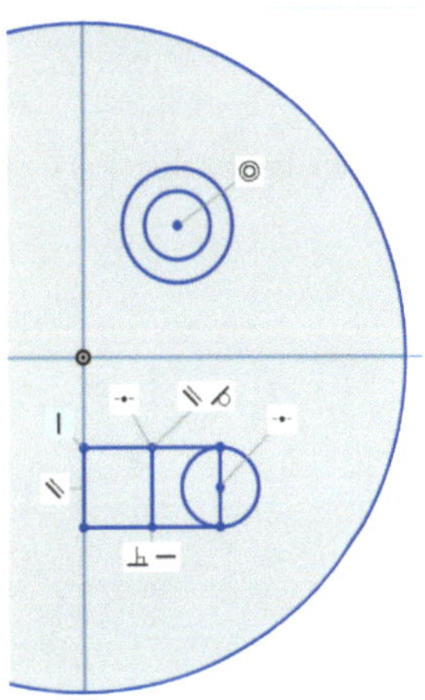

Select the Midpoint Constraint, click the line's bottom endpoint, and click the rectangle's bottom edge.

Click the line's top endpoint and click the rectangle's top edge.

Click the bottom circle's center and the rectangle's right edge.

Select the Tangent constraint, click the bottom circle, then click the rectangle's top or bottom edge.

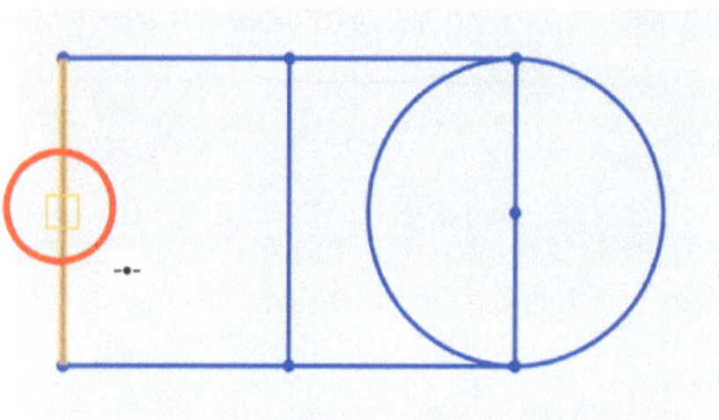

To make the horizontal line down the middle of the teeth type [L] for Line.

Move your cursor along the left edge of the rectangle until it snaps to the midpoint and displays an orange square .

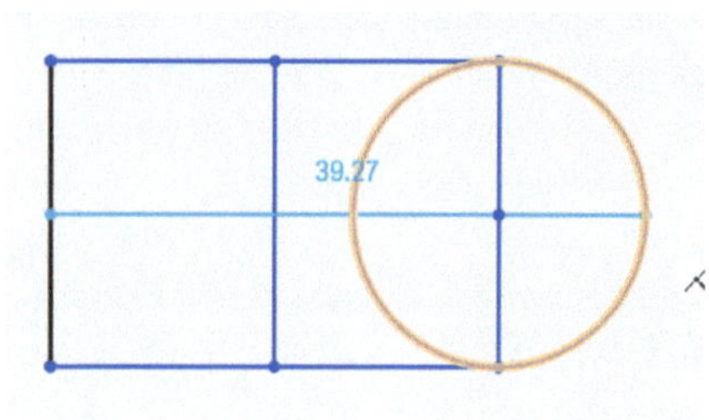

Click, move your cursor horizontally to the right, click on the right side of the circle and press Esc.

Q? What letter of the alphabet does the Coincident constraint look like?

....

You can manually add constraints to Sketch Features, but Onshape will also try to work out (infer) what constraints it thinks you want and suggest them to you with an orange icon. This can be helpful, but can also be added accidentally.

To make the Emoji, you need to trim away the left half of the circle. The Trim tool can be found with the shortcut [M].

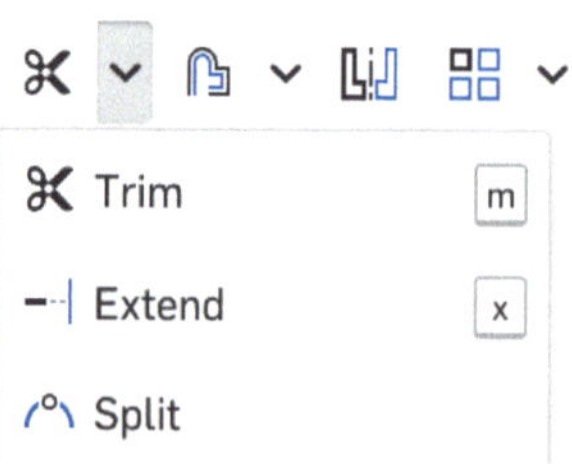

There are two ways to Trim sketch elements, either hover your cursor over a section of the sketch to highlight it in orange and click, or click and drag through a part of a sketch like an erasing tool.

Q? Which other tools in the dropdown can you use to break the circle into arcs?

....

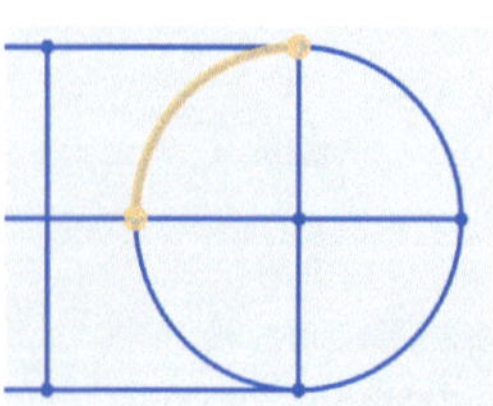

Trim away the circle's two left arcs to leave you with the following shape which resembles the Grimace Emoji's toothy mouth.

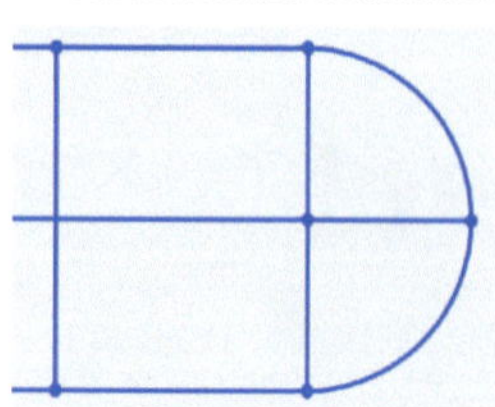

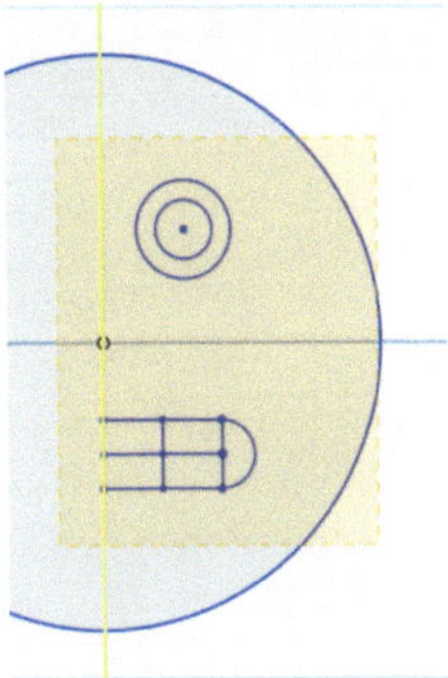

Use the search box to find the Mirror tool. Follow the prompts to mirror the sketch features.

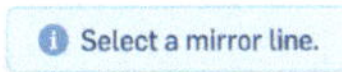

When prompted, select the vertical axis as the mirror line.

Then click and drag a selection box around the eye and mouth features.

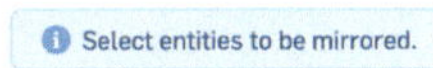

Because you applied a Mirror operation, dozens of Symmetry constraints were added which can clutter your project.

Navigate to the Sketch Dialogue Box and check Show Constraints to see all constraints in the sketch.

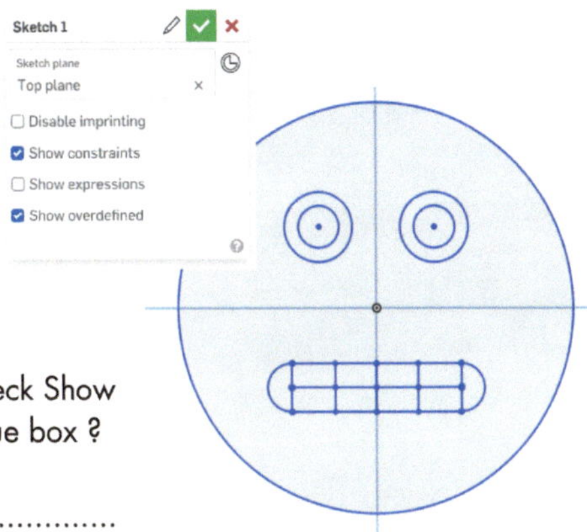

Q? What happens when you uncheck Show Constraints from the Sketch dialogue box ?

....

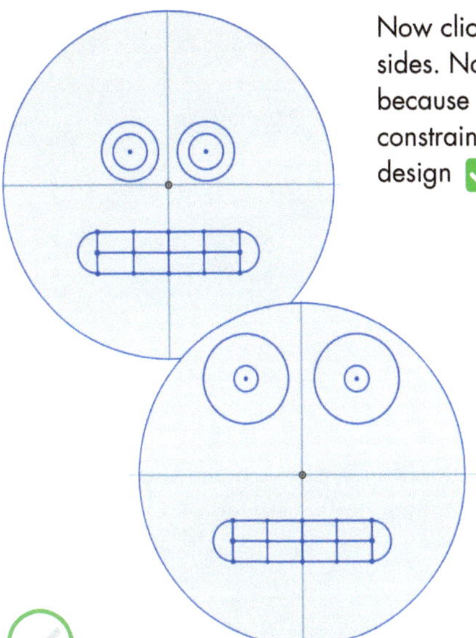

Now click and drag Sketch elements from both sides. Notice how they move symmetrically because they are mirrored but that the constraints keep a sense of "order" to the design ✅.

Q? The conventional wisdom is to constrain and fully define sketches. Would you be able to move things around if you had done that?

Circle the answer: YES NO

Congrats on making your first 2D Design, now let's learn what we can do with it!

2D Sketch Application

Once you have a 2D Sketch, you are able to export the flat file for tools that cut 2D shapes like laser, plasma, water-jet, and vinyl cutters.

Laser cutting is a high-precision manufacturing process that uses a focused beam of light to cut or engrave materials with incredible accuracy. Lower-power machines (around 20W) are commonly used for engraving or cutting thin materials like plywood, acrylic, or cardboard, while industrial laser cutters (over 1kW) are powerful enough to slice through steel, glass, and other dense materials with ease.

All these tools work with the same principle, a cutter follows a 2D path of lines and arcs to make a finished part.

These tools use different 2D file types depending on the model, but a DXF (Drawing Exchange Format) is the most commonly used.

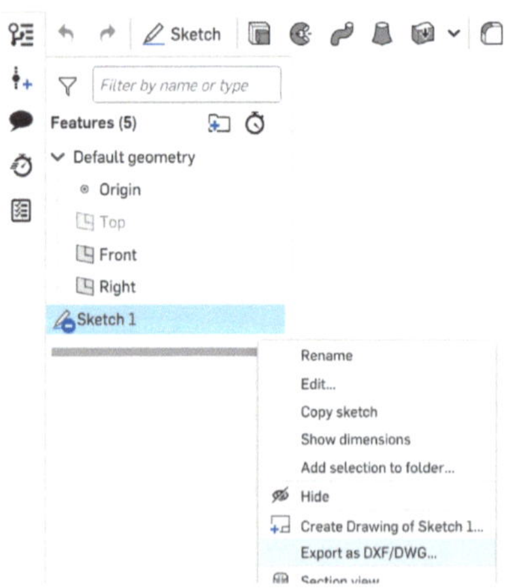

To export a laser cut-able DXF file from Onshape:

Navigate to the Feature List, right click on the sketch (Sketch 1) and select Export As DXF/DWG.

Name the file and press Export.

Export

This 2D file can now be saved onto you computer for future use.

Although DXFs and DWGs are standard 2D file types, you will need to download a DXF viewer app to verify that the profiles are correct before cutting your material.

Teacher Notes

Constraints are rules applied to sketch entities to control their behavior and relationships. They help create predictable, parametric designs that are easy to modify. Understanding constraints is crucial for creating robust and flexible models.

Geometric Constraints:

- **Coincident**: Objects share the same location
- **Concentric**: Circles or arcs share the same center
- **Parallel**: Lines or planes are always equidistant and never intersect
- **Tangent**: A line or curve touches another curve at one point without intersecting
- **Horizontal**: A line or plane is parallel to the horizon
- **Vertical**: A line or plane is perpendicular to the horizon
- **Perpendicular**: Lines or planes intersect at a right angle
- **Equal**: Objects have the same size or value
- **Midpoint**: The point that divides a line segment into two equal parts
- **Normal**: A line or plane that is perpendicular to another surface at a point
- **Pierce**: An object penetrates or passes through another object
- **Symmetric**: Objects are identical on opposite sides of a line or plane
- **Fix**: A constraint that prevents an object from moving or changing
- **Curvature**: The rate at which a curve changes direction

All these can be added manually or automatically using inferencing.

Dimensional Constraints:

- **Distance/Length:** Specifies the length of a line/distance between entities
- **Angle:** Defines the angle between two lines
- **Radius/Diameter:** Sets the size of circles and arcs

Line colors:

Blue: Under-Defined / Un-Defined

Black: Fully-Defined / Defined

Red: Over-Constrained / Conflicting

Assessment Ideas:

- Create exercises where students must fully constrain a given sketch
- Have students identify and fix over-constrained or under-defined sketches
- Challenge students to create a sketch that can be easily modified by changing key dimensions

Reinforce & Stretch

Try to remake the symmetrical Emoji Face project with another emoji, ideally your most used emoji.

Practice this approach: add your sketch elements first and fast, then add constraints, and lastly dimensions.

If you need inspiration, try one of these (easy > hard):

Q? What does the keyboard shortcut [S] do?

....

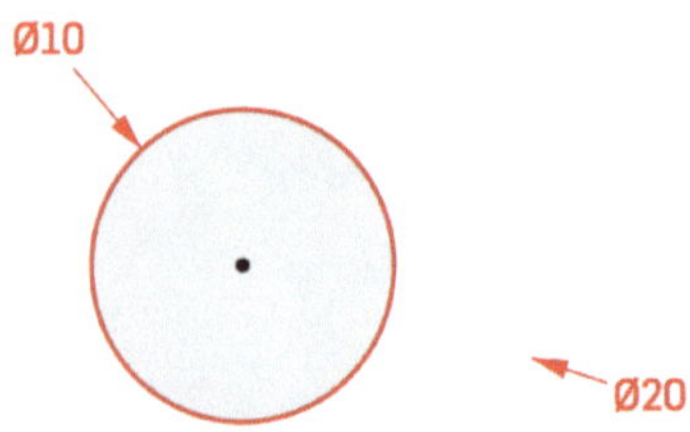

Try to deliberately Over Constrain (add too much information) the Sketch and see what happens.

You can do this with both dimensions and constraints.

Q? What do you think it means if the Sketch goes red and it says "Sketch could not be solved"?

....

Try to remove constraints in the sketch. For example, the Coincident constraint between the large circle and the Origin, and see what happens.

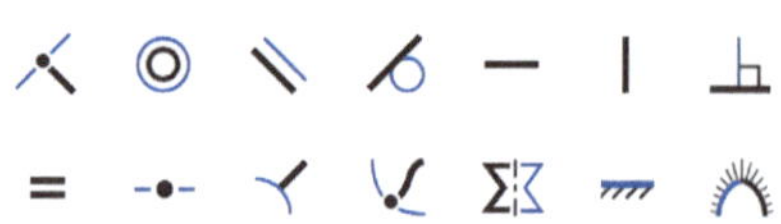

Q? Can you copy and paste sketch entities? (Ctrl/Cmd + C, Ctrl/Cmd + V)?

....

Q? Which new terms can you fill out in the glossary in the back of the book?

Rubric

Criteria	Excellent (4)	Good (3)	Fair (2)	Needs help (1)
Constraints	Understands and correctly applies all constraints	Understands and can apply most constraints	Can apply a limited number of constraints	Has difficulty applying constraints
Mirror	Understands and can apply mirror to symmetric sketches	Can apply mirror to symmetric sketches	Can mirror with limited understanding	Has difficulty mirroring sketches
Sketch Mastery	Understands how to sketch and resize various shapes	Understands how to sketch and resize some shapes	Understands how to sketch and resize 1 shape	Difficulty understanding how to sketch and resize shapes
Dimensions and Constraints	Has mastery over when to apply dimensions vs constraints	Understands when to apply dimensions vs constraints	Lacks understanding of when to apply dimensions vs constraints	Has difficulty applying dimensions and constraints
DXF for Laser	Can export a laser cutable .DXF file	Can export a laser cutable .DXF file with some difficulty	Can export a laser cutable .DXF file with some help	Unable to export a laser cutable .DXF file
Problem Solving	Confidently explains how the emoji was created using the CAD terms above	Can mostly explain how to create the emoji	Can explain how to create parts of the emoji	Has difficulty explaining how to create the emoji

Tool Review: Constraints

Constraints control the position and relationship between different elements in a 2D sketch. They allow CAD designers to define specific rules and conditions that govern how parts, features, and components interact.

Constraints can be used for a variety of purposes in CAD, including:

- To fix the location and orientation of parts relative to one another
- To establish relationships between features, such as aligning edges, matching sizes, or maintaining tangency
- To control how a model responds to changes in parameters, ensuring that the overall design intent is maintained

While constraints are useful, there are some potential pitfalls:

- Constraints that contradict each other can cause the model to become unstable or fail to update correctly
- Constraints can create complex dependencies between different elements of the model. Changes to one part may have unintended consequences on other parts, which can make the design process more challenging

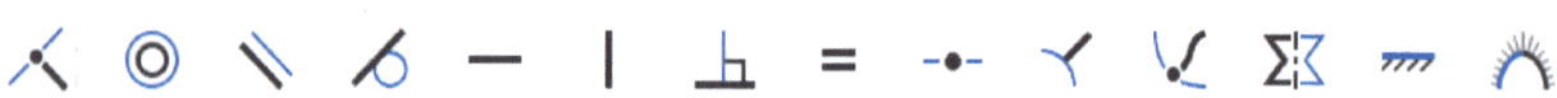

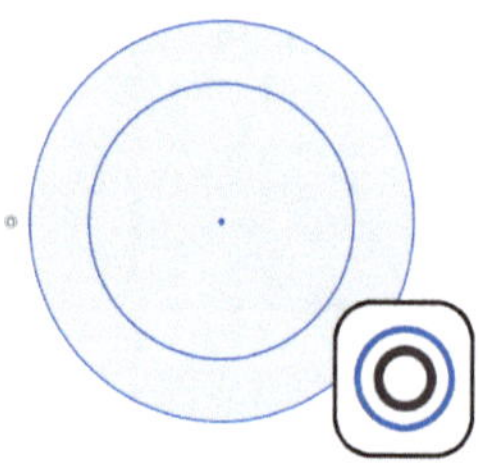

In some sketches, you can use two different constraints and get the same result.

You can make 2 circles that share the same center by using the Concentric constraint or using the Coincident constraint and selecting both circle's centers.

Manual Constraints are constraints that you deliberately add yourself. You select the geometric elements and explicitly choose what type of constraint to apply from the toolbar.
Examples include:

- Adding a perpendicular constraint between two lines
- Setting a specific dimension
- Making two circles equal diameter
- Fixing a point in space

Automatic (Inferred) Constraints are added by the CAD software as you sketch. It detects likely geometric relationships based on your input and shows them with orange visual indicators.
Common inferences include:

- Horizontal/vertical lines when sketching near 0° or 90°
- Parallel lines when drawing near existing lines
- Concentric circles when drawing close to another circle's center

Tool Practice: Constraints

Copy the link into your browser or scan the QR code and make a copy. Work your way along the tabs at the bottom to practice the Constraining tools.

t.ly/rZwlw

...or go to the Public Library, and search for "CADclass sketch constraints" and open the file made by the user ***CADclass***.

Select Make a Copy to Edit.

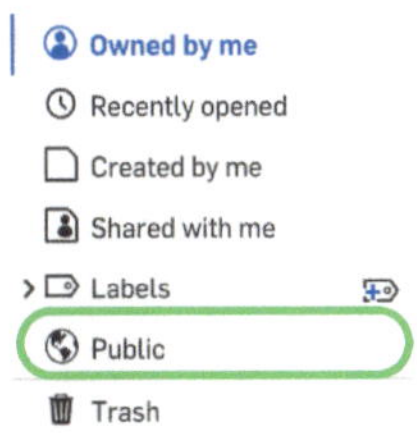

Tool Practice #1-3: Coincident, Concentric, & Horizontal / Vertical

Using the Coincident constraint, correct the following profiles so they are fully enclosed. Using the Concentric constraint connect the profiles so they share the same center. Using the Horizontal / Vertical constraint, align the lines of the polygon and then perform the same operation to the endpoints on the right.

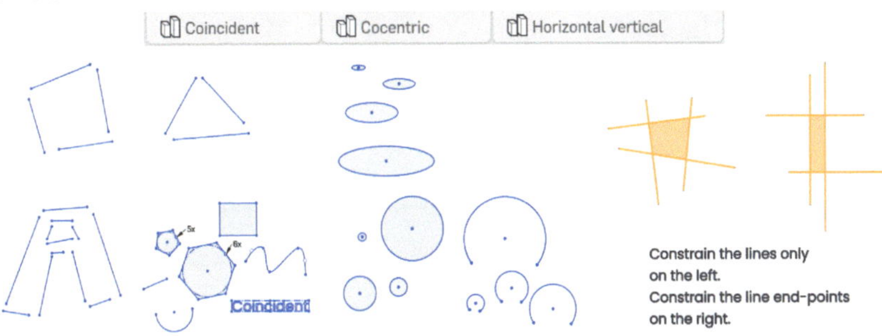

Tool Practice #4-6: Tangent, Perpendicular, & Midpoint

Using the Tangent constraint, connect a series of lines to the central circle. Using the Perpendicular constraint set a series of lines to be 90 degrees to each other; both floating lines and enclosed polygons. Using the Midpoint constraint, set a series of lines to be at the midpoint of varies points.

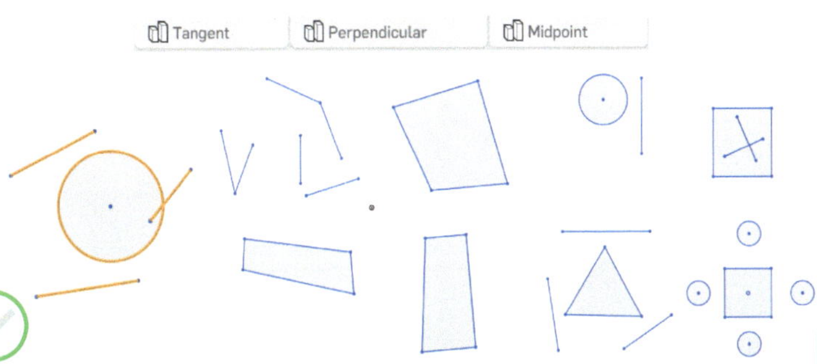

Constraints Review

Name the Constraints and draw the icon

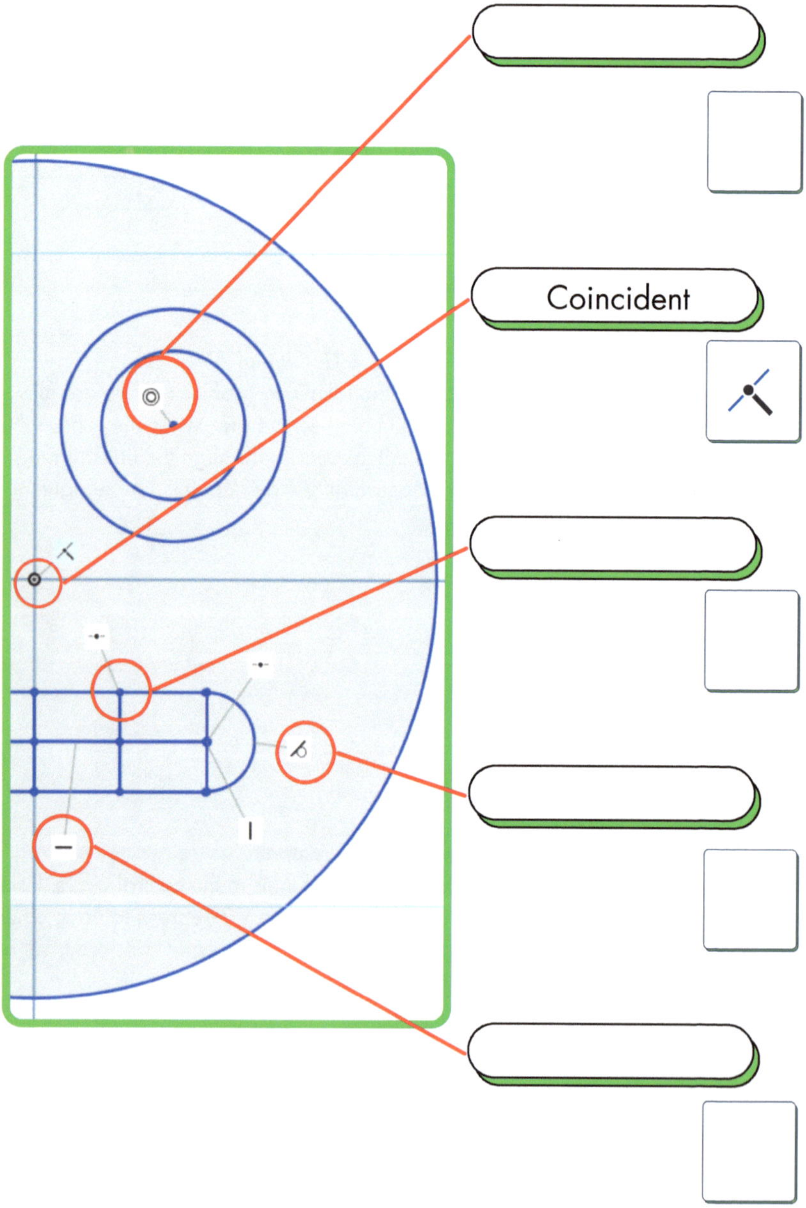

Solutions

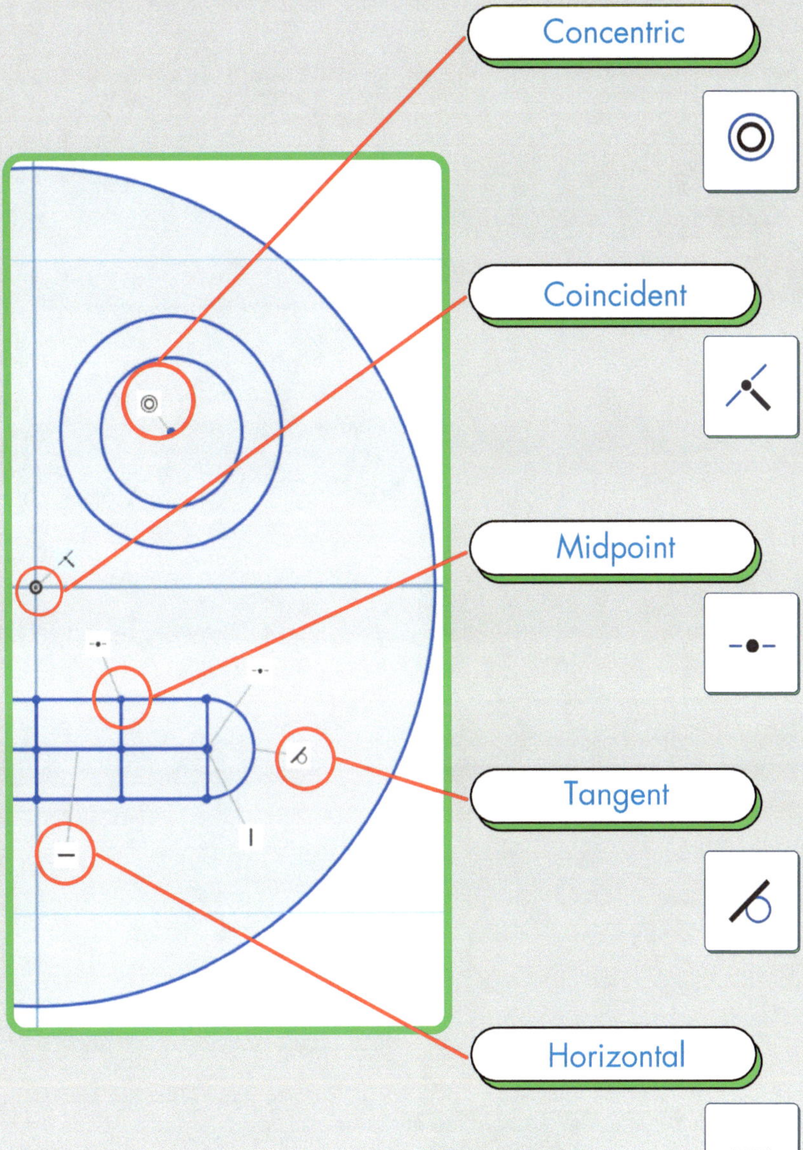

TIP: Hold the SHIFT key to disable auto-inference of constraints

TIP: When you are sketching, indicators showing the contraint inferance appear next to the mouse cursor as the curves snap to inferences.

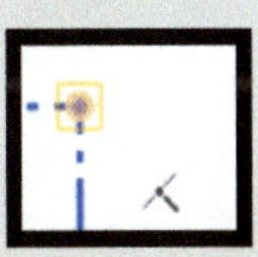

True or False?

Q: Onshape will try to automatically infer constraints and suggest them to you with orange icons?

Q: When starting a circle at the Origin, both its location and size are automatically defined?

Q: A good rule of thumbs is: use more dimensions and fewer constraints when sketching?

Q: Once a sketch is fully constrained and defined, you can still move elements around freely?

Q: The Tangent constraint can be used to make a circle touch the edge of a rectangle at one point?

Solutions

Q: Onshape will try to automatically infer constraints and suggest them to you with orange icons?

A: True. This can both help, and hinder.

Q: When starting a circle at the Origin, both its location and size are automatically defined?

A: False (only location is defined, size remains undefined).

Q: A good rule of thumbs is: use more dimensions and fewer constraints when sketching?

A: False - we recommend more constraints, fewer dimensions

Q: Once a sketch is fully constrained and defined, you can still move elements around freely?

A: False (fully constrained means elements can't move freely).

Q: The Tangent constraint can be used to make a circle touch the edge of a rectangle at one point?

A: True

Constraints Review

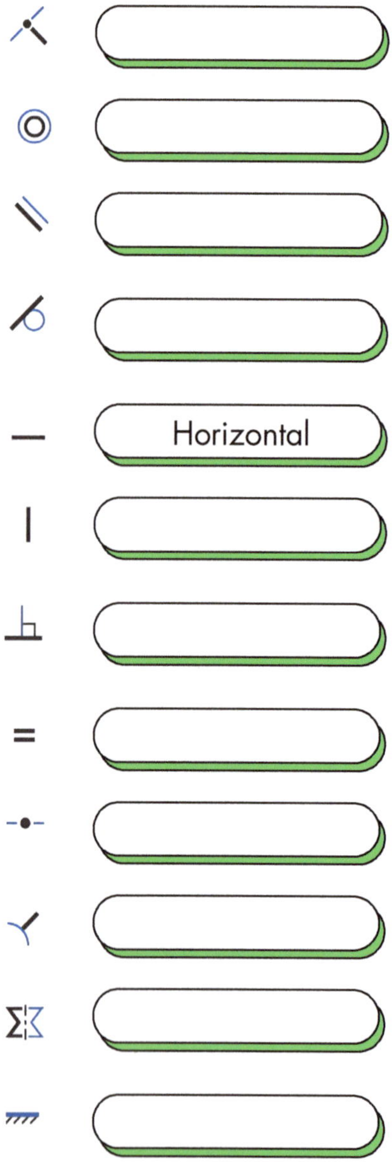

Solutions

Coincident 

Concentric 

Equal 

Tangent 

Horizontal 

Vertical 

Perpendicular 

Parallel 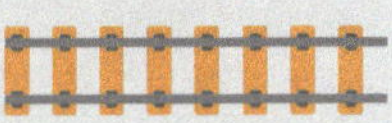

Midpoint 

Normal 

Symmetry 

Fix/Unfix 

Challenge

Your next challenge in turning 2D Drawings into 3D Models is to design a custom Laser-Cuttable project made entirely from one sketch. Because Laser, Plasma, and Vinyl Cutters all create physical objects from 2D designs you can turn any sketch geometries into projects without going into the 3D workspace.

Using the tools you learned in the Emoji Face project: Sketch Elements, Coincident, Tangent, Vertical, and Midpoint constraints, you'll model the classic Robot Emoji.

You technically only need the 2D sketch for this project but to make this more of a challenge, practice extruding the correct profiles into 2 mm thicknesses being careful which profiles you extrude as New or Add. Finally, add specific colors to match the original Robot Emoji.

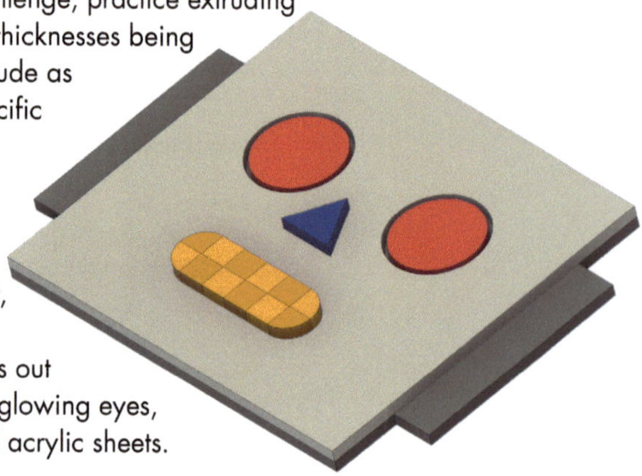

As you are making this project, imagine you are going to be making each the metal sections out of polished aluminum and the glowing eyes, nose and mouth out of colored acrylic sheets.

Search the Public Library for "CADclass Robot Template". Open it and make a copy and add these constraints.

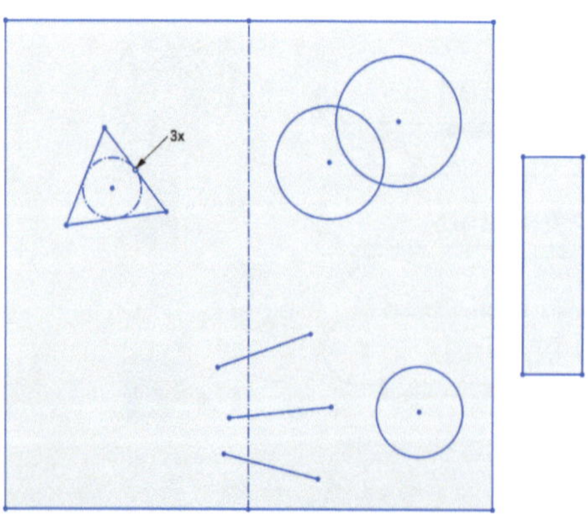

- Nose: A triangle > add a Coincident constraint to the Origin
- Eyes: 2 circles > require a Concentric constraint
- Ear: a rectangle > add a Coincident constraint to the edge of the face
- Mouth: 3 lines and a circle > make lines horizontal and constrained to the mirror line and tangent to the circle
- A construction line to use as a mirror

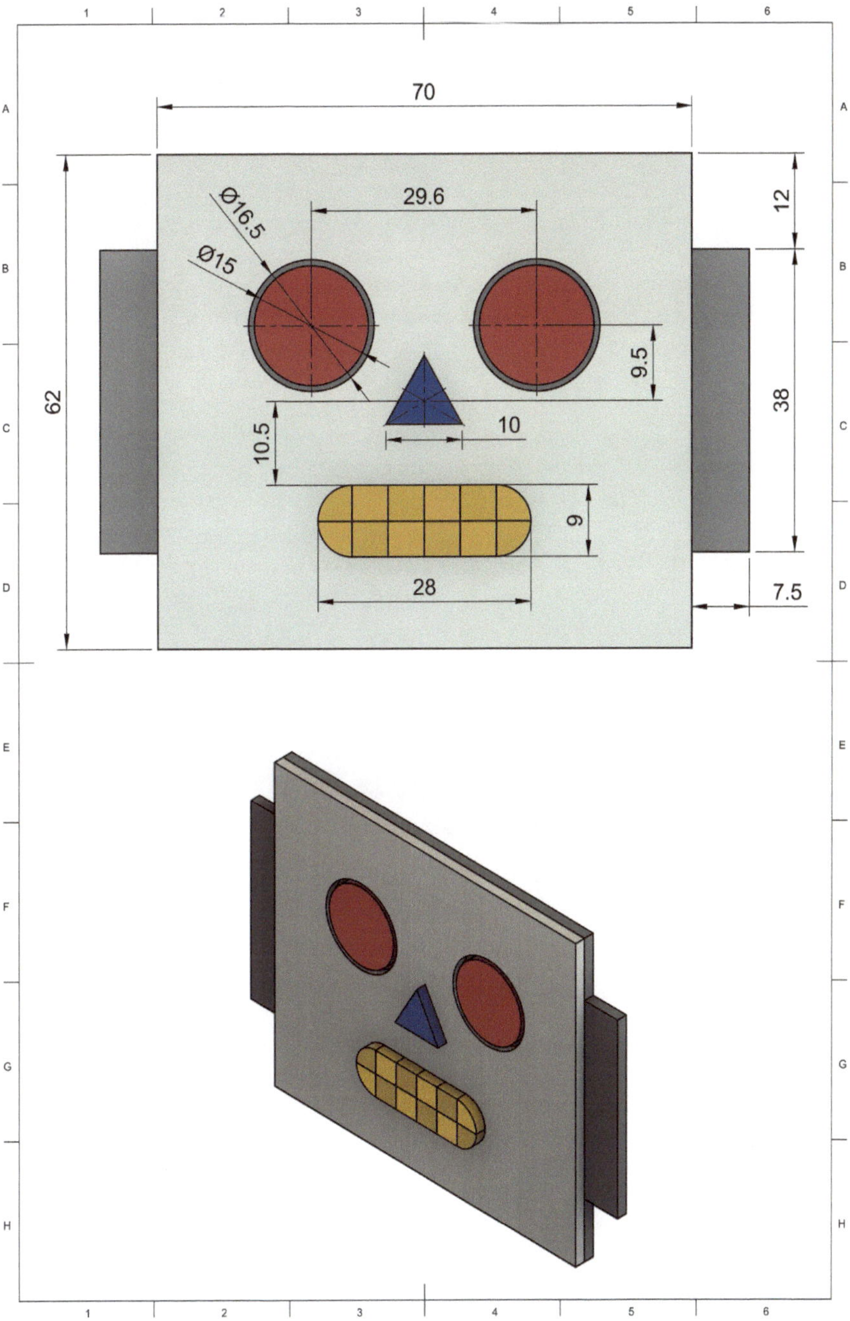
70
Ø16.5
Ø15
29.6
12
62
9.5
38
10.5
10
9
28
7.5
1
2
3
4
5
6
A
B
C
D
E
F
G
H

Active Engagement

This chapter scaffolds learners through a complex CAD project. It breaks down the iconic Saturn V rocket into segments, teaching important concepts like Extrusions, tapered angles, patterns, and appearances through a real-world example. Here are practical ways educators can enhance this activity:

Have students research different rocket designs:

- Sketch their observations of geometric shapes in rockets. Notice the repetition of parts, like the boosters.
- Identify common features and discuss why certain shapes are used in aerospace

Create a physical modeling component:

- Use paper rolls or cardboard to demonstrate tapered shapes
- Build simple rocket models to understand how components fit together
- This helps students visualize 3D relationships before working in CAD

Extend the learning through variations:

- Challenge students to modify the design for different purposes
- Ask them to calculate volume or material requirements
- Have them optimize the design for 3D printing

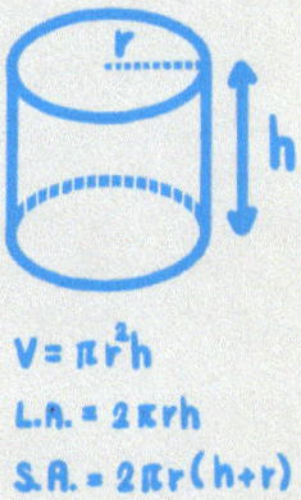

TESTING ESTES A8-3 ENGINE!
t.ly/AOxdG

Move from digital to physical:

- 3D print the rocket at scale, this may require splitting the rocket into parts and joining it post-printing.
- Extrude (cut) a cavity for a rocket motor and launch it! For example the Estes A8-3 engine.

Making these designs real brings CAD to life. When students can touch, test, and share their creations, CAD class becomes an engaging experience they'll remember long after graduation.

SATURN V ROCKET
Onshape Fundamentals Workbook

saturn v rocket.

Project #4
Sketch
Extrude
Project
Taper Extrude

Fillet
Circular Pattern
Artificial Reality

where makers are made.

Estimated Time: 1.5 hrs
Onshape Fundamentals
Workbook

Saturn V Rocket

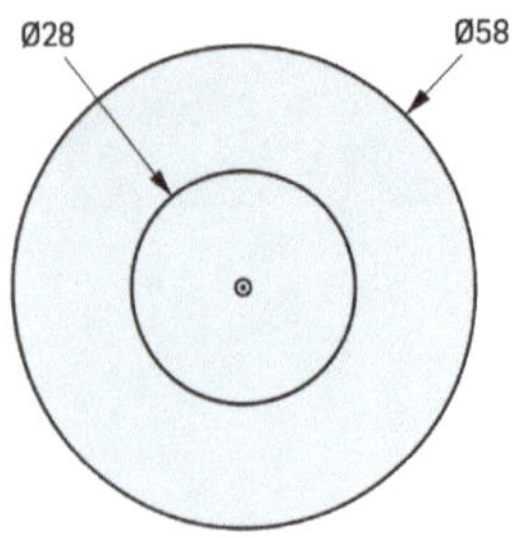

Create a new Document called "CADclass Saturn V Rocket". Create a new Sketch on the Top Plane and sketch a 24 mm and a 58 mm circle [C] at the Origin. Confirm the Sketch ✅.

Q? Were any constraints applied automatically? (check using Show Consraints) If so, which ones?

....

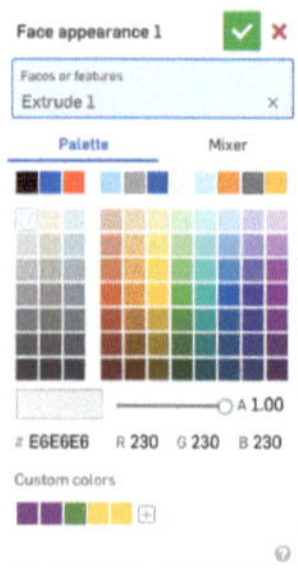

Get an Isometric view of your sketch and Extrude the ring profile upwards 365 mm. Right click it and click Edit face appearance. Select the lightest gray color ✅ .

Q? Can you make a shortcut to this specific color e.g., set a "Custom color"?

....

Set all RGB values to 255 for the color white and click the + below Custom Color to make a White appearance option. Note that you can use this custom color in this project, but it can be hard to select in the Appearance Dialogue Box.

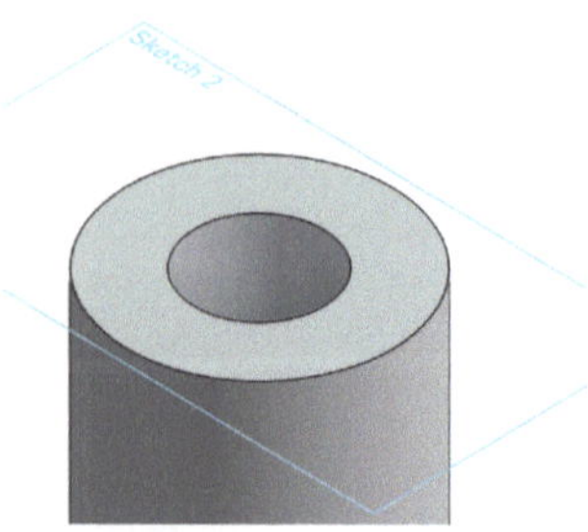

The main body of the Saturn V Rocket is a series of stacked straight and tapered cylinders that alternate in color and size.

The next extrusion will be a tapered black extrusion to cap off this hollow tube. Make a new Sketch on part's top face.

Change to a top-down view, press [U] for Use, and click on the inner circle which projects an edge of a part onto the active sketch plane.

This will allow you to select and therefore Extrude both the ring profile and the inner circle at the same time. Confirm the sketch ✅ .

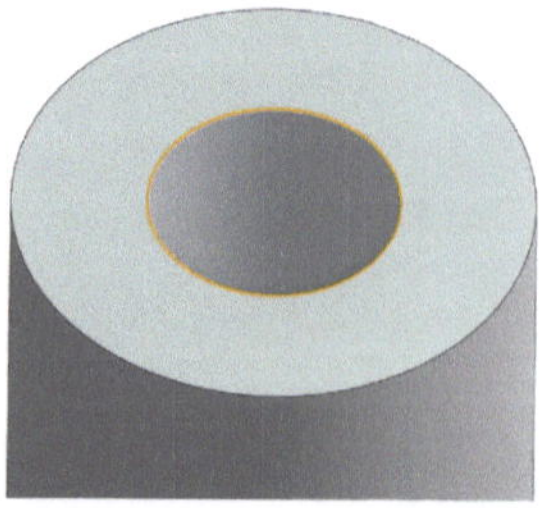

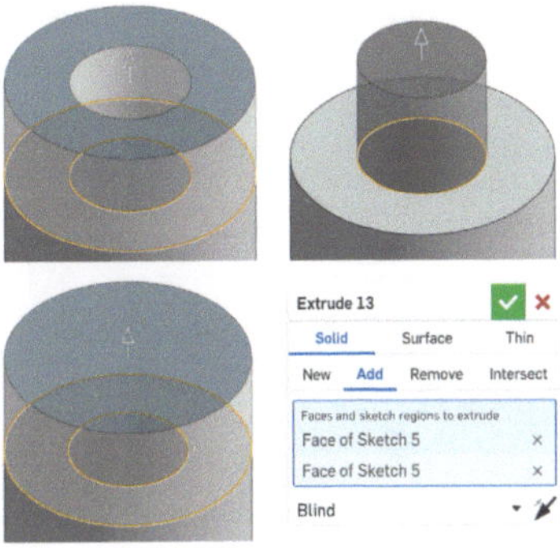

Press [Shift + E] for Extrude then click on the faces of both the inner circle and outer ring profile.

Notice how both faces are listed in blue boxes in the Extrude dialogue box.

Extrude the ring and the inner circular profiles up 32 mm, set the Draft to 16 deg, and change it to Opposite Direction to taper inwards.

Q? What happens if you adjust this slider at the bottom of the Extrude Dialogue box?

....

Confirm the Extrude.

Press the Appearance Panel icon in the menu on the right middle of the page.

Click the Add face appearance button in the top right corner of the pop-out box.

Click the tapered face and click black, then confirm the appearance.

Q? What is the difference between applying an Appearance to an Extrude feature vs to a Face?

....

Extrude the top face of the Rocket body up 66 mm and confirm.

You can Extrude any flat face without having to make a new Sketch every time.

On the real Saturn V Rocket, this cylinder has a black ring at the top, so you need to use the Split tool to cut the face into a top and bottom. Remember, you can always search for a new tool using Search Tools.

Q? Look at the dropdown in the Plane dialogue box. Offset is the default, what other types of planes are there?

....

Navigate to Plane, select the top face, pull the arrow down, and set the distance to 13 mm, and click Confirm.

Navigate to Split. Select Face at the top of the Dialogue Box. Select the cylindrical face, click Entities to Split With, click the new Plane, and Confirm.

Click the eye icon next to Plane1 in the Feature List to hide the Offset Plane.

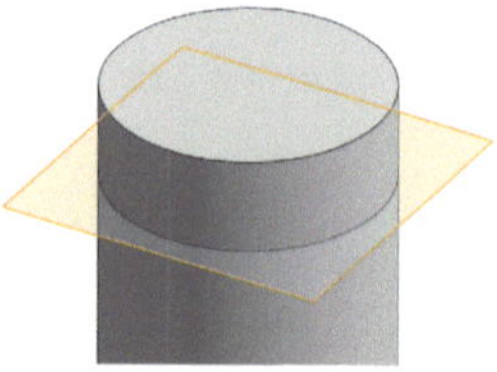

Apply a black color to the new ring at the top via the Appearance panel.

Q? Can you change the color of sketches in the Appearance Panel, or just Parts and Surfaces?

....

Extrude the following set of cylinders and drafted cylinders:
To speed up these steps, double-press Enter after entering the dimension to finish each extrusion.

Extrusion 4: 57 mm, 9 deg
Extrusion 5: 23 mm
Extrusion 6: 7 mm, 35.7 deg
Extrusion 7: 15 mm, 6 deg
Extrusion 8: 3 mm, 30 deg
Extrusion 9: 27 mm
Extrusion 10: 5 mm, 25 deg

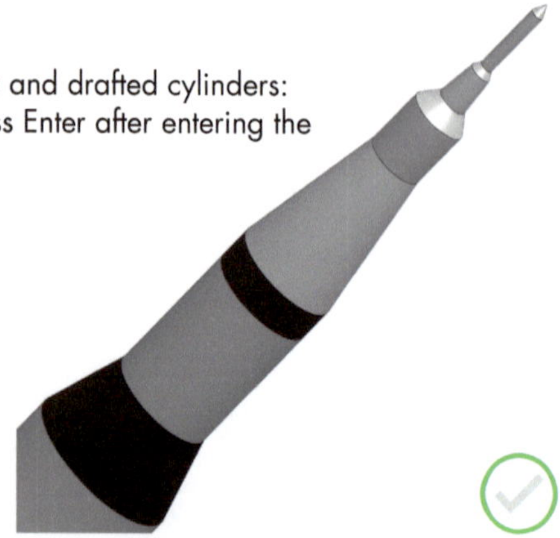

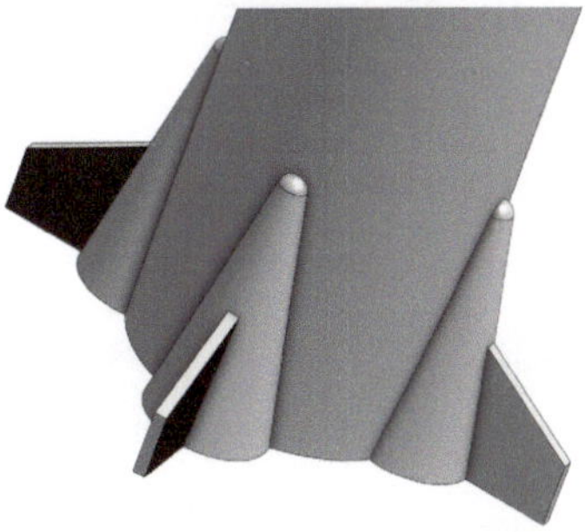

The next part of this project is to make the four fins and four thrusters at the Rocket's base.

Since the four thrusters and fins are equally spaced, you can create one set and then use the Circular Pattern tool to make the rest.

Orbit to the underside of the rocket and create a new Sketch on the Rocket's bottom face.

Sketch a 25 mm circle near the X-axis, Horizontally constrain the circle's center to the Origin, and Coincidently constrain the circle's center to the outer circle's diameter.

Confirm the Sketch.

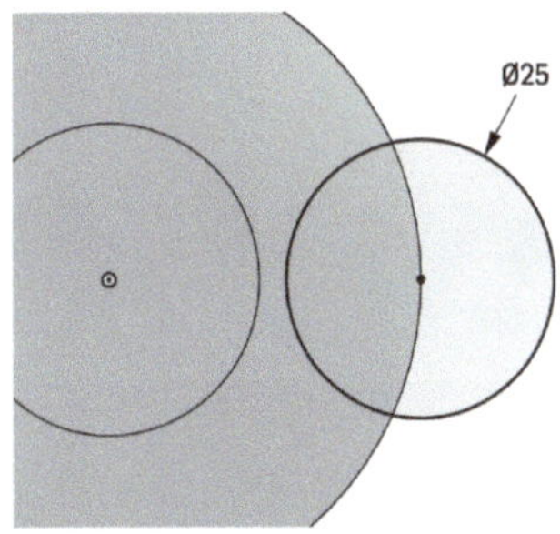

To verify if any of your sketches are fully Defined, look a the Sketches in the Feature List and check for a **blue** stop sign.

If there is a blue stop sign icon, the sketch is Undefined. If not, it is Defined, like in Sketch 2.

Type [Shift + E] for Extrude, select the 2 profiles that make up the circle, click [Shift + 7], click and drag the arrow upwards 52 mm.

Set the Draft to 11 deg and change the direction. Change the Operation from Add to New. **If this operation is set to Add, the later patterning step will not work.**

Q? What would happen if you accidentally set the Extrude type to Remove?

....

Press [Shift + F] for Fillet and select the tapered cylinder's top edge (not face).

Set the Fillet size to 2.9 mm which will give the top face of the thruster a domed effect.

Any more radius on this section will cause a self-intersecting error.

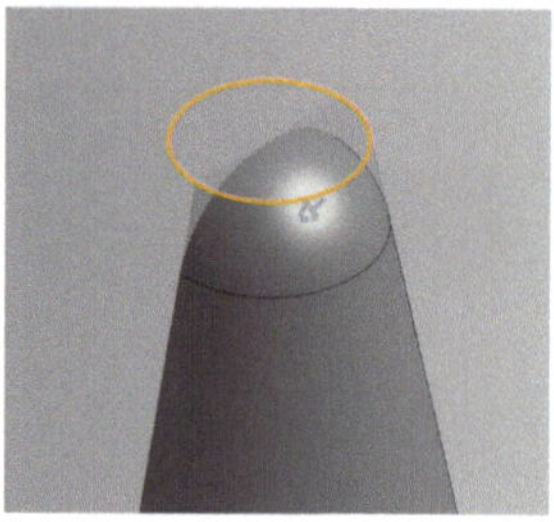

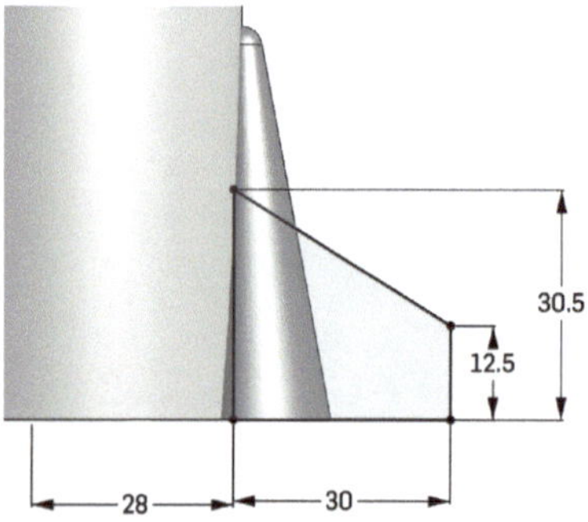

Create a new Sketch on the Front Plane, sketch four lines, and set the bottom horizontal line Coincident to the Origin.

Add the dimensions shown and verify the area inside the profile is light gray. Confirm the Sketch ✅.

Q? Can you Extrude profiles that aren't light gray?

....

Extrude the profile, check Symmetric, set the Depth to 2.4 mm, and set the Extrude type to New.

Q? Where else can you Start an Extrude?

....

Just like the Thruster extrusion, if it set to Add, the later patterning step will not work. Confirm the Feature ✅.

Orbit to the fin's other side, add a Black appearance to the back face of the fin, and collapse the appearance tool.

Fun Fact! On the real Saturn V Rocket, these colors were used to track the rocket's rotation and to help with thermal expansion.

Click the pulldown button button on the Linear Pattern tool and select the Circular Pattern tool.

You can also find these tools with the Search tool [Alt + C].

Keep the Pattern type set to Part Pattern and select the Thruster and the Fin Parts.

Click Axis of Pattern and click on the Rocket's outer cylindrical face. Increase the Instance count to 4 and confirm ✅.

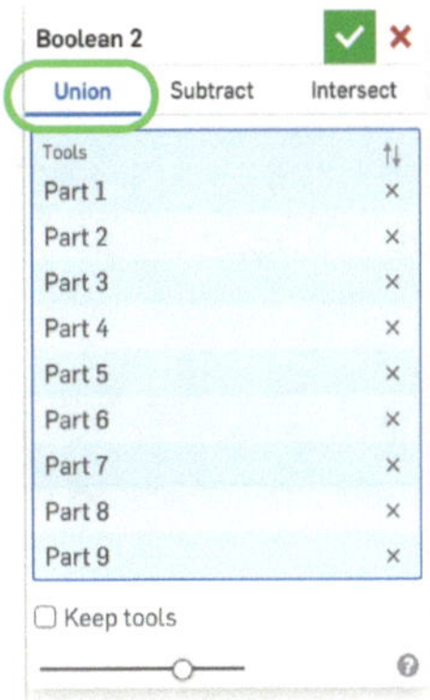

Notice the Parts list in the bottom left of your screen has now increased from Part 1 to Part 9.

To joint all these pieces into one singular Part, select the Boolean tool and verify it is set to Union.

Select on the top Part in the Parts List, hold down Shift, select Part 9 to highlight all Parts and confirm ✅.

Congratulations, your Saturn V Rocket model is complete!

You can view your project in AR (Augmented Reality), on the Onshape app. If you have an iPhone, download and open the app, open your file, tap the View Cube, scroll down and select AR View.

Point your phone's camera at a flat surface, tap to place the design and see your design in 3D!

Follow the instructions so you can rotate, scale, and pan around to see and share all the details of your part!

Reinforce & Stretch

Re-do the Rocket exercise from scratch, doubling all dimensions, so 58 mm becomes 116 mm, and 24 mm becomes 48 mm.

This variation helps you practice scaling while reinforcing your understanding of proportional design.

Q? When extruding, what happens if Type is set to To Surface?

....

Q? What other ways could you make this stack of normal and drafted cylinders?

....

Redesign the Rocket's thrusters and fins to have smaller dimensions.

Update the Circular Pattern tool to increase the number of instances from 4 to 6, evenly spacing the new, smaller components around the Rocket for a sleeker design.

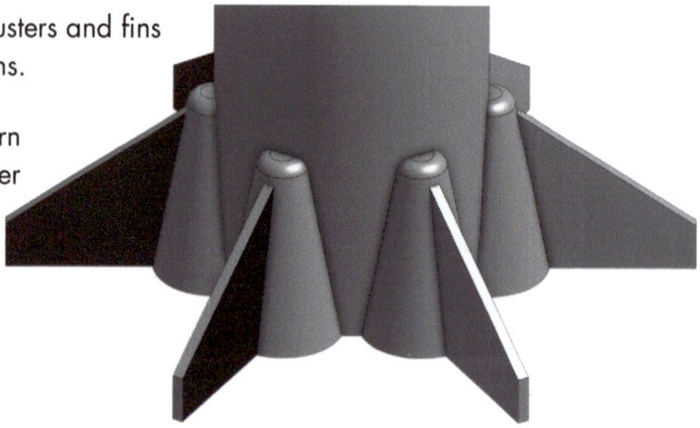

Q? What do the two other types of pattern do?

....

Q? What does the little gray question mark in the bottom right of a dialogue box do?

....

Q? Which new terms can you fill out in the glossary in the back of the book?

Rubric

Criteria	Excellent (4)	Good (3)	Fair (2)	Needs help (1)
Fully Constrain	Understands how to fully constrain sketches (black lines)	Understands how to constrain most simple sketches	Can constrain a single simple sketch	Has difficulty constraining 1 simple sketch
Modify 3D Tools	Understands how to modify 3D parts using tool dialog boxes	Understands how to modify a single 3D part using dialog box	Understands where to find dialog boxes but has trouble using	Has difficulty finding and using dialog boxes
Pattern Features	Has a detailed understanding of how to apply and use the pattern tool	Can use the pattern tool for rocket fins	Understands what pattern does but has difficulty in Onshape	Has difficulty applying and understanding patterns
Split Part	Can modify Part and apply appearances using the Split Face tool	Can modify a Part using the Split Face tool	Can find and use the Split Face tool with instructor help	Has difficulty using the Split Face tool
Augmented Reality (AR)	Can view an augmented reality	Can view in AR with some difficulty	Can view in AR with lots of help	Unable to view in AR
Problem solving	Asks insightful questions and solves issues independently and creatively	Asks for help and tries to solve issues	Tries to solve problems but often gets stuck	Is often stuck and cannot get un-stuck

Tool Review: Pattern

Pattern is a powerful tool for creating multiple copies of Sketches, Features, or Parts in a structured arrangement. It saves time and ensures consistency.

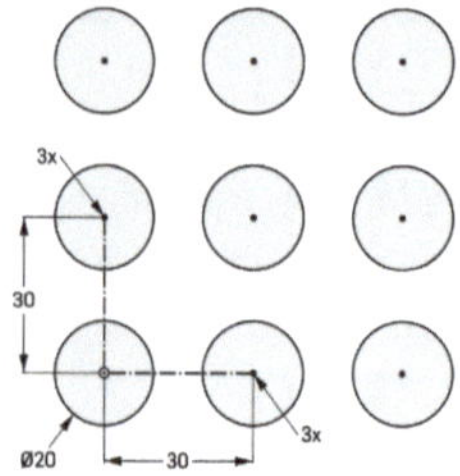

The 2D Linear Pattern tool lets you quickly copy sketch entities in straight rows and columns.

You can control the quantity of entities and the spacing between them in two directions, making it perfect for hole arrays, slots, or shapes aligned in grids.

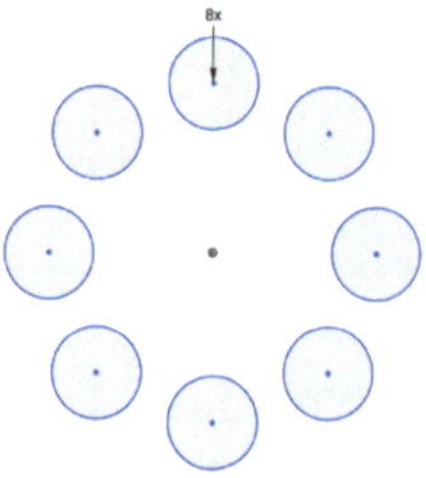

The 2D Circular Pattern tool copies sketch entities around a central point or axis in a circular layout.

You set how many instances you want and the angle they cover. This is ideal for evenly spaced holes, spokes, or repeated features around a circle, like a gear or sprocket.

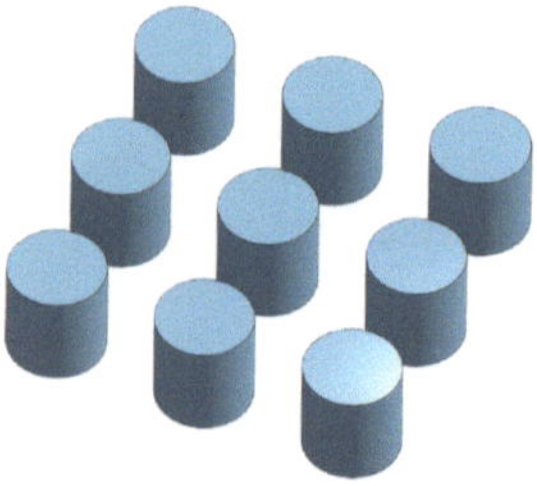

The 3D Linear Pattern tool duplicates parts, features, or faces in one or more straight directions in 3D space.

You control how many copies to make and the distance between them. You can also skip instances to hide individual parts.

The 3D Circular Pattern tool creates duplicates of parts or features around a central axis in 3D.

You define the number of instances and whether they cover a full circle or just a portion. This is great for things like fan blades, lug nuts, or radial patterns on wheels.

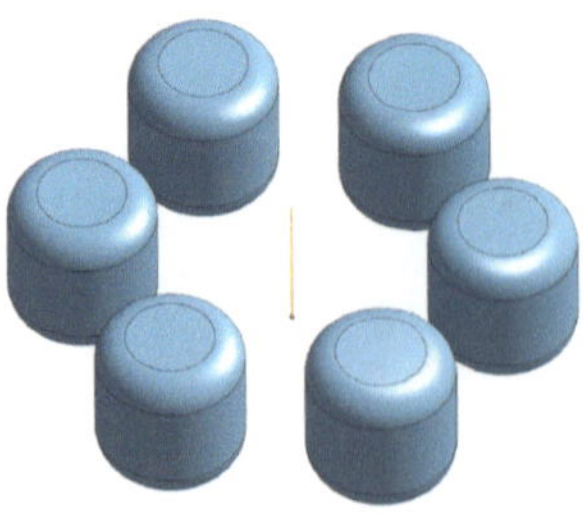

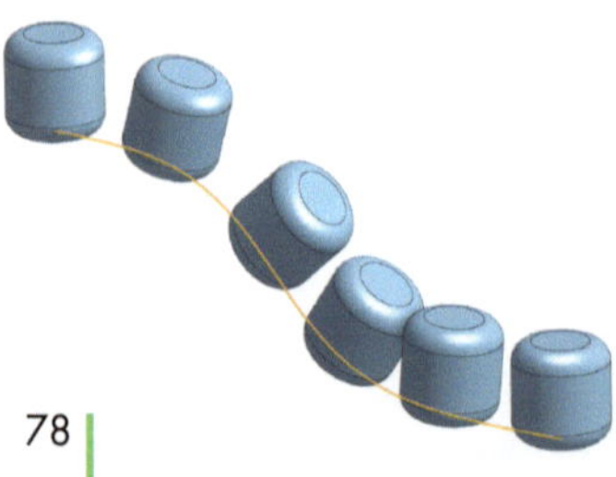

The Path Pattern tool copies parts or features along a curve, like a spline or edge.

It's ideal for making repeated geometry that follows a bend or spiral, such as stitches, treads, or decorative details along a custom path.

Tool Practice: Pattern

Copy the link into your browser or scan the QR code and make a copy. Work your way along the tabs at the bottom to practice the Pattern tool.

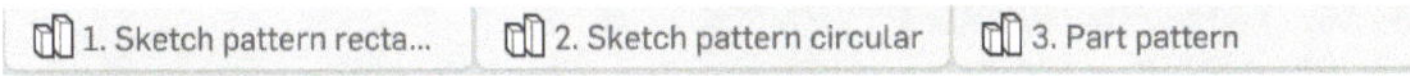

t.ly/osW1o

...or go to the Public Library, and search for "CADclass pattern" and open the file made by the user ***CADclass***.

Select Make a Copy to Edit.

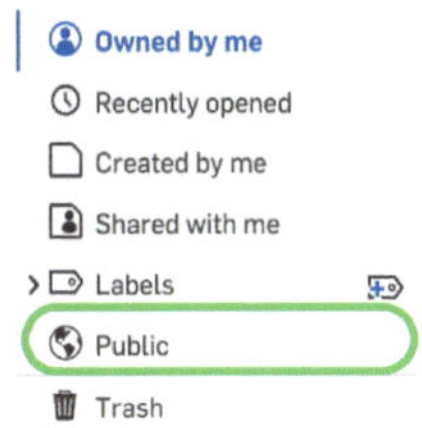

Tool Practice #1

Using 4 simple profiles, use the 2D Linear Patterning tools to create: a simple square grid with no gaps, a crosspatch pattern, a famous car brand badge linearly, and a hexagonal honeycomb pattern with non X and Y directions.

Tool Practice #2

Using 4 simple profiles, use the 2D Circular Patterning tools to create: 6 circles equally spaced about a central point, sun rays emanating from a sun, curved profiles about a single point, and a line and circle about a single point.

Tool Practice #3

Using 4 simple Parts, use the 3D Patterning tools to create: a linear grid of parts, a multi-level chessboard, a circularly patterned part, and a path of tall cylinders.

The solutions are in a folder in the final tab, if required. The final Part pattern (orange) requires a new pattern tool for you to try - Curve pattern!

Solution

True or False?

Q: Extrude can only be used to add material, not to remove it?

Q: You can Extrude directly from a flat face without creating a new Sketch every time?

Q: When using the Extrude tool you can specify a draft angle to create tapered surfaces?

Q: You can apply appearances to individual faces as well as parts?

Q: You can use the "Use" tool to create Sketch geometry based on existing 3D features?

Solutions

Q: Extrude can only be used to add material, not to remove it?

A: False. Extrude can Add, New, Remove, or Intersect.

Q: You can Extrude directly from a flat face without creating a new Sketch every time?

A: True. Very Handy!

Q: When using the Extrude tool you can specify a draft angle to create tapered surfaces?

A: True. Just like when you made the Rocket.

Q: You can apply appearances to individual faces as well as parts?

A: True. Just like when you made the donut.

Q: You can use the "Use" tool to create Sketch geometry based on existing 3D features?

A: True. This is kind of a "pro-tool" tool. Now you know it too!

Review

?	
Isometric view shortcut	?
?	Confirm Sketch icon
?	Extrude
Circle	?
?	U
	?
	?

Solutions

Show/Hide icon	
Isometric view shortcut	Shift + 7
	Confirm Sketch icon
Shift + E	Extrude
Circle	C
Use	U
	Apperance Panel
	Extrude

Challenge: Saturn V Rocket

Your next challenge is to turn a 2D drawing into a 3D model by designing a custom metal gear, a classic CAD exercise that combines Patterning and Boolean functions into one project.

Using tools from the Saturn V Rocket project: Extruding, Applying Appearances to faces, and Patterning, you'll model a 25-tooth cast gear with heat-treated teeth for added strength.

The history of gears is a fascinating mix of math, chemistry, metallurgy, and engineering. Despite being used as far back as 2700 BCE, the ideal gear tooth shape wasn't discovered until 1694, a major milestone in mechanical design.

On some gears, you might notice the teeth are a different color than the rest of the gear. This color change is a sign of heat treatment, which enhances the hardness, surface quality, and wear resistance of the gear's mating surfaces.

During heat treatment, intense heat creates thin oxidation layers on the metal. These layers interact with light, producing a visible rainbow-like coloration on the gear teeth.

In a similar method to the Saturn V Rocket Project start with the center of the gear and add the teeth on later.

As you extrude the body of the gear, you can also include the axle hole and the rectangular keyway for the shaft that runs through the bore hole of the gear.

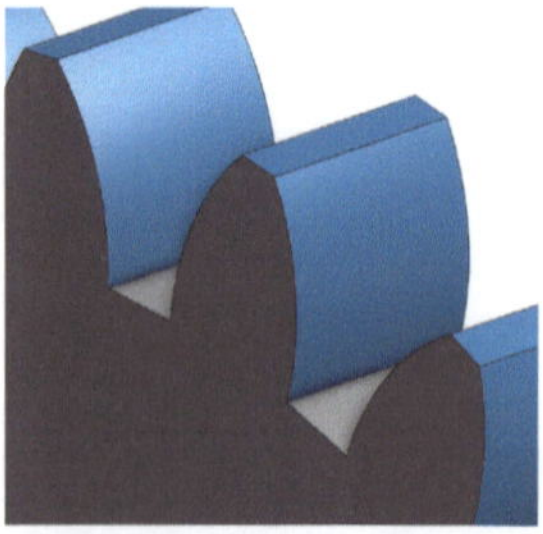

- Sketch and Extrude the gear body, not including the gear tooth, 5 mm
- Sketch and Extrude the gear tooth as a New Part
- Add a blue appearance to the 3 faces of the gear tooth representing heat treatment
- Circularly Pattern the gear tooth part about the center hole of the gear
- Use the Boolean tool to join all 26 Parts together into one

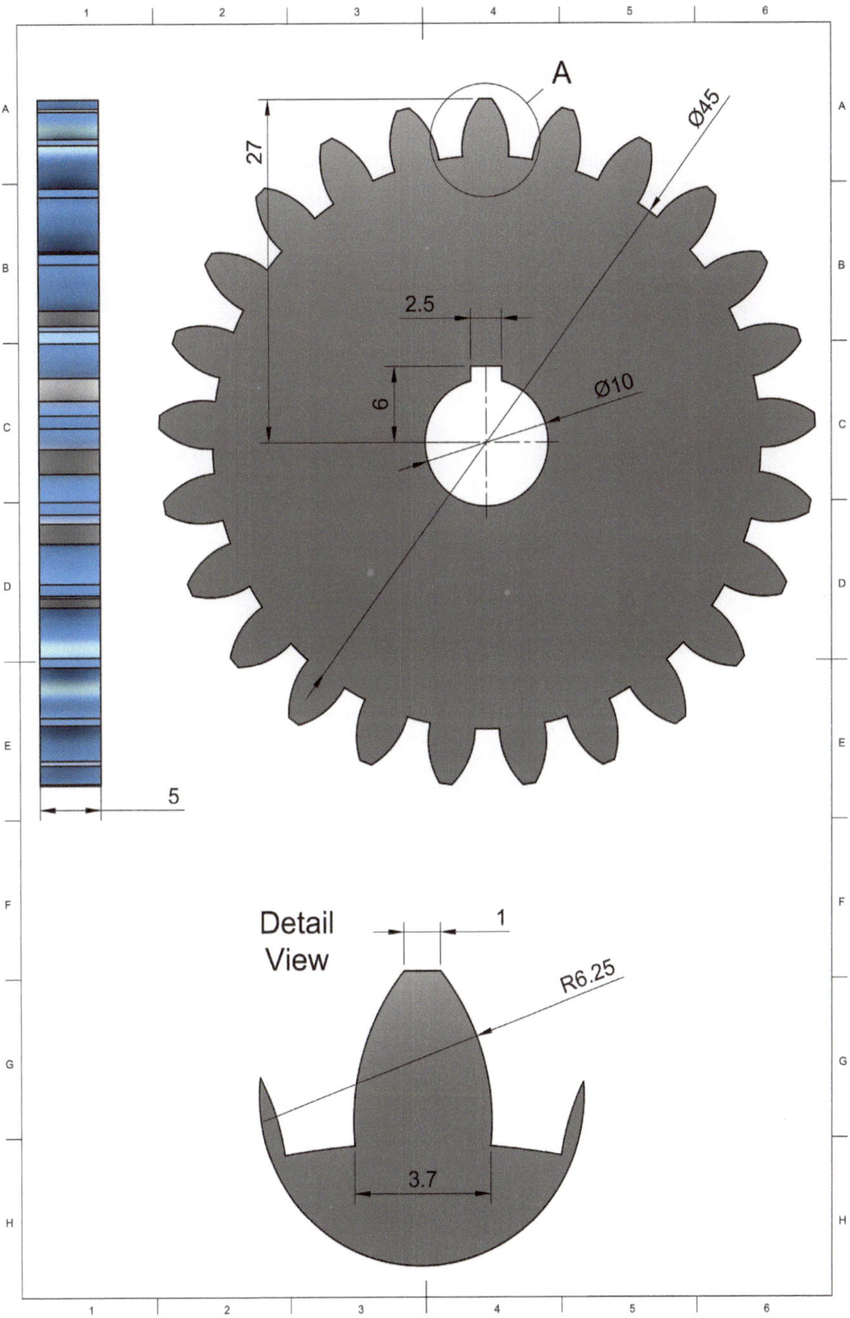
A
Ø45
27
2.5
6
Ø10
5
Detail View
1
R6.25
3.7

Design Intent: 2D > 3D

We're starting to master the fundamentals of Onshape, building a solid foundation in real-world CAD skills.

Remember, the core workflow follows a logical path: start with a fully constrained 2D sketch, turn it into a 3D part, then modify and refine that part using tools like Fillets, Patterning, and Draft Extrusions.

Along the way, you'll face plenty of fun challenges and creative twists that put your skills to the test!

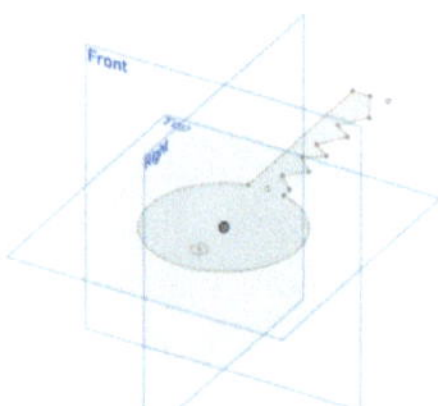

1.Sketch

2.Extrude (new)

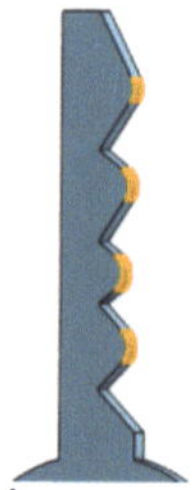

3.Fillet

4.Sketch

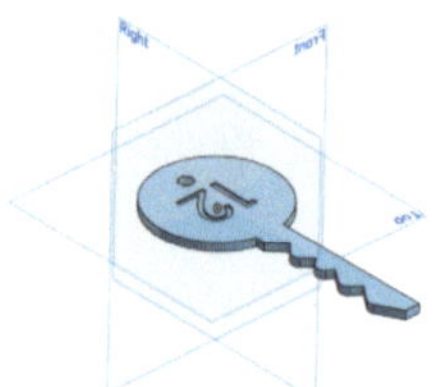

5.Extrude (remove)

6.Chamfer

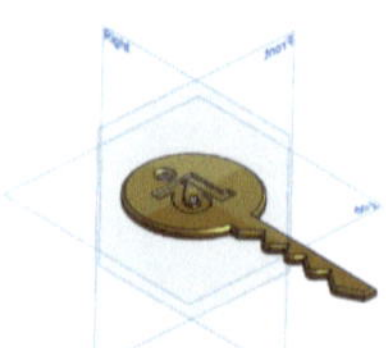

7. Appearances

8.Materials

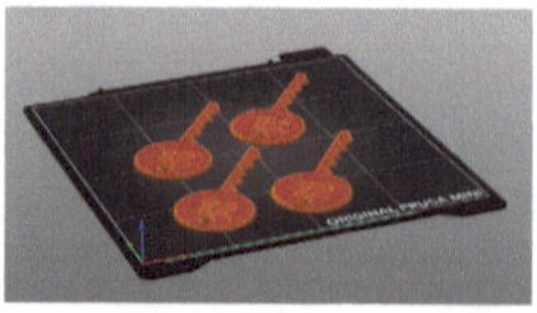

9.Export

Design Intent: 2D > 3D

Storyboard the sketches, features, and tools used to create this (use some, or all of these boxes, as necessary).

Solutions

Option 1

1. Sketch a Circle
2. Extrude with a taper
3. Sketch on top face, Extrude with a taper, repeat
4. Shell
5. Sketch a Circle on bottom face
6. Pattern Sketch feature
7. Extrude (cut)

- This method involves basic operations like Extrude and cut
- The method allows for more customization in the shape of the pot, as you can adjust the dimensions and profiles of the various Extruded shapes.
- Option 1 requires more steps to complete, potentially leading to more opportunities for errors.
- While suitable for simple shapes, this method can become more complex for intricate designs.

Option 2

1. Sketch a profile
2. Revolve
3. Shell
4. Sketch a Circle on bottom face
5. Extrude (cut)
6. Pattern Extrude feature

- This method involves fewer steps, potentially reducing the risk of errors.
- If the pot is highly symmetrical, revolving a 2D profile is an efficient approach.
- Creating a 2D profile can be easier to visualize and understand than multiple 3D operations.
- The shape of the pot is more constrained by the initial 2D profile.
- Requires a symmetrical profile: This method is best suited for shapes that are symmetrical around an axis.

Both methods are valid approaches for creating a plant pot in Onshape.

The "best" method depends on the specific design requirements and the designer's preference.

Design Intent: 2D > 3D

Storyboard the sketches, features, and tools that could be used to recreate this toy brick with an open bottom (use some, or all of these boxes, as necessary).

Solutions

Option 1

1. Sketch a Rectangle
2. Extrude
3. Sketch circle on top face
4. Pattern Sketch feature
5. Extrude
6. Sketch a Rectangle on bottom face
7. Extrude (cut)

- This method allows for more variation in the brick's dimensions, as you can adjust the width and length of the rectangle.
- Option 1 involves more steps than Option 2, potentially increasing the risk of errors.

Option 2

1. Sketch a Square
2. Extrude
3. Sketch circle on top face
4. Extrude
5. Pattern both Extrude features
6. Shell

- Fewer steps are involved, which can save time.
- The Shell function means all wall need to be the same thickness, unless you add another step.

Both methods are valid approaches for creating a toy brick in Onshape. In some cases, a combination of both might be used to achieve the desired result.

Design Intent: 2D > 3D

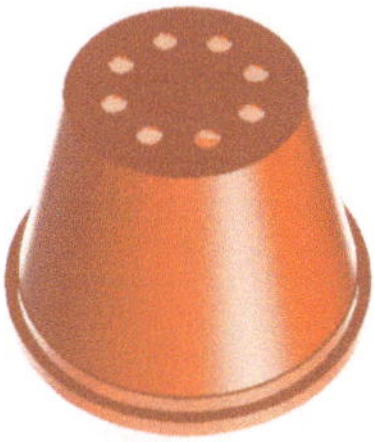

1. 2D Sketch (Profile)
2. Constrain & Dimension
3. Revolve (New Part)
4. Shell
5. 2D Sketch (1 x Hole)
6. Circular Pattern
7. Extrude (Cut)

1. 2D Sketch (Profile)
2. Constrain & Dimension
3. Extrude (New Part)
4. 2D Sketch (1 x Stud)
5. Extrude (Join)
6. Rectangular Pattern
7. Shell

Active Engagement

The carabiner scaffolds progression by introducing sweep operations - a more advanced CAD concept - through a practical, real-world object. It combines previously learned skills (sketching, constraints) with new concepts (sweeps, modifications) in a project that students can produce via 3D printing. Here are some key pedagogical elements and suggestions for enhancement:

Product Analysis:

- Begin by having students examine real carabiners
- Discuss the engineering principles behind their design
- Identify safety considerations and load-bearing requirements
- Have students measure and document real carabiner dimensions

Develop Manufacturing Awareness:

- Compare different manufacturing methods (3D printing vs. metal) and costs on Xeomerty **www.xometry.com**
- Discuss why certain features are needed for different processes e.g. no overhangs in 3D printing
- Analyze how design changes affect printability

Timeline Learning:

- Plan timelines of the design process before CAD-ing
- Practice reorganizing features in different ways
- Explore the cause-and-effect of feature ordering
- Document common failure points and solutions

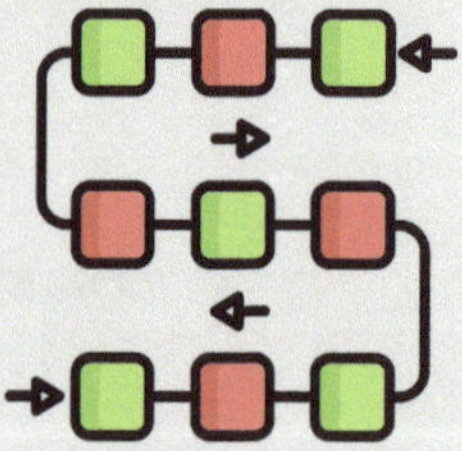

Product Showcase:

- Create a gallery of carabiners in action: print 2 of each carabiner, one to test and one to keep. Make a display board of all the parts after they were tested to the point of failure.
- Grab photos of all student's backpacks hung up on by the carabiner
- Alter the opening slots so they bear weight better

CARABINER
Onshape Fundamentals Workbook

carabiner.

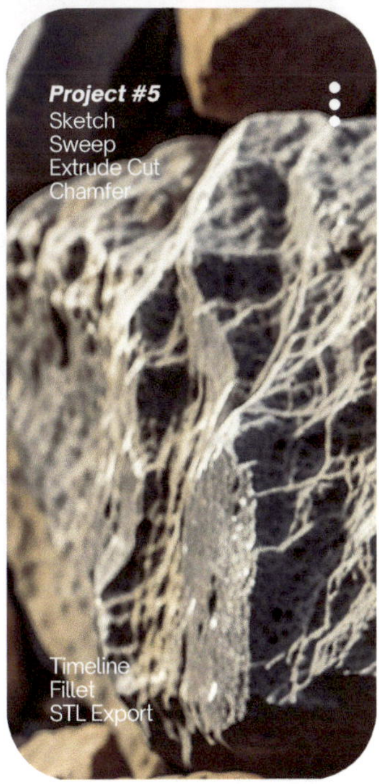

Project #5
Sketch
Sweep
Extrude Cut
Chamfer

Timeline
Fillet
STL Export

where makers are made.

Estimated Time: 2 hrs
Onshape Fundamentals
Workbook

Carabiner

Create a new document in your CADclass.org Folder called CADclass Carabiner.

Sketch two circles [C] on the Top Plane above one another.

Hold down Ctrl/Cmd, select both circle's centers and the Origin, and add a Vertical constraint [V] to all 3 points.

Select the Coincident constraint and click the lower circle and the Origin, so the bottom-most point of the circle passes through the Origin.

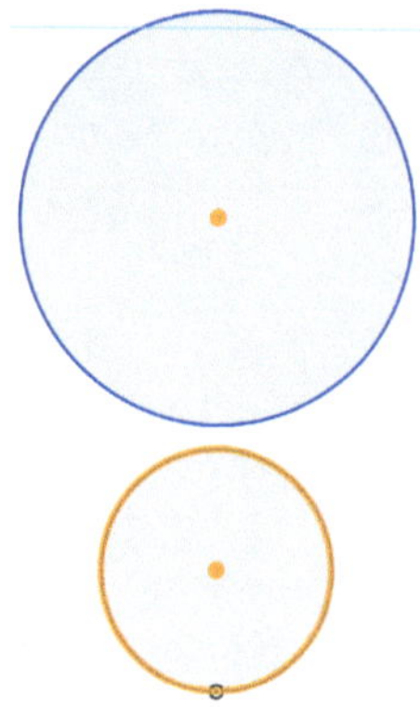

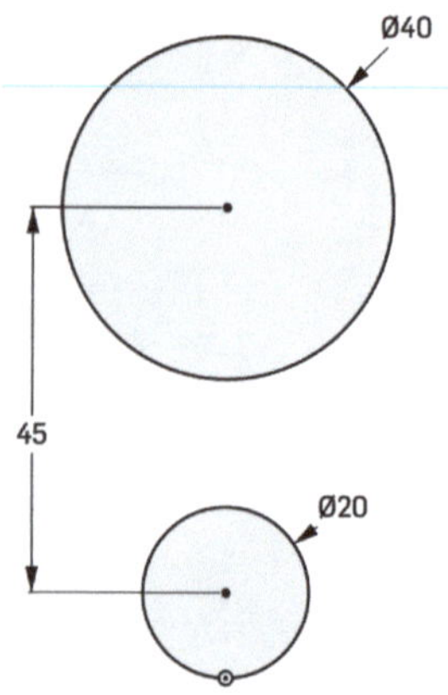

Add the following dimensions to the sketch.

Q? How do you know if your sketch is fully defined?

....

If any of the geometry is blue, click and drag the undefined geometry to see how it can move and add dimensions or constraints to correct it.

Type [L] then [Q] for a Construction line between the two circle's centers. Type [Q] to return to normal Sketch lines and make an angled line that joins the top and bottom circle to the left of the Construction line.

Select the Mirror tool, click on the vertical Construction line, then the angled Sketch line to make a symmetric angled line.

Q? Why do all Mirrored sketch geometry have inherent symmetry?

....

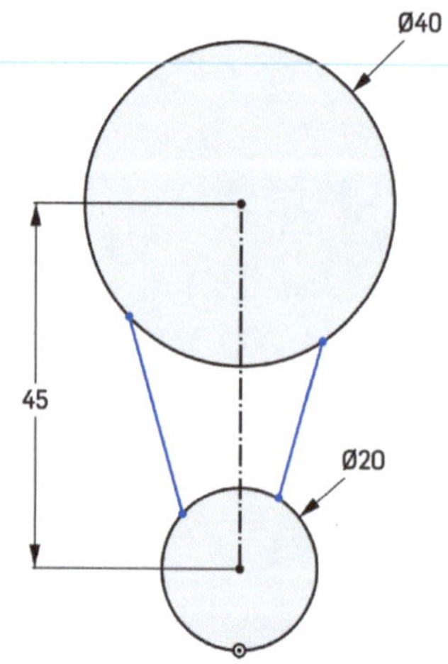

Add a Tangent constraint [T] between the top circle and the left angled Sketch line.

With the Tangent tool still enabled, add another constraint between the bottom circle and the same angled Sketch line.

Because the Mirrored line has inherent symmetry, the Tangent constraint is added to the other angled line.

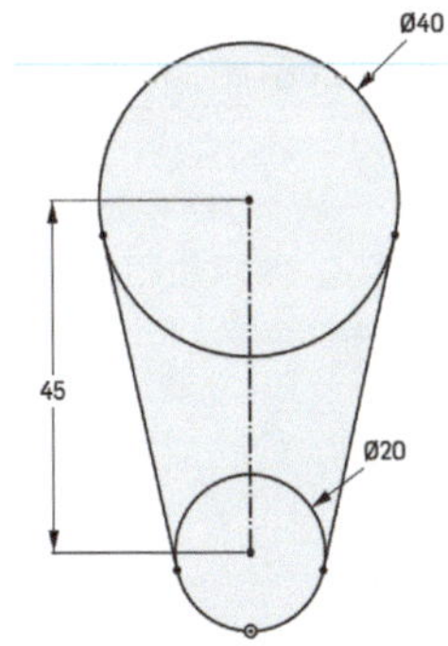

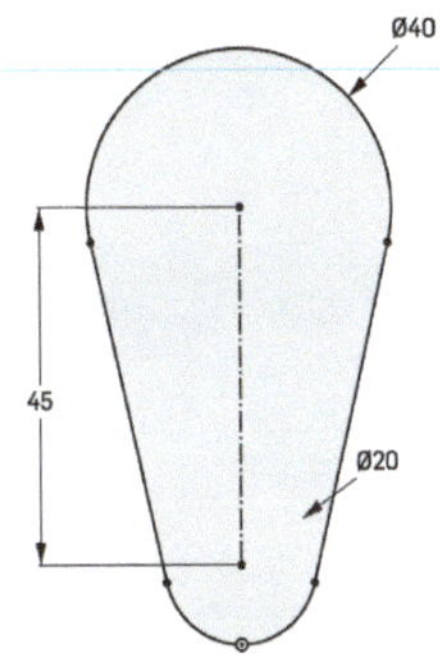

The tool that will be used to make the 3D Part requires this profile to be a continuous shape. You'll need to remove the inner arcs.

Select the Trim tool [M] and click and drag your cursor through the inner arcs to remove them, but keep the Construction line.

Confirm the Sketch ✅ and get an Isometric view.

New Sketch on the Right Plane, then [N] . Create and dimension a Center Point Rectangle [R] from the Origin. Confirm the Sketch ✅.

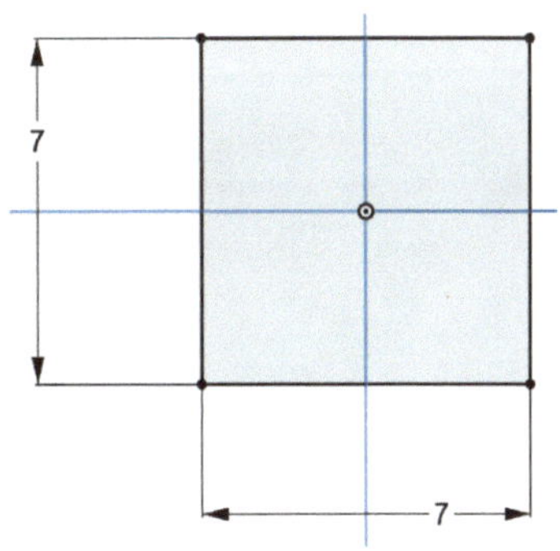

Q? Click the tape measure tool in the bottom right of the page, then click diagonal corners of the square. What is the distance between the points?

....

There are two ways to fully define this sketch that take the same amount of time.

1 - Dimension both lines to 7 mm.
2 - Dimension one side and use the Equal constraint.

Q? Which way do you think is "better" and why?

....

The main tool used in this project to make the general Carabiner model is the Sweep tool. This tool requires two sketches: a profile, and a path to trace that profile along. In this project, Sketch 1 is the path, and Sketch 2 is the profile.

Navigate to the Sweep tool, click the rectangle profile as the profile, click the red Sweep Path box, and click on the lines of the Carabiner for the path. Confirm.

Q? Does it matter in what order the path segments are selected?

....

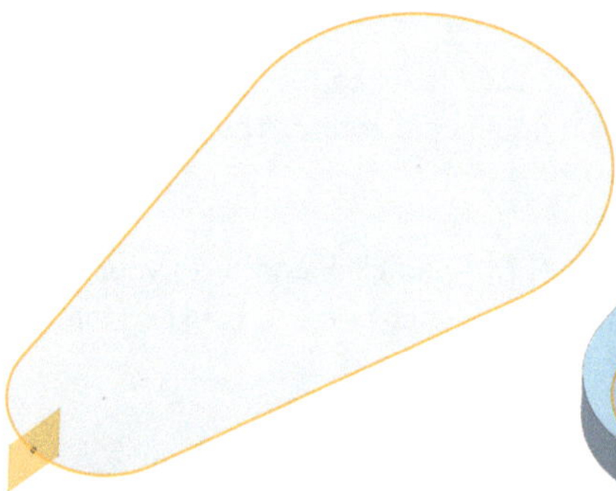

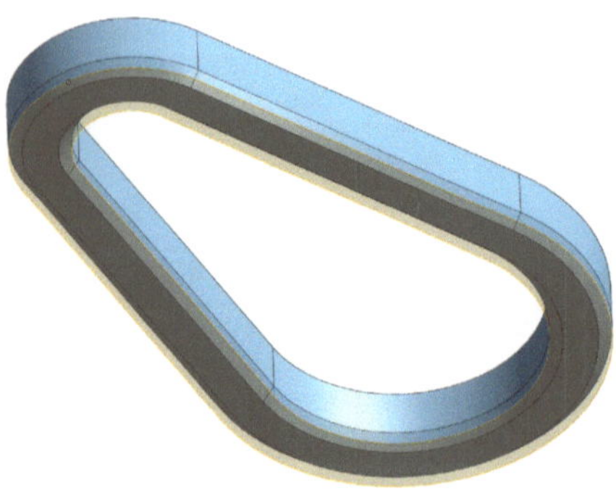

Select the Chamfer tool, select the bottom face, and set the Distance to 1.5 mm.

Q? What happens if you set it to 20 mm?

....

Q? What happens if you change the angle of the Chamfer 80 deg?

....

In manufacturing, sharp edges are usually removed; Fillets (rounded) and Chamfers (angled) are the most common techniques for removing them.

Because this Carabiner is designed to be 3D Printed, it is beneficial to Chamfer the underside of the part to prevent drooping and to Fillet the rest of the part.

Next in the design, you will make a bending relief cut out, and the latch mechanism of the Carabiner.

Make a new sketch on the Carabiner's top face and sketch a Construction line [L] and [Q] from the white Origin dot up to the edge of the carabiner.

Expand the Offset pulldown menu to select the Slot tool, select the Construction line and press Enter.

Double click the dimension, type 1, and press Enter. Confirm Sketch ✅.

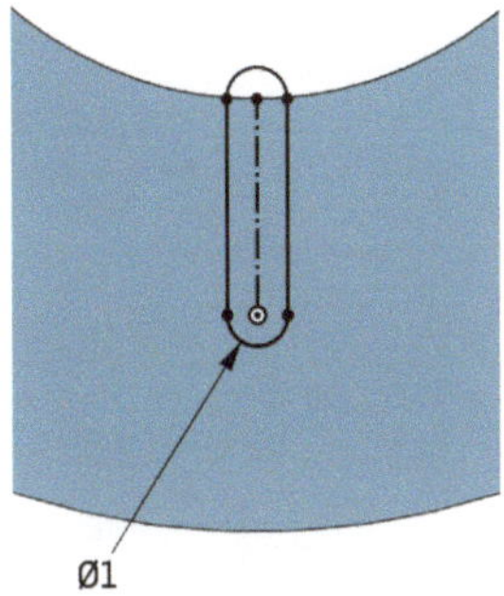

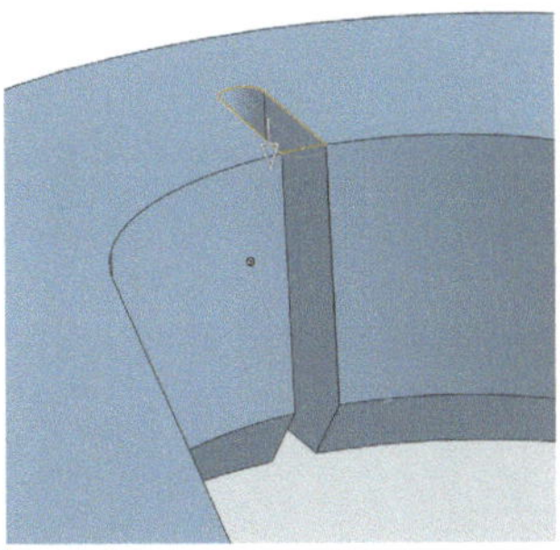

Click the View Cube's corner for an isometric view. Extrude Remove the slot and Change the End Type from Blind to Through All.

Q? What happens if you set the Extrude extent from Through all to Up To Face? Do you think that affects your design later?

....

Make a new Sketch on the Carabiners Top Face, press [U] for the Use tool, and select the top inner arc of the Part.

The right endpoint of the arc will be the starting point of the sketch for the latch mechanism.

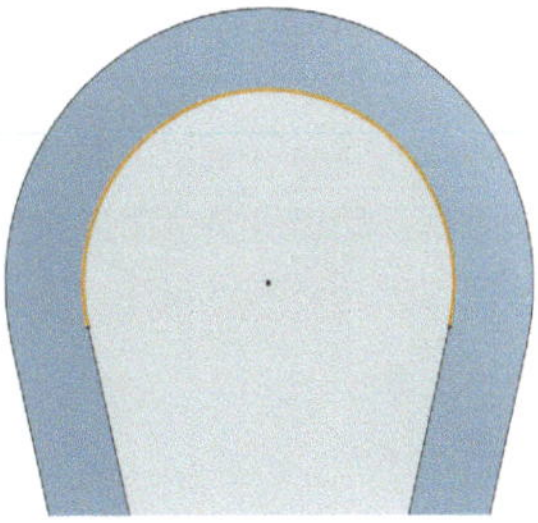

Make a Z shape of three Construction lines, [L] then [Q], from the right endpoint of the arc. Add an Equal constraint [E] to the two horizontal lines and set the angled line to be Parallel [B] to the angled edges of the Part. Dimension the horizontal lines to be 8 mm apart.

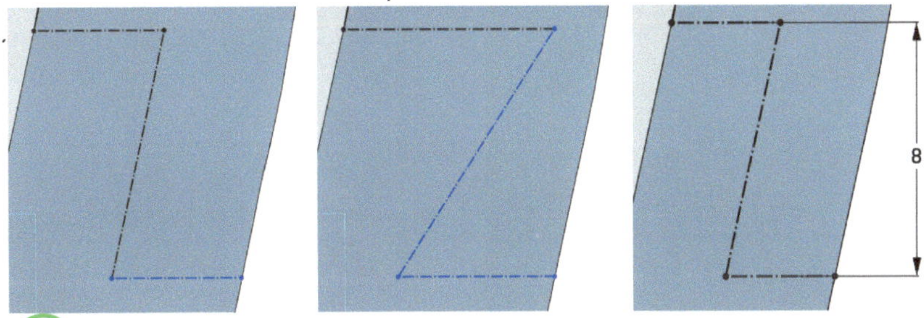

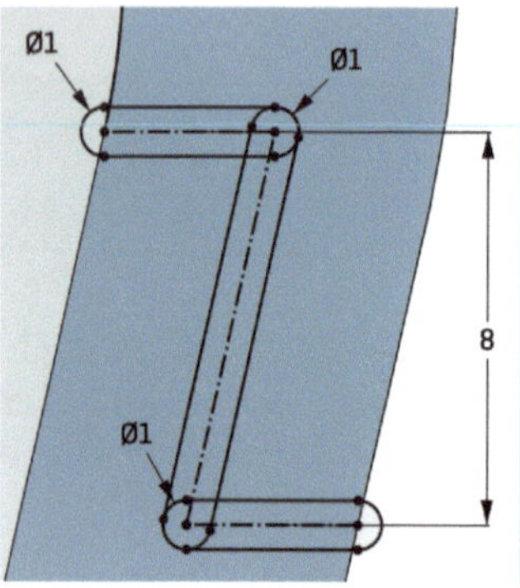

Select the Slot tool, click on the top Construction line, and confirm it with the left mouse button.

Using the same dimension as the previous Slot, you can keep it at 1 mm in diameter.

Next click on the middle angled line, confirm it with the left mouse button, click the bottom horizontal line, confirm the last slot, and finally confirm the Sketch ✅.

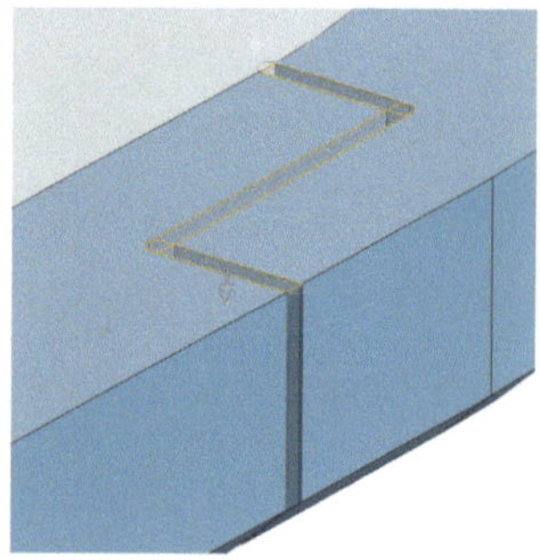

Get an Isometric View of the Sketch and Extrude Remove the 5 profiles through the entire Part ✅.

Q? Did you use a dimension or an Extent Type?

....

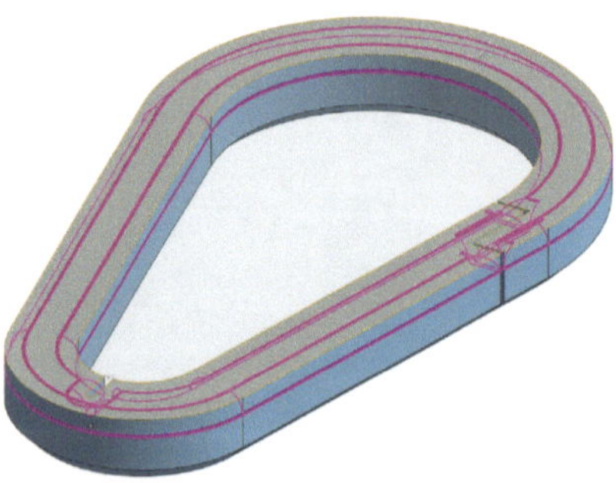

Add a 2 mm Fillet to the top face.

Uh oh... When you do this, you get an error because of the sharp geometry.

Q? Is there a number that does not cause this error?

....

One way to fix this is to confirm the fillet, navigate to the Feature List, and click and drag the Fillet 1 feature to above the most recent Extrude feature.

This reorders the "timeline" of the project and make a Fillet on the top face first, then Extrude Removes the latch mechanism.

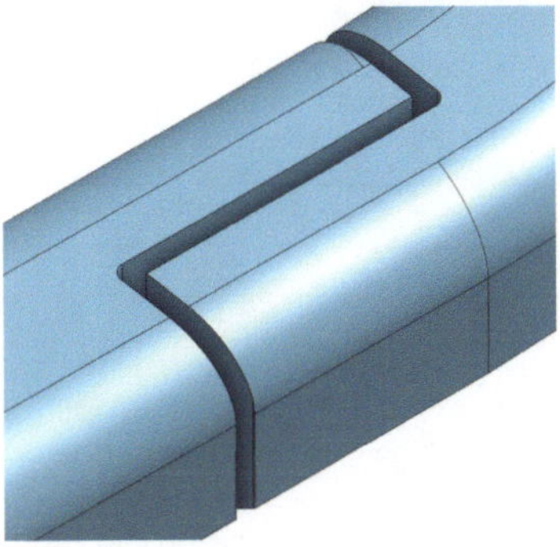

Double-click Fillet 1 to edit it, set the radius to 1.5 mm, and click to confirm.

Then click, drag, and move Fillet 1 back below the Extrude (the present).

Q? What does this information say about how the feature list works?

....

Right click on Part 1 in the Parts List and select Edit Appearance to set the 3D printable Carabiner to a 3D printing filament you have on hand, or to your favorite color.

Giving your CAD model an accurate visual appearance based on the real-world material you plan to use helps make the designs easier to visualize.

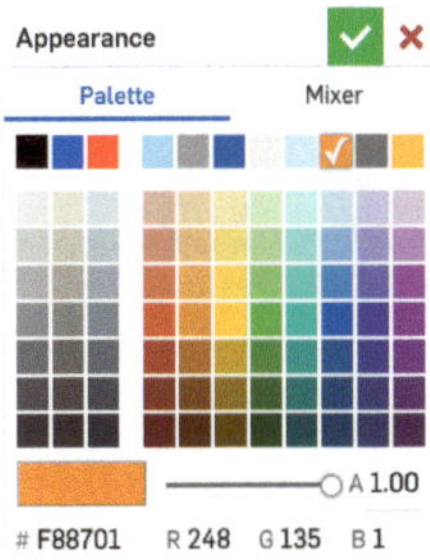

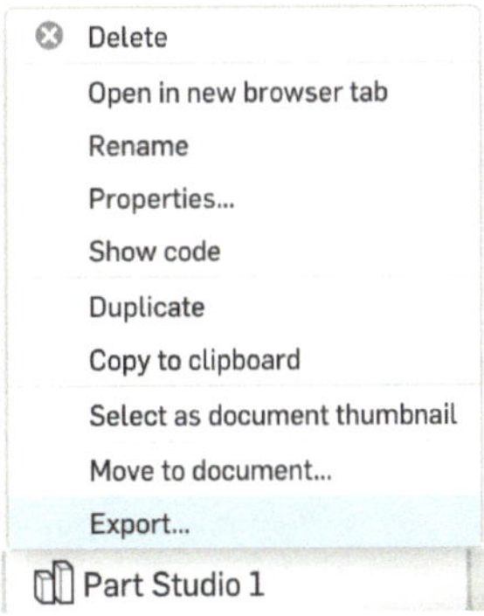

To save the file as an STL for 3D printing, you can export it and change the file type.

Right click on the Part Studio 1 tab at the bottom of your page and select Export. Name it Carabiner, change the Format to STL, and press Export. This format will be understood and accepted by most slicing softwares.

For those new to 3D printing, slicing is the process of turning a 3D model into a 3D printable file.

Reinforce & Stretch

Change the diameters of the circles and the distance between them in Sketch 1, and significantly increase the size of the square profile.

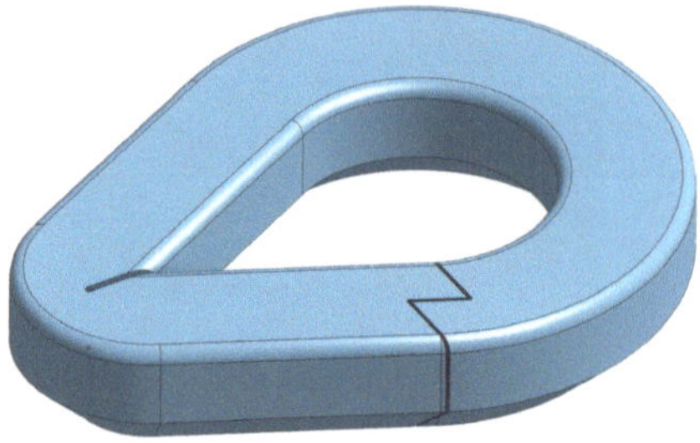

Notice how these adjustments radically affect the final shape and proportions of the model.

Q? As you move them, do any of the constraints stop you? Can the profile be too big for the path?

....

- Sweep Path Sketch
- Sweep Profile Sketch
- Sweep Feature
- 3D Print Chamfer Underside
- Stress Relief Sketch

Right-click and Rename to give all Sketch and features in the Feature List clear and logical names.

This helps you stay organized and makes it easier to understand your model later, especially if you are working on your file with others.

Q? Did you notice some features were hidden (gray eye) in the browser list? Did you do that or did the program do it automatically?

....

Drag and rearrange the features in the Feature List to scramble their order.

See what unusual or unexpected results you get, some features may break, change shape, or even disappear depending on the order they're applied.

- Sketch 1
- Sketch 2
- Sweep 1
- Chamfer 1
- Sketch 5

Q? What happened when you moved a feature that didn't have the necessary information from the previous feature e.g. an Extrude without a Sketch?

....

Q? Which new terms can you fill out in the glossary in the back of the book?

Rubric

Criteria	Excellent (4)	Good (3)	Fair (2)	Needs help (1)
Multi-Plane Sketches	Understands why it's necessary and how to create sketches on different planes	Understands how or why but not both	Somewhat understands how or why	Has difficulty with concept and execution
Sweep	Can join sketches with the sweep tool using different profiles and paths	Can join a single profile and path	Understands the concept but has difficulty applying it	Has difficulty using and understanding the sweep tool
Chamfer & Fillet	Understands how and why to modify 3D bodies using chamfer and Fillet tools	Understands how to use the Fillet and Chamfer tool	Understands how to use either the Fillet or the Chamfer tool	Has difficulty using Fillet and Chamfer tools
Inferred Constraints	Understands when inferred constraints are created and how to delete them	Understands inferred constraints but has trouble removing them	Understands some inferred constraints	Has difficulty understanding inferred constraints
Editing Timeline Features	Can make modifications to features in the Feature List and change the order	Can make some modifications using the Feature List	Understands where to find the Feature List but struggles to edit	Has difficulty identifying editing features in the Feature List
Problem solving	Can ask insightful questions and solve issues independently and creatively	Asks for help and tries to solve issues	Tries to solve problems but often gets stuck	Is often stuck and cannot get un-stuck

Tool Review: Sweep

Sweep creates 3D objects by tracing a 2D profile along a 2D path. It works by following the path's direction, adding complexity to shapes. You can control the profile, path, and even twist angles for more advanced designs.

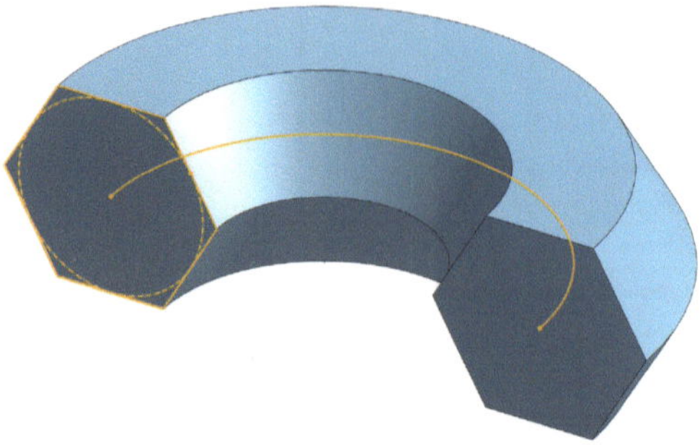

A sweep profile can be joined back up with itself or be disconnected. The Carabiner project joins back up with itself but the object shown here does not.

This object is a hexagon swept along a semi-circle and is left "open".

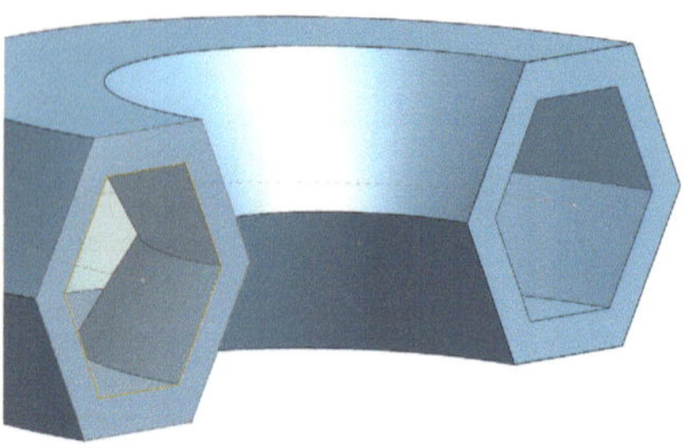

Like the other 3D modeling tools, you are able to make new parts, but also remove volume.

In this example, an offset profile from the original hexagon is Remove Swept along the same path as the example above.

You can also change the Orientation of the Profile from None to Keep Profile Orientation or Lock profile direction.

Instead of the profile following the path perpendicularly, it keeps the profile parallel to the original profile.

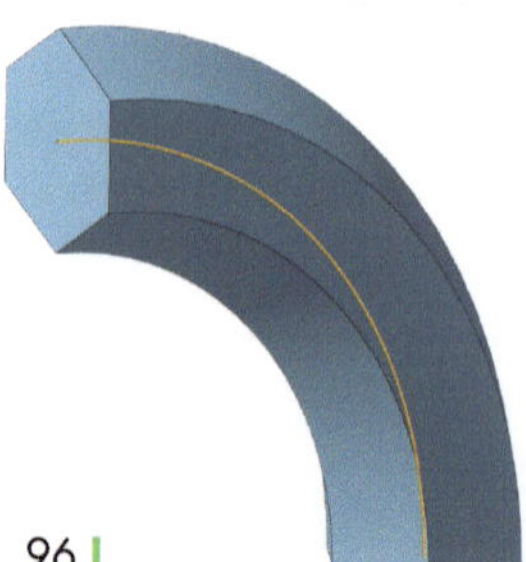

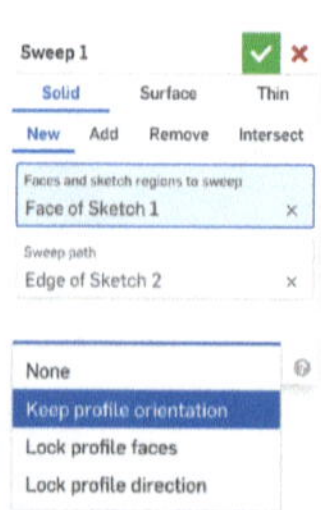

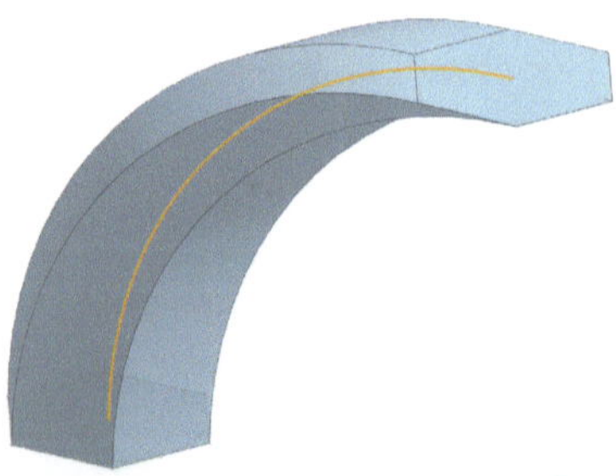

Tool Practice: Sweep

Copy the link into your browser or scan the QR code and make a copy. Work your way along the tabs at the bottom to practice the Sweep tool.

t.ly/aDL92

...or go to the Public Library, and search for "CADclass Sweep" and open the file made by the user ***CADclass***.

Select Make a Copy to Edit.

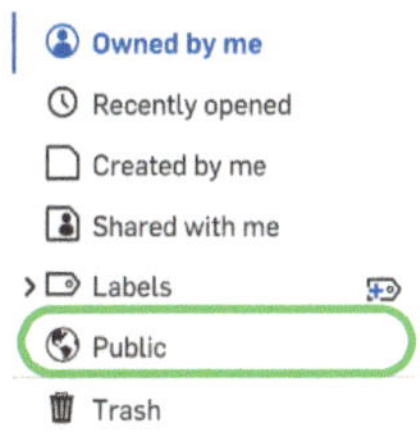

Tool Practice #1

Sweep a circle along a curved and straight path to create a simple paperclip with a unique color.

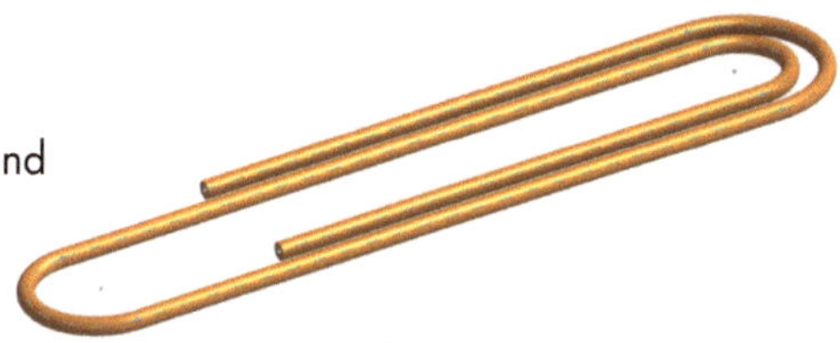

Tool Practice #2

Sweep a hexagonal profile about a 3 dimensional helical path.

A Helix consisting of only a single curve is a common geometric shape that is strangely not often found in other CAD programs.

Tool Practice #3

The Sweep 2 operation has an error and the potential swept part is red meaning it cannot be solved.

Figure out what needs to be edited in the file so the Profile can be successfully swept around the Path.

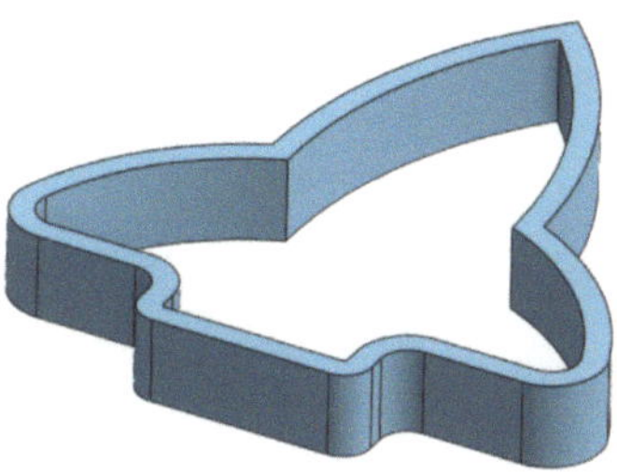

True or False?

Q: A Sweep operation requires only one Sketch to create a 3D object?

Q: You can create your own shortcut keys?

Q: The there is view option which looks like a wireframe model (no shading)?

Q: A Fillet applies a radius to an edge, while a Chamfer applies a 45 deg bevel?

Q: The Feature List allows users to reorder Features to change the order that parts are generated?

Solutions

Q: A Sweep operation requires only one Sketch to create a 3D object?

A: False. A Sweep needs a Profile and a Path

Q: You can create your own shortcut keys?

A: True. Help menu > Keyboard shortcuts > click the Customize keyboard shortcuts

Q: The there is view option which looks like a wireframe model (no shading)?

A: True. It is called Translucent

Q: A Fillet applies a radius to an edge, while a Chamfer applies a 45 deg bevel?

A: True.

Q: The Feature List allows users to reorder Features to change the order that parts are generated?

A: True, it is a time travelling device

Review

onshape

Line

M

Dimension

Measure

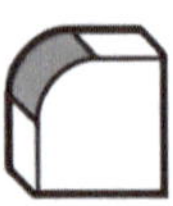

Solutions

Show/Hide icon	
Split	
onshape	Dashboard
L	Line
M	Trim
Dimension	D
	Measure
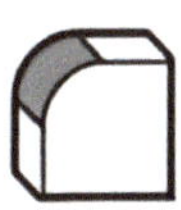	Fillet

Challenge

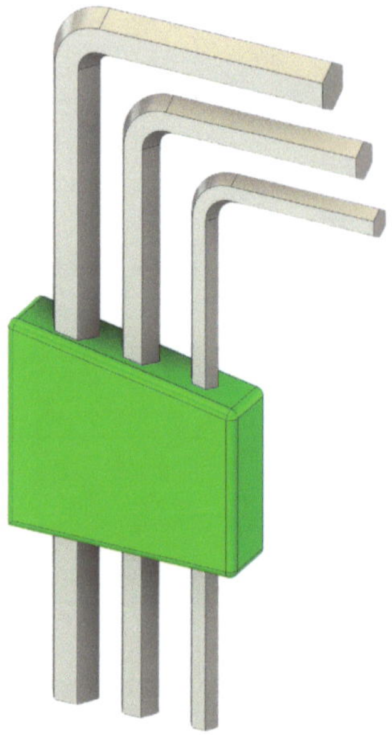

Your next challenge is to turn a 2D drawing into a 3D model by designing a set of Hex Keys, a set of tools that are found in every workshop in the world!

Using tools from the Carabiner project: Sweep, Fillet, and Chamfer, you'll model a 3, 4, and 5 mm hex wrench set with a holder.

Hex keys, also known by their brand name, Allen wrenches, date back to the early 1900s and were popularized by the Allen Manufacturing Company, hence the name.

Their compact, L-shaped design became a standard for driving screws with hexagonal sockets, offering a reliable, slip-resistant grip in tight spaces.

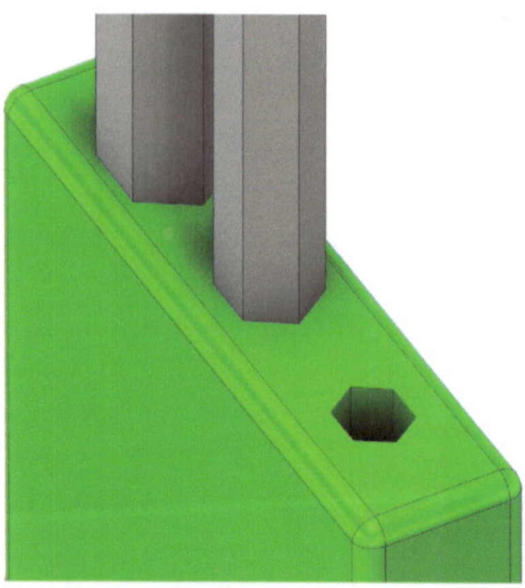

This is the first multi-part challenge in the course, but don't worry, the extra parts don't make it harder, and your logical approach to the project remains the same.

The general workflow is to sketch the profiles of all three hex wrenches in one sketch, create all three paths in another, then perform three separate Sweep operations before moving on to design the tool holder.

- Sketch the Profiles on the Top Plane (Hint: try the Polygon tools)
- Sketch the Paths on the Front Plane (Hint: try to add a sketch radius)
- Sweep the 3 Hex Wrenches
- Sketch the Tool Holder profile
- Symmetrically Extrude Add to 8 mm
- Hide Parts 1 - 3
- Add 1 mm Fillets to outer edges of the Tool Holder
- Show Parts 1 - 3
- Open the Boolean Subtract tool
- Set Parts 1 - 3 as the Tools, Part 4 as the Target, and Keep the Tools

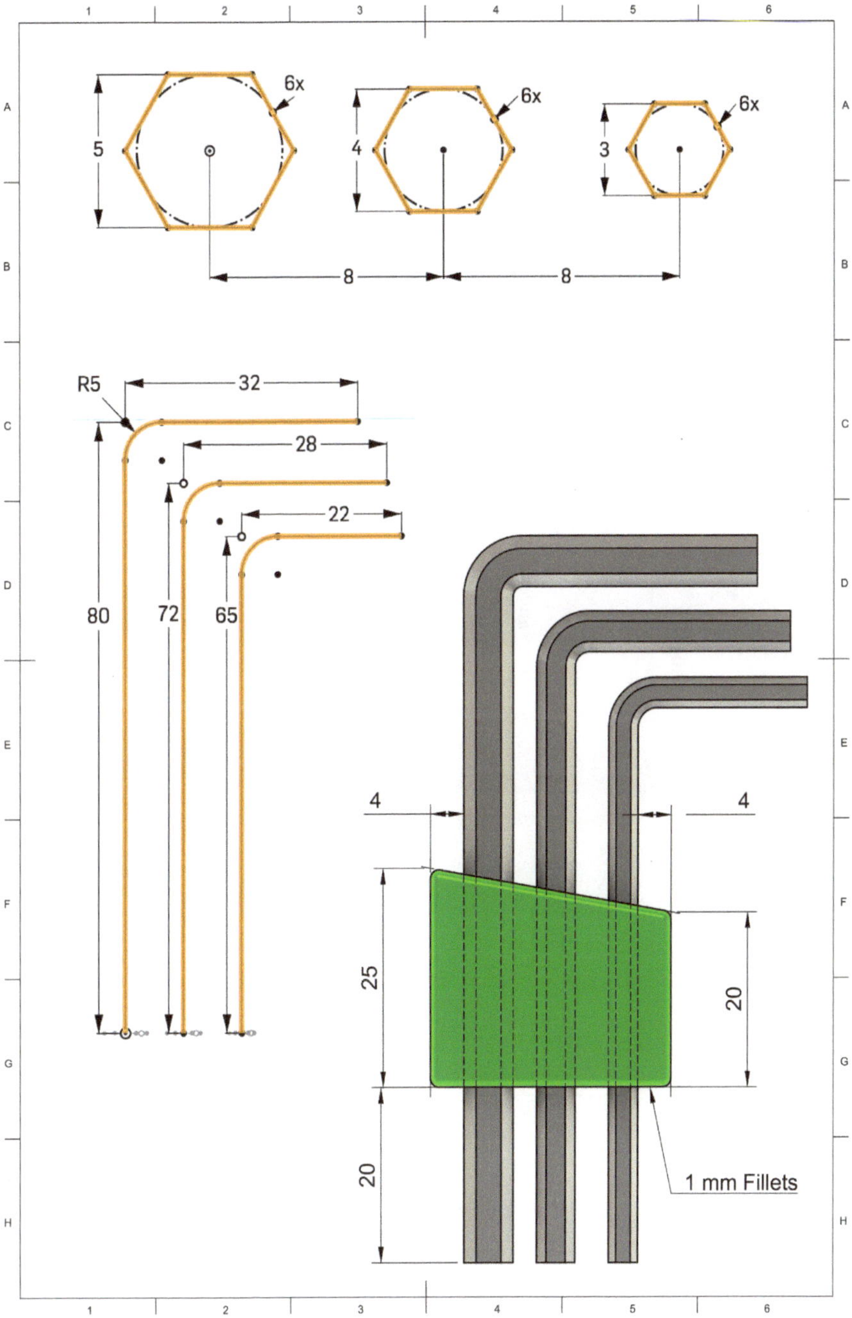

6x
6x
6x
5
4
3
8
8
R5
32
28
22
80
72
65
4
4
25
20
20
1 mm Fillets

Active Engagement

This chapter uses the narrative and real-world connection, opening with a description of surfing that connects technical CAD concepts to tangible experiences in a fun scaled-down way. This approach helps students understand the relationship between 2D design and 3D objects in a meaningful context.

Create Collaborative Design Challenges:

- Teams design boards for different purposes (longboard vs shortboard)
- Groups analyze how profile changes and spacings affect lofted outcomes
- Peer review of designs using specific criteria
- Documentation of design decisions
- This develops critical thinking and communication skills

Extended Learning Opportunities:

- Design custom fins
- Create board decoration patterns using decals
- Develop mounting systems
- Design complementary products

Teaching Lofting:

- Use transparent materials to show internal profiles
- Demonstrate how profile order affects shape
- To teach Offset Planes use physical spacing boards
- Explore other shapes that could be lofted e.g a banana

Implementation of Design Thinking:

- Research different board designs
- Document user needs and requirements
- Create design criteria and constraints
- Test and iterate designs
- This teaches systematic design approaches.

FINGER SURFBOARD
Onshape Fundamentals Workbook

finger surfboard.

Project #6
Sketch 1-4
Loft
Sketch
Symmetric Extrude
Fillet
Hole
STL Export

where makers are made.

Estimated Time: 1.5 hrs
Onshape Fundamentals
Workbook

Finger Surfboard

Create a document called "CADclass surfboard" in the CADclas.org folder.

In this project, you'll make 4 offset Planes from the Right plane and 4 separate sketches on those planes.

Navigate to Plane, and make an Plane offset 24 mm from the Right Plane. Confirm ✅.

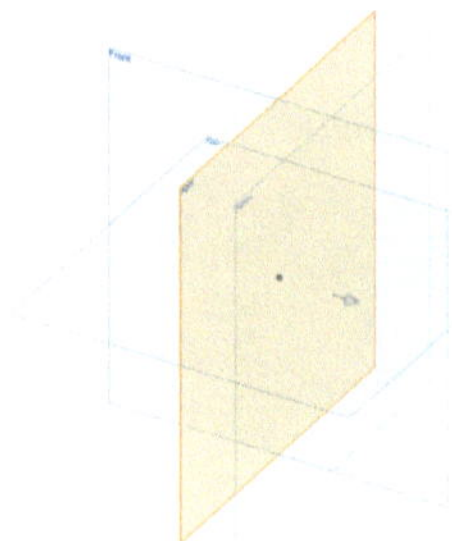

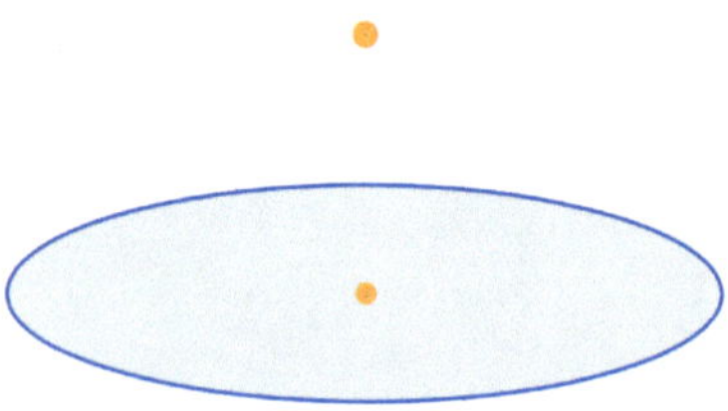

Create a new Sketch on this Plane, navigate to the Circle pulldown, and select the Ellipse tool. Draw an ellipse below the origin.

Add a Vertical constraint between the Origin and the ellipse's center.

Dimension the ellipse's width, height, and distance from the Origin as shown.

Confirm the Sketch ✅.

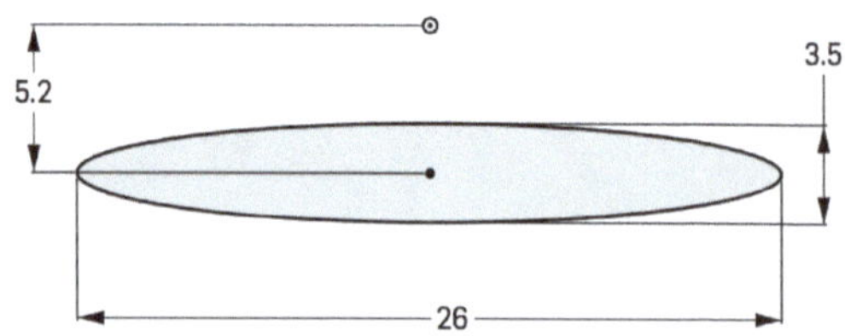

Repeat this process again for the second offset Plane and Ellipse. To make the next Sketches easier to see, Hide Plane 1 and Sketch 1, as they will be behind your next sketch.

Make a new Plane 72 mm from the Right plane, sketch an Ellipse, apply a Vertical constraint between the Origin and the ellipse's center, and dimension the ellipse's width, height, and distance to the Origin. Confirm the Sketch ✅ .

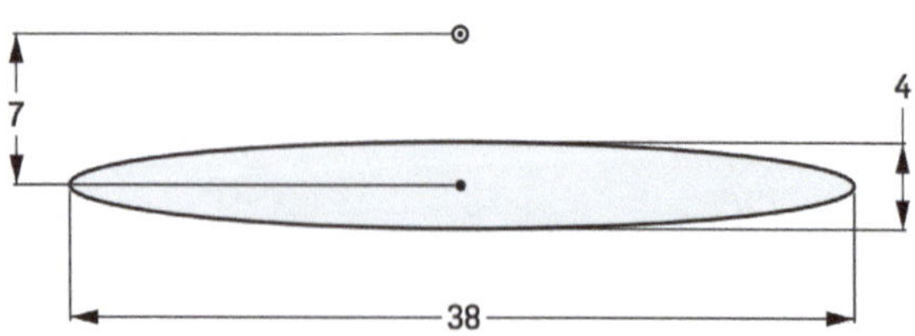

Repeat this process 2 more times:

1. Hide the previous Plane and Sketch.

2. Construct a Plane offset from the Right Plane.

3. Make a new Sketch on this Plane.

4. Draw an ellipse below the Origin, Vertically constrain it, and add the height, width, and center to the Origin dimensions.

Ellipse #	Plane Offset Distance	Ellipse Width	Ellipse Height	Origin to Ellipse Center
3	116.0	29.6	4.0	6.0
4	140.0	18.0	4.0	4.2

Navigate to the Loft tool, click the ellipses in Sketch 4, 3, 2, 1, and then the workspace Origin in that order.

The Surfboard shape will appear as you go.

Q? What other Operations other than New are available in Loft?

....

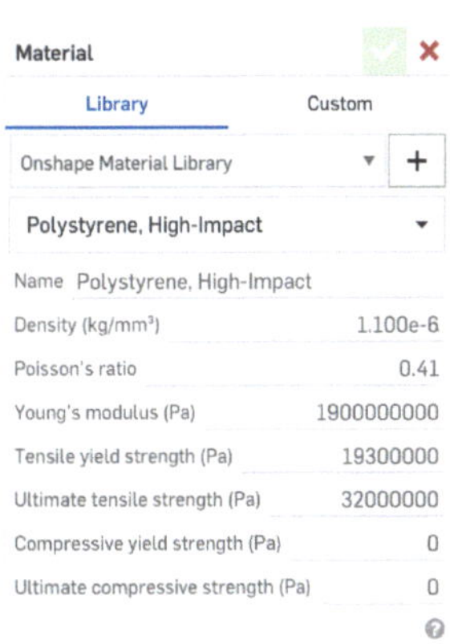

Confirm Loft 1 ✅ then add an interesting color to the board.

Right-click on Part 1 and select Assign material. Search for Polystyrene, High-Impact, and confirm.

Click the Scales icon in the bottom right then click the surfboard.

Q? What is its mass of this Surfboard?

....

Create a new Sketch on the Front Plane to make the fin next. First, type [U] for the Use tool and select the Surfboard's bottom edge.

This will allow you to make a surfboard fin profile that will snap to the underside of the Part.

Select the Spline tool, click on the edge on the underside of the Surfboard, click on three more points as seen in the figure, and finally click on the underside edge again to enclose the profile.

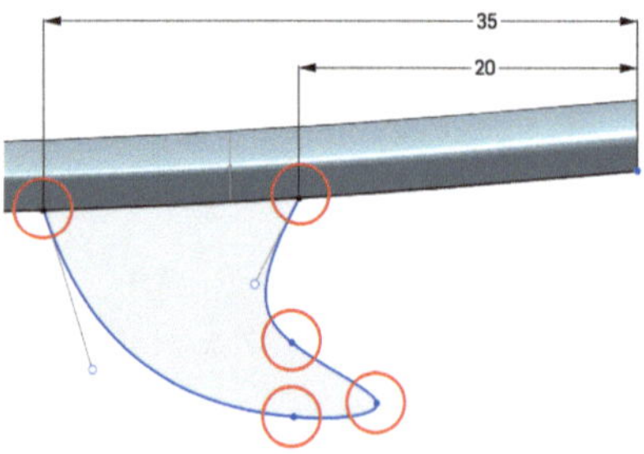

Press Esc to finish the spline.

Click and drag the white points to adjust to curvature of the spline to make it more realistic. Confirm the Sketch ✅.

Q? How else could you draw a fin?

....

Orbit your view to the underside of the Surfboard.

Symmetrically Extrude the profile 2.4 mm. Check the Operation is Add and Confirm ✅.

If the fin is a different color to the board, edit the Extrude feature and change the Operation from New to Add.

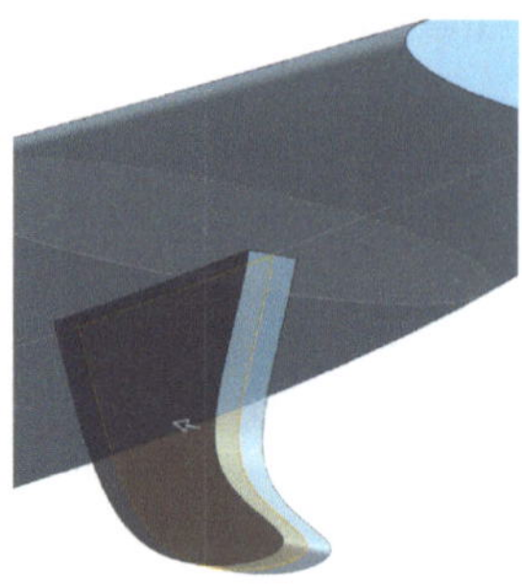

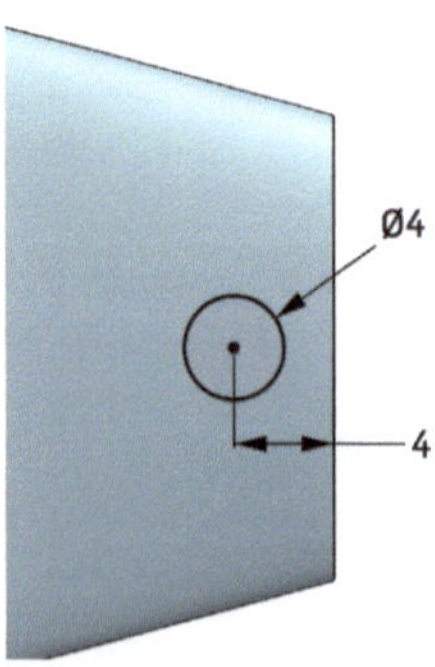

Create a new Sketch on the Top Plane and draw a circle on the right side of the surfboard shape.

Horizontally constraint to align the circle with the Origin, add the required dimensions, and confirm ✅.

This circle represents the hole for threading fishing line, so you can attach the surfboard to your finger, just in case it tries to ride the waves without you!

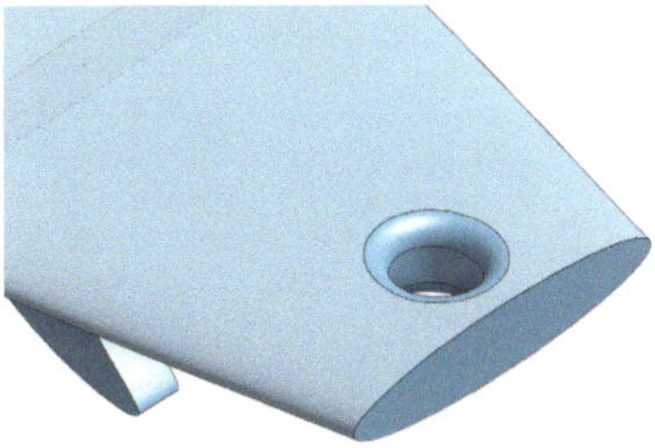

Extrude Remove the circle through the surfboard and add a 1 mm Fillet to the hole's inner surface.

Q? What's the name of another tool you could use to do the same thing?

....

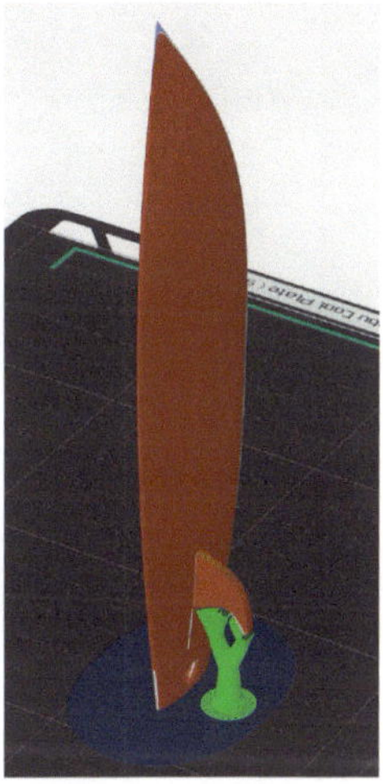

Right-click Part Studio 1 and export it as an STL to be 3D Printed in the vertical orientation with support.

Because the Surfboard wants to be as light as possible, it should be printed with 2 perimeters or walls and 0% infill. To prevent it from falling over, add a 10 mm brim to the first layer.

Q? Go to Help in the Onshape Help menu ? (in the top right corner): Search for "Glossary." What is the first term in the glossary list?

....

Thread some fishing line through the hole and around your finger, slap some grip tape on the top, hang your hand out the window, and shred your new Finger Surfboard on your next road trip on the air!

Reinforce & Stretch

Adjust the size and placement of the Loft's profiles to create a more exaggerated and unusual version of the Finger Surfboard.

If you 'break' the Part, you will have to revert some of the dimensions to fix the file.

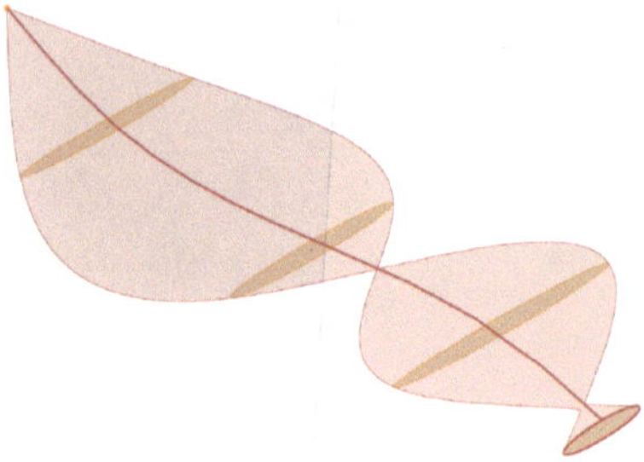

Q? What happens if you re-order features in the Feature List?

....

Change the order of the profiles when Lofting from profile to profile to point. Experiment by reversing the order, and then randomizing the order of profiles.

Q? What do you think the "Guides and Continuity" option in the dialogue box means?

....

Make a test model where you perform a Lofting Cut that removes the volume inside a Lofted Part.

Then try this on the Finger Surfboard Part so you can make it a hollow part.

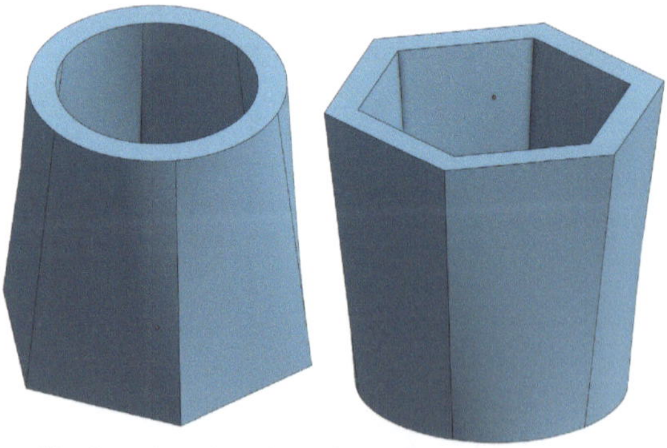

Q? Is there maximum size profile that "breaks" the loft tool?

....

Q? Which new terms can you fill out in the glossary in the back of the book?

Rubric

Criteria	Excellent (4)	Good (3)	Fair (2)	Needs help (1)
Loft	Understands how to join 3+ sketches on 3+ planes using loft	Understands how to join 2 sketches on 2 planes using loft	Understands the concept	Has difficulty using and understanding loft
Offset Plane	Thoroughly understands the concept and use of offset planes	Understands how to offset a plane from another plane	Understands simple examples	Has difficulty understanding and applying offset planes
Independent Features	Able to create many types of custom features such as holes and fins	Able to create a few custom features	Able to create 1 custom feature	Has difficulty creating a custom feature
Rename and Organize	Able to rename sketches, Part's, and Feature List features	Able to rename and reorganize some features, Part's, or sketches	Able to rename at least 1 item	Has difficulty renaming
Explore	Understands how to design surfboard using other 3D tools (not loft)	Able to design parts of the surfboard using other tools	Able to explain how but has trouble doing it	Has difficulty designing the surfboard using other tools
Problem Solving	Can ask insightful questions and solve issues independently and creatively	Asks for help and tries to solve issues	Tries to solve problems but often gets stuck	Is often stuck and cannot get un-stuck

Tool Review: Loft

Loft creates 3D shapes by smoothly joining 2 (or more) 2D profiles or cross-sections. These profiles are usually separated on parallel Offset Planes. Loft is commonly used to create complex curved surfaces or objects with varying cross-sections.

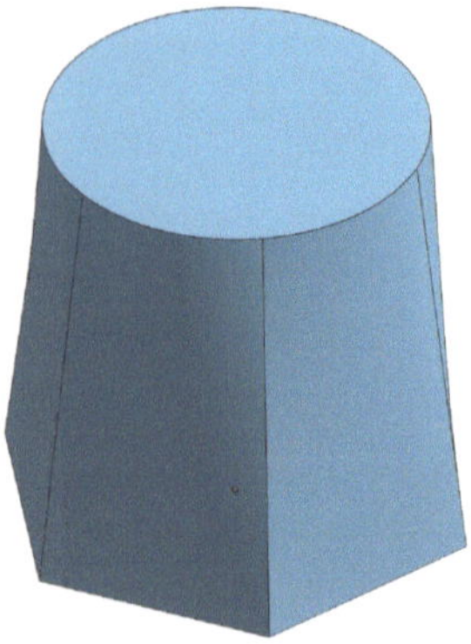

Lofting can create complicated 3D objects from simple sketches and is especially useful for making real-world connectors between any two objects (think dust-collection port and vacuum). These 3D objects can be made by joining 2 or more profiles, points, or a combination of both.

The planes that the profiles are sketched on, don't need to be parallel. You can make a series of Sketches on Planes "Along a Path".

When you Loft and still have the Dialog Box open, you can select "Show Isocurves" to show a mesh overlay on the loft faces.

This shows the progression from one profile to the other and how the facets of the Part stretch as it is lofted from one profile to another.

Note that this also works if you have a Solid Loft, a Surface Loft or a Thin walled Loft.

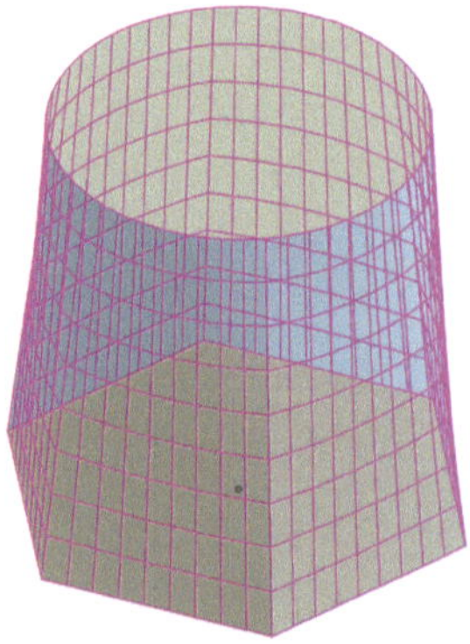

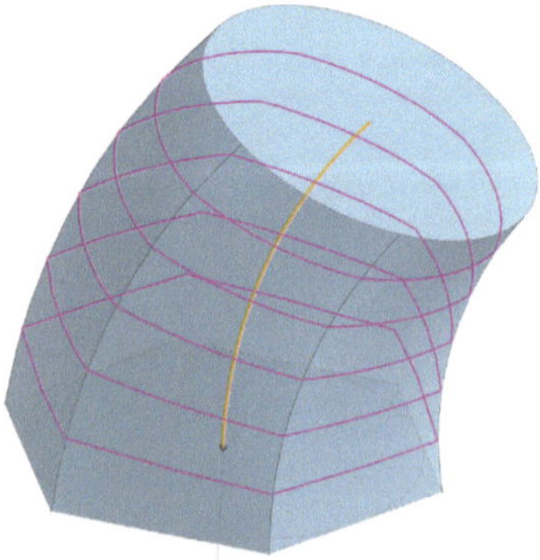

The examples above are Lofting which joins two profiles along the shortest distance, a straight line where the profiles are parallel to each other.

But you can also use Path, curved or straight lines that act as guides for lofting to move along, similar to the Sweep tool.

Here you can see a hexagon Lofting to a circle along an Arc.

Like with all Onshape 3D create tools, the Parts you make can be solid new parts, surface parts that have no thickness, thin parts that have a wall thickness.

You can also Loft Remove an intricate volume from an existing Part.

Tool Practice: Loft

Copy the link into your browser or scan the QR code and make a copy. Work your way along the tabs at the bottom to practice the Loft tool.

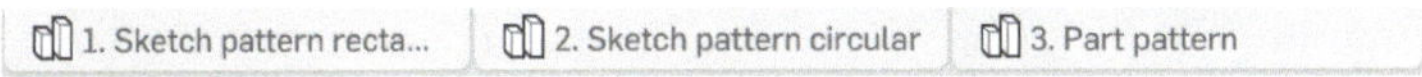

t.ly/MIA2d

...or go to the Public Library, and search for "CADclass loft" and open the file made by the user ***CADclass***.

Select Make a Copy to Edit.

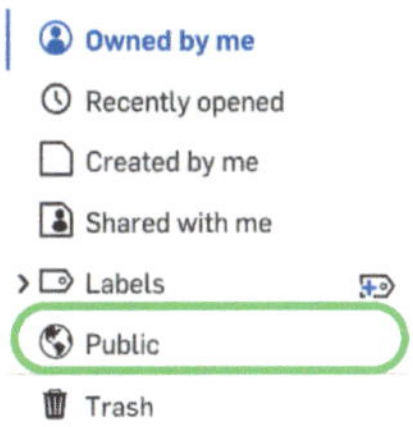

Tool Practice #1

Using the Loft tool, connect the top surface of the green prism to the rectangular profile to make the roof of a plastic house.

Tool Practice #2

Loft between a series of parallel profiles to join to two opposing parts to make a yellow banana.

Alter the appearance of the fruit to make it more accurate.

Tool Practice #3

Perform a series of lofting operations to create a traffic cone with the correct appearance.

This can be tricky as the profiles form the previous feature can interfere with the current lofting operation.

True or False?

Q: You can only loft between profiles?

Q: You can only Loft between profiles that are parallel to each other?

Q: The geometry from the Use tool and Intersect tool are the same thing?

Q: Appearances only come in different shades of colors?

Q: Extrude Cutting volumes are always green?

Solutions

Q: You can only loft between profiles?

A: False. You can Loft between profiles and points.

Q: You can only Loft between profiles that are parallel to each other?

A: False, Lofting can be between planes that are angled to each other.

Q: The geometry from the Use tool and Intersect tool are the same thing?

A: True. They are both functionally the same. 2D geometry from 3D bodies.

Q: Appearances only come in different shades of colors?

A: True.

Q: Extrude Cutting volumes are always green?

A: False, it is a transparent void.

Review

	Shift + E
	U
	Circle
3 Point is a type of...	
Shift + W	

	Ellipse

Solutions

Extrude	Shift + E
Use	U
?	Help
C	Circle
3 Point is a type of...	Arc
Shift + W	Revolve
	Loft
	Ellipse

Challenge

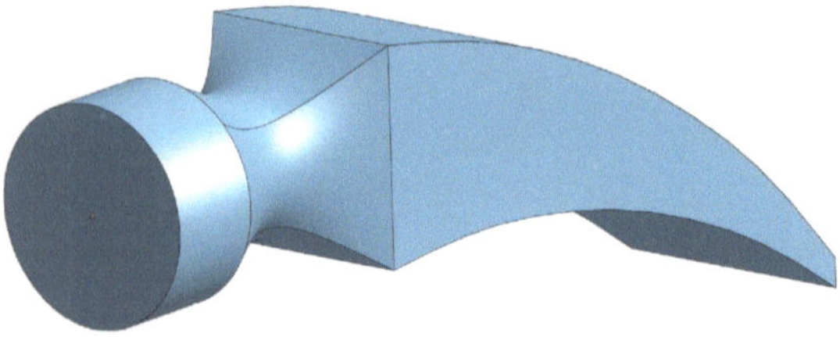

Your next challenge is to turn a 2D drawing into a 3D model by designing a class Hammer Head, a tool so ubiquitous, it represents making, inventing, and tinkering!

Using tools from the Finger Surfboard project: Offset Planes, Lofting, and Extruding you'll model a complex lofted shape from a handful of profiles.

Early versions of this tool were just stones tied to sticks, but they evolved into forged metal as blacksmithing techniques and metallurgical sciences advanced. Over centuries, blacksmiths refined the hammer into a precise tool, shaping everything from swords to railroad spikes with nothing but heat, muscle, and skill.

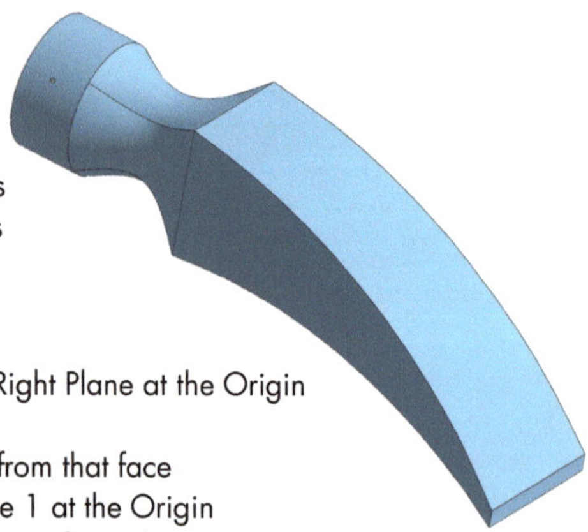

This project will utilize a series of Features, planes and sketches to create a complex 3D shape. A good approach to this challenge is to think of the cross-section profiles of the Hammer Head as you progress down its length.

- Sketch a 30 mm circle on the Right Plane at the Origin
- Extrude it 15 mm
- Make an Offset Plane 15 mm from that face
- Sketch a 20 mm circle on Plane 1 at the Origin
- Make another Offset Plane 15 mm from Plane 1
- Sketch a 30 x 30 mm Center Rectangle on Plane 2 at the Origin
- Make another Offset Plane 90 mm from Plane 2
- Sketch a 4 x 35 mm Center Rectangle on Plane 3 at the Origin
- Vertically constrain and dimension the center of the rectangle to the Origin
- Make a sketch on the Front plane of a horizontal line and a tangent arc
- Loft the 30 mm circle to the 20 mm circle to the 30 x 30 mm Center Rectangle
- Loft the Center Rectangles to each other, check Path, and select the tangent Arc to guide the Lofting operation
- Optional Step: Cut out the forked section of the hammer, change the material, add necessary fillets to sharp edges, and model wooden handle.

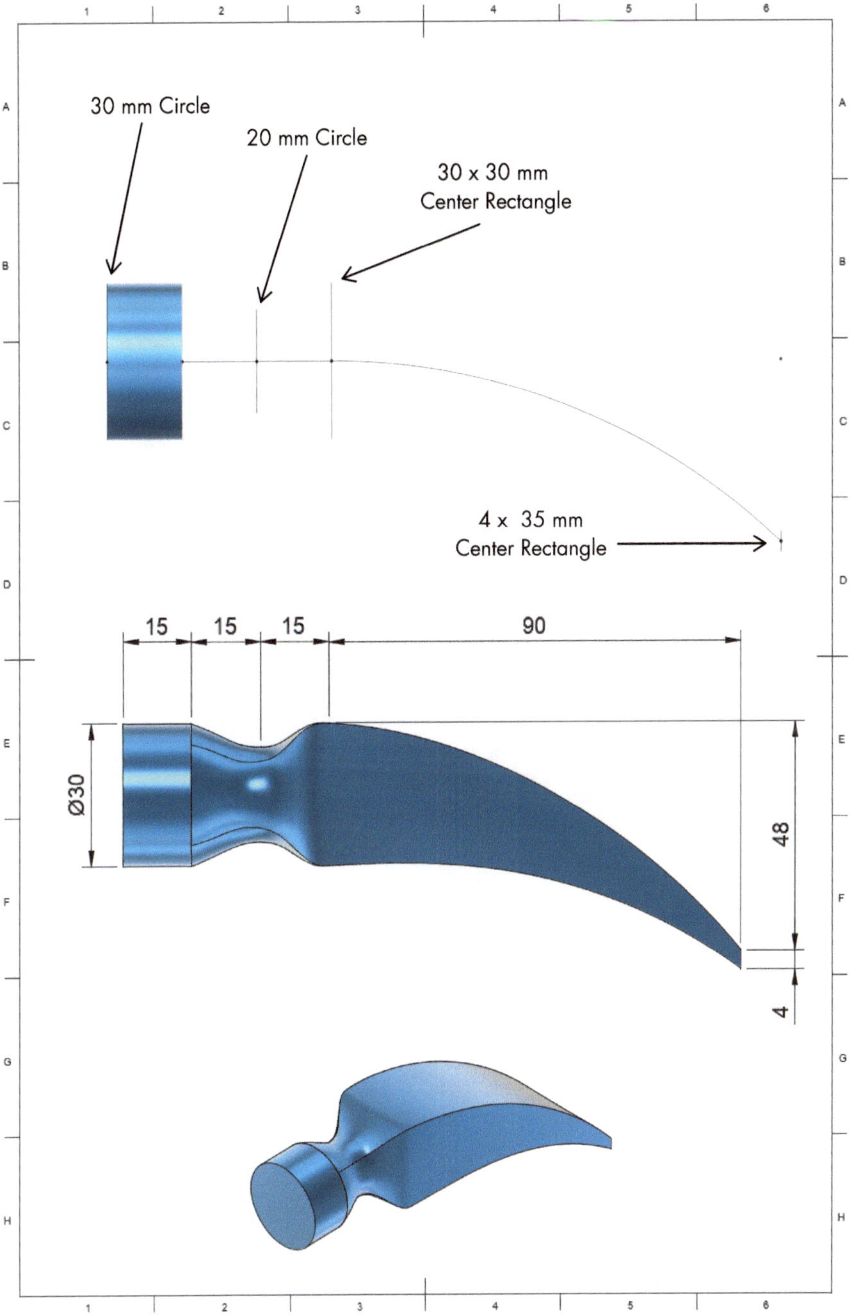
30 mm Circle
20 mm Circle
30 x 30 mm
Center Rectangle
4 x 35 mm
Center Rectangle
15
15
15
90
Ø30
48
4

Active Engagement

A pizza cutter is an excellent product for teaching the fundamentals of assemblies because it perfectly balances simplicity and functionality, making it relatable and engaging for new learners. The "mezzaluna", invented by Italian Silvio Pacitti in 1708 as a rocking herb cutter, evolved into the rotary pizza cutter in the late 19th century when it became a continuous circular cutting motion that proved more efficient for slicing through delicious cheese-covered pizzas. Pizza cutters are readily available in a range of low-cost designs, if you want to curate a handling collection.

Simplicity with Purpose:

- A basic pizza cutter has just three main components (handle, pin, and blade), making it approachable for without being overwhelming
- Each part serves a clear function that students can easily understand
- Each part can be simplified, or re-designed to showcase student creativity

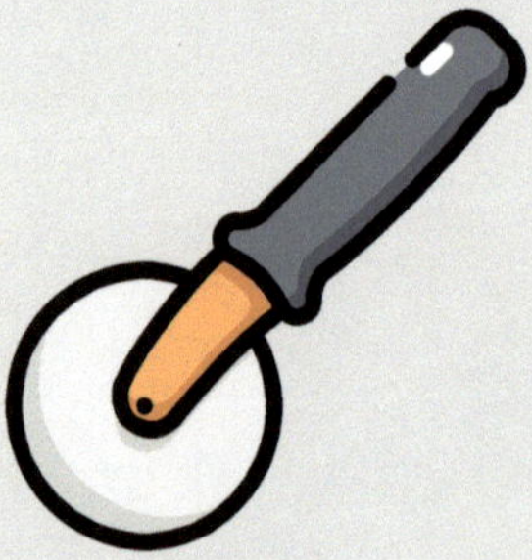

Mechanical Relationships:

The pizza cutter requires and demonstrates fundamental mechanical assembly principles:

- The pin and blade need to be fixed together (Fasten mate)
- The blade needs to spin freely within the handle (Revolute mate)

Key CAD Concepts:

- Creating basic shapes: The handle can be a cylinder or custom shape, the blade is a thin disc, and the pin is a simple cylinder
- Mates: Parts need to connect with proper relationships
- While keeping the basic functionality, students can personalize their designs with different handle shapes, materials, or ergonomic features
- CAD > CAM: The handle is a 3D printable part allowing for physical prototyping and real-life testing

PIZZA CUTTER
Onshape Fundamentals Workbook

pizza cutter.

Project #7
Assembly
Part Studio
Triad Manipulator

Revolute Joint
Mate
Joint Origins

where makers are made.

Estimated Time: 3 hrs
Onshape Fundamentals
Workbook

Pizza Cutter

Create a document called CADclass Pizza Cutter in the CADclass.org Folder.

Click the + in the bottom left corner and create 2 new Part Studios, so there are 3 in total. Right click on Part Studio 1 and rename it "Pizza Cutter Handle", then rename Part Studio 2 as "Pizza Cutter Pin", and Part Studio 3 as "Pizza Cutter Blade".

Click on Pizza Cutter Handle and create a Sketch on the Front Plane.

Sketch a horizontal Construction line and add a Slot with a 25 mm diameter. Verify there is a Coincident constraint between the slot's centerline and the Origin, and add the following dimensions. Confirm the Sketch ✅.

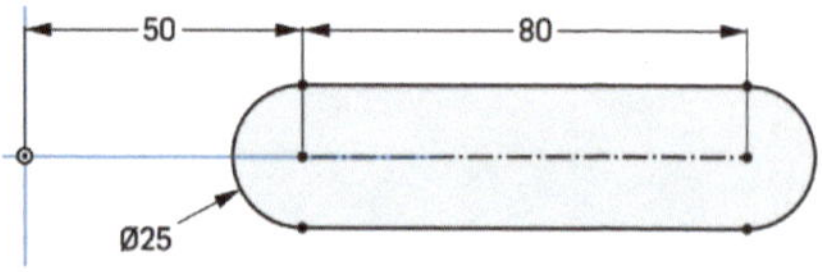

Extrude the profile 2 mm, verifying the arrow's direction of extrusion is pointing towards you.

This is important, as the Part will be mirrored in a later step about the Front plane.

Create a new Sketch on the front face of the Handle, not the Front Plane.

Sketch another Horizontal Construction line and add a Slot from the Origin to the right center of the previous slot. Add a 5 mm circle at the Origin. Add the dimensions shown. Confirm Sketch ✅.

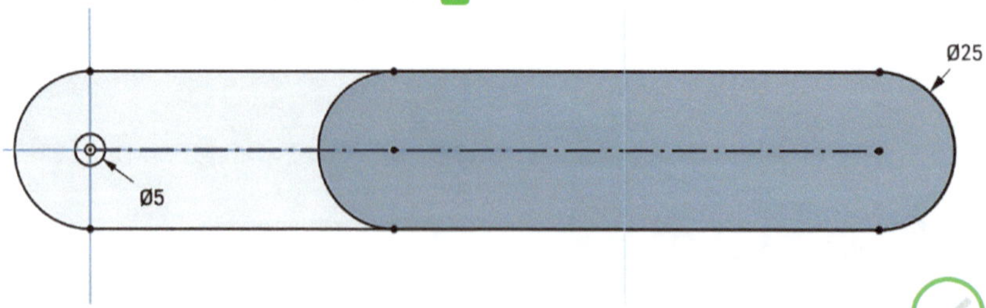

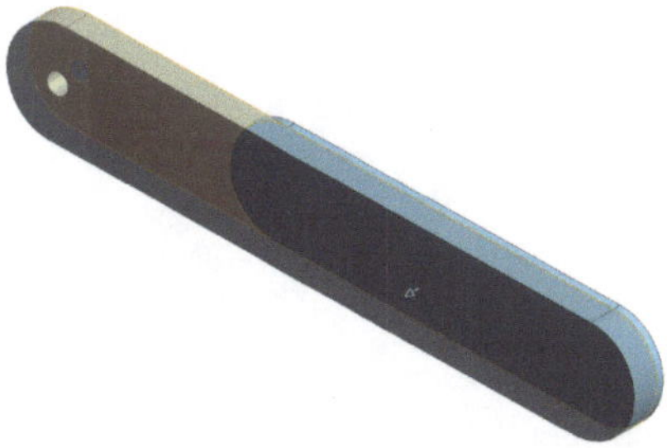

Extrude the two profiles that make up the slot 7 mm, not including the circle.

This will leave you with a hole for the Pizza Cutter's Axle.

Make a new Sketch of a Rectangle on the front face. Coincidently constrain with the top and bottom edges.

Add the dimensions and Confirm the Sketch.

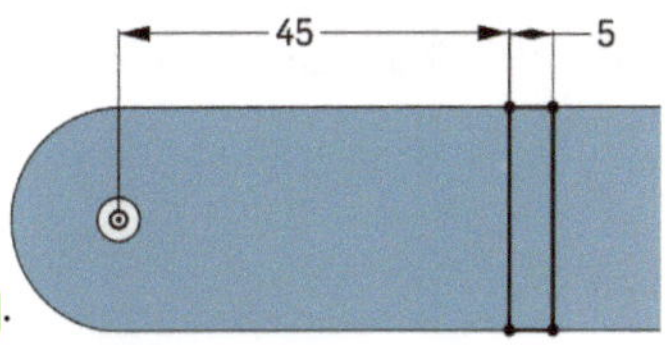

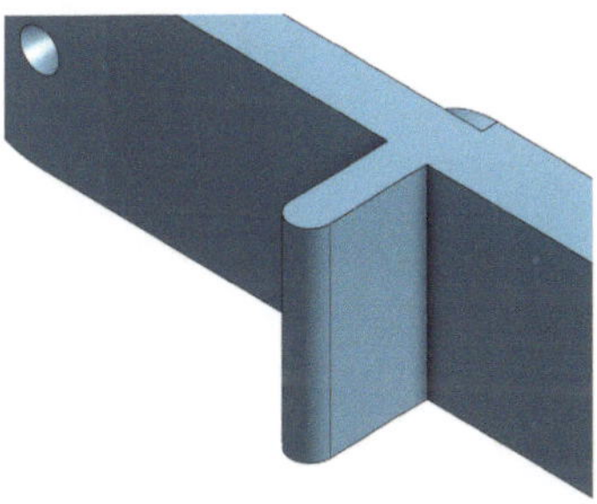

Extrude this rectangular profile 15 mm out to make the hand shield.

Fillet the front vertical edges 2.5 mm as shown below so the front face is domed.

Mirror the Part about the back face / Front Plane. Highlight the entire Part and add a 1.5 mm Fillet to remove all sharp edges from the Handle.

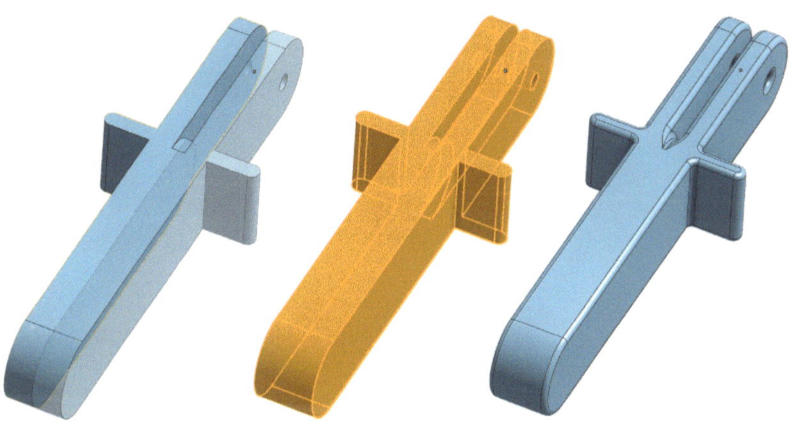

Edit the appearance to something bright and bold.

This is # AE55BC or R:174 G:85 B:188.

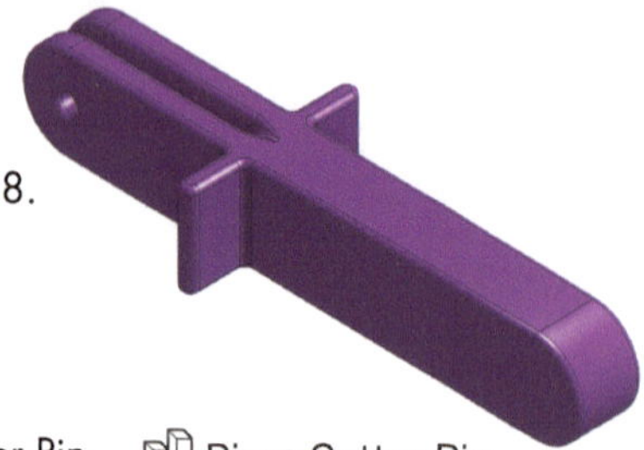

Congratulations, this Part is all done!

Click Part Studio you renamed Pizza Cutter Pin. Pizza Cutter Pin

Q? What happens if you click, hold and drag the Part Studio tabs along the line of tabs?

....

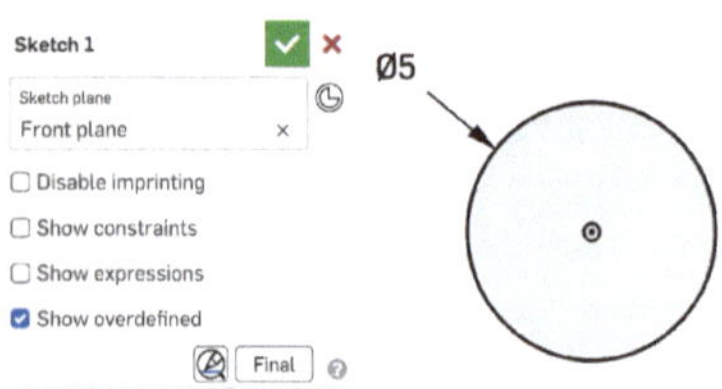

Start a new Sketch on the Front plane and create a circle from the Origin 5 mm in diameter ✓.

This will be the pin that will pass through the hole in the handle holding the blade in place while allowing it to rotate.

Symmetrically Extrude the circle 30 mm and confirm the sketch ✓.

You might notice this is waaay too long, don't worry, its on purpose and we'll fix it later.

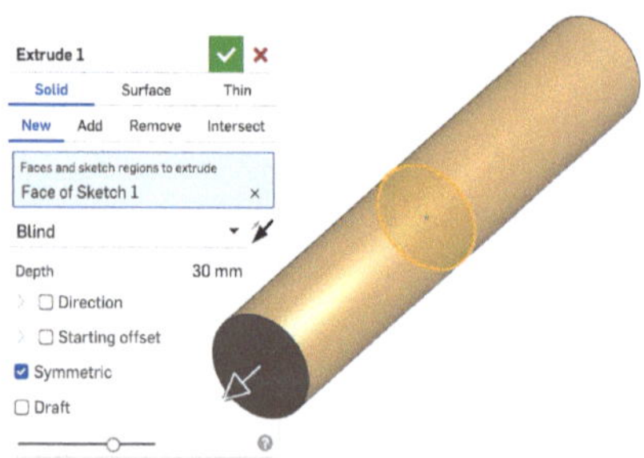

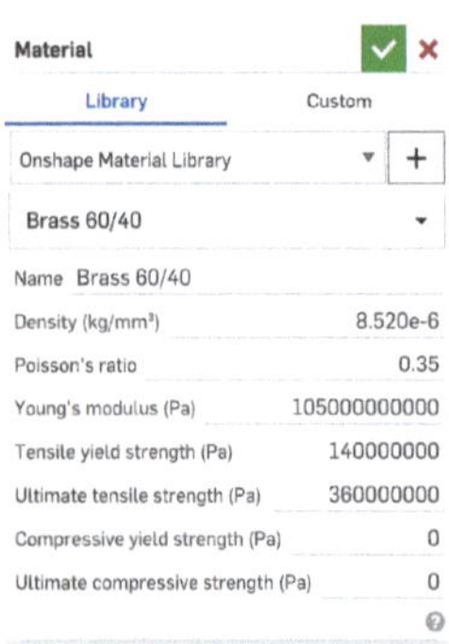

Right click on Part 1 and select Assign Material. Search for Brass, and select Brass 60/40 ✓. Edit the appearance to match the gold-like color of brass too.

Q? Click the scale ⚖ in the right corner and click the pin, what is it's Mass?

....

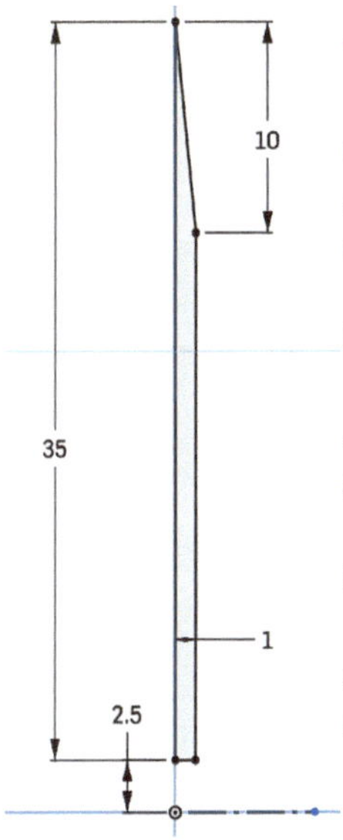

The Pin component is done!

Click on the Pizza Cutter Blade tab and create a new sketch on the Right Plane and make the following sketch using Sketch and Construction lines.

Set the left vertical line Coincident with the Origin.

Add the following dimensions and Mirror the profile about the left vertical line and Confirm the Sketch ✅.

Revolve the two profiles about the horizontal line.

Add a metal appearance of your choice to look better and more accurate.

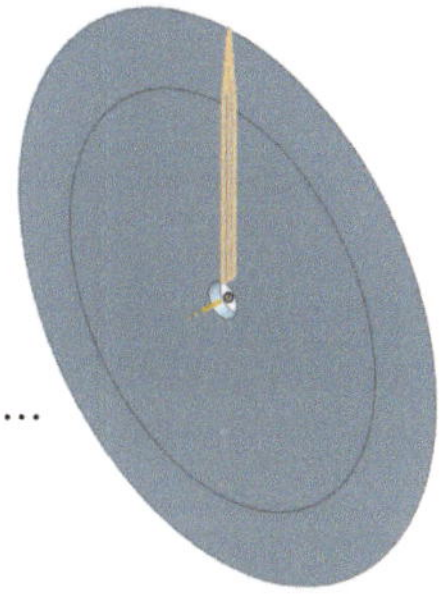

Q? How else could you make this blade?

....

Create a new sketch on the front flat face of the blade.

Search for the Text tool and click and drag to draw a text-box and type in your chef name.

If your text-box needs to be resized you may need to apply a Fix constraint to one corner, then you can click and drag to resize it. Confirm sketch ✅.

Extrude the text by 0.2mm.

Because Onshape is a browser-based CAD program, computational efficiency is paramount and all appearances are simple solid colors. With the text being extruded, you will see that the blade is rotating when you apply a rotating mate in a later step.

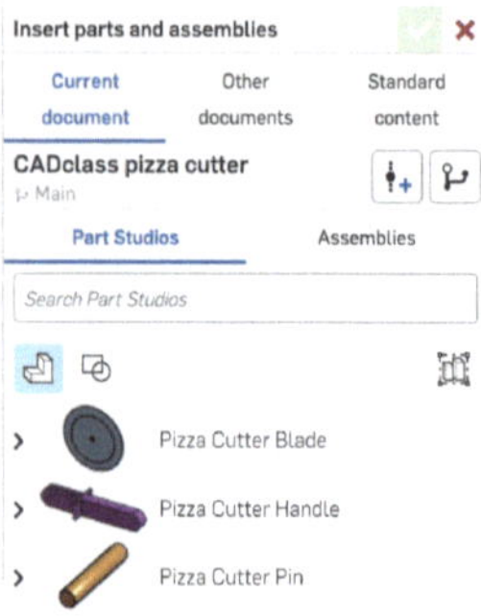

Navigate to the Assembly tab at the bottom of the screen. Click Insert, then select the Pizza Cutter Blade and the Pizza Cutter Pin (don't worry where they are placed for now). Confirm ✅.

Click on either of the parts and notice the Triad Manipulator, which can be used to reposition parts along or around an axis.

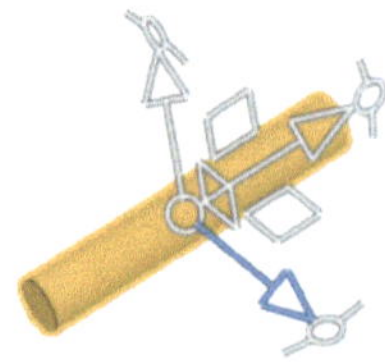

The best practice when assembling is to (1) use the Triad Manipulator to move your parts to approximately the desired position before adding mates but (2) not to reposition them so they are going to interfere with visibility when adding mates.

Move your parts so they are similar to this:

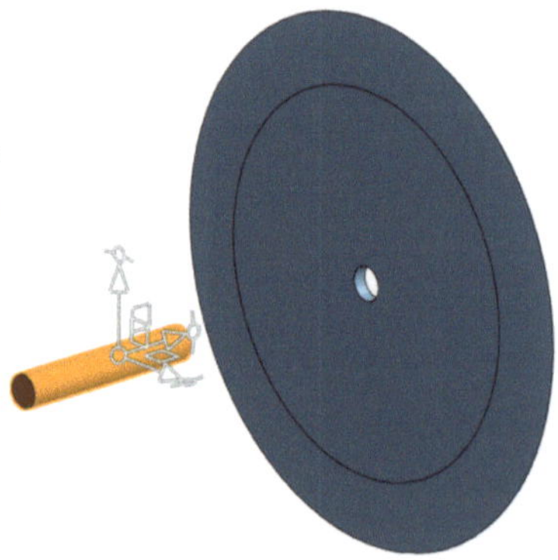

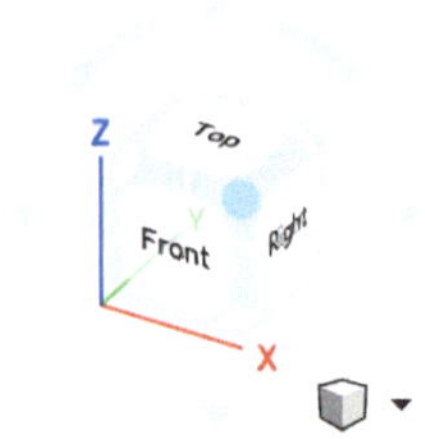

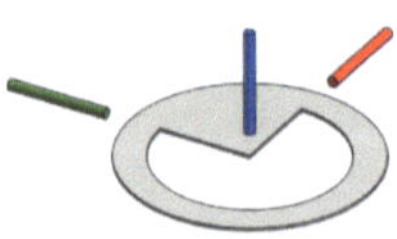

This is the icon for the mate connector. Note that it has the same axes and color system as the View Cube.

Select the Fastened Mate and hover the cursor over the pin. Notice the disc that appears.

This is a mate connector: an anchor point. They are typically "implicit," meaning they are generated automatically based on geometry.

Implicit mate connectors will automatically be generated (inferred) at the ends and midpoints of lines and curves, at the centers of circles, along the axes of cylinders, and at the centroids of faces. Be warned they can be a bit fiddly to place, but it gets easier with practice. Press Undo if required.

Move your mouse so it infers the middle of the pin cylinder as in the image and click to place the mate connector.

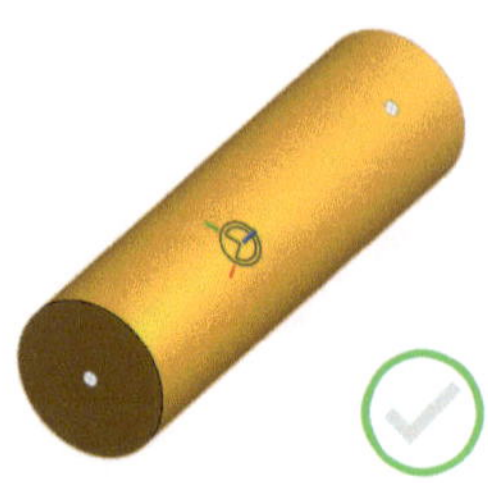

Then move your mouse so it infers the middle of the cylinder void in the Pizza Cutter Blade as in the middle image and click to place the mate connector. This can be tricky, so try zooming in and changing the view angle.

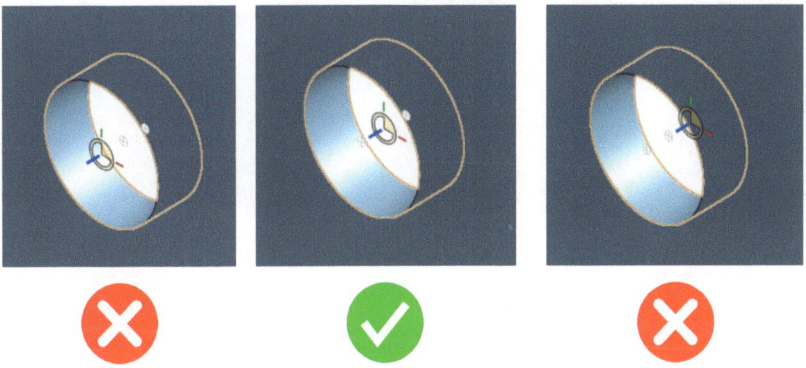

Click the green checkbox in the small dialogue box to Commit Current Mate.

This action adds the mate and also tries to add another.

If it's proving tricky, try clicking the Offset box, and change the values.

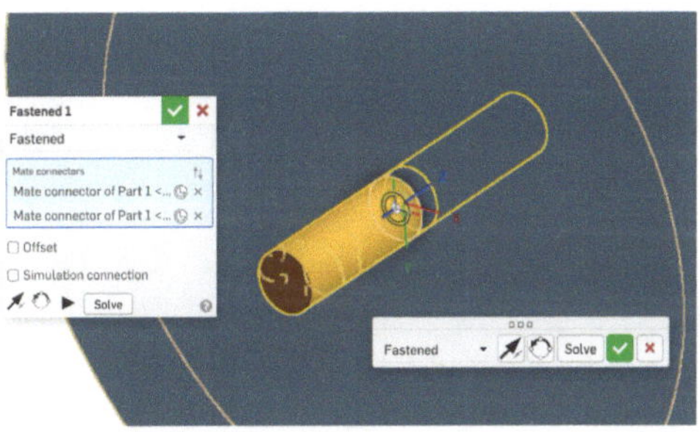

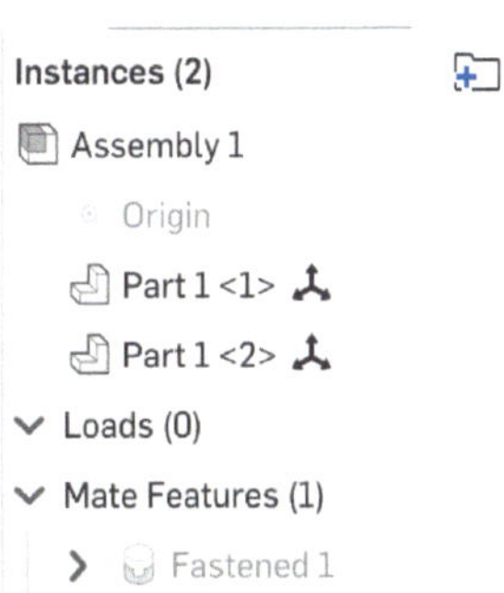

Then click the red **X** in the Fasten 2 dialogue box to confirm you don't want to add another mate. This will close the dialogue box.

Look at the list on the left-hand side.

Notice the 2 parts listed in the assembly and also the mate feature you just created.

Like the Part Studio, you can right-click each of these to edit them, or if you double-click a part it will take you into the Part Studio to edit it.

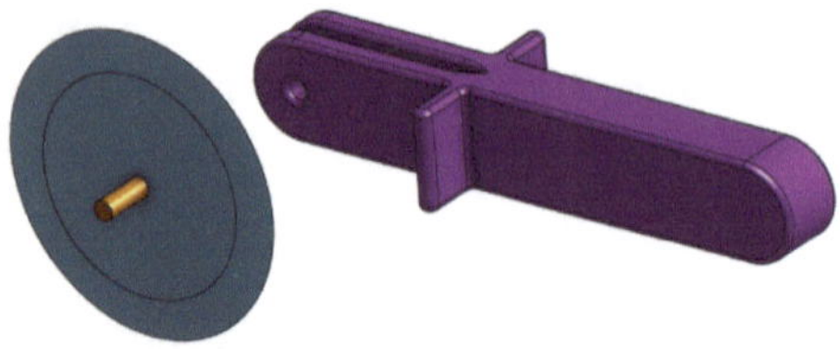

Click Insert, then select the Pizza Cutter Handle.

Click to place it near the other Parts and click Confirm.

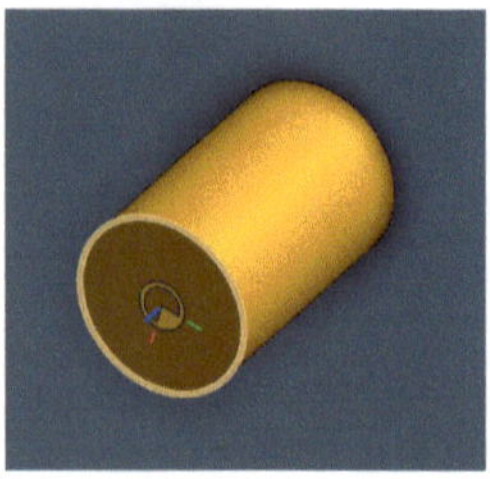

Navigate to Revolute Mate and click the end face of the pin and click the centre of the hole in the end of the handle.

If the connector is snapping to the inside edge of the fillet, try holding [Shift] while you move your cursor from the flat face of the handle over the hole.

Click the green checkbox in the small dialogue box to Commit Current Mate then click the red checkbox in the Fasten 2 dialogue box.

Oh no, there's a problem! The pin is too long for the handle.

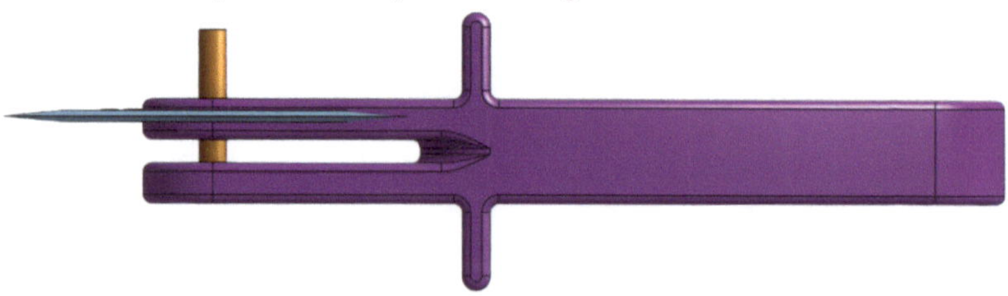

We can solve this in 2 ways: (1) go back to the Pizza Cutter Pin Part Studio and edit Extrude 1 to be 18 mm or (2) in the Assembly Tab, double click the Pizza Cutter Pin part in the Instance List and edit it in Context. Press Go to assembly when complete.

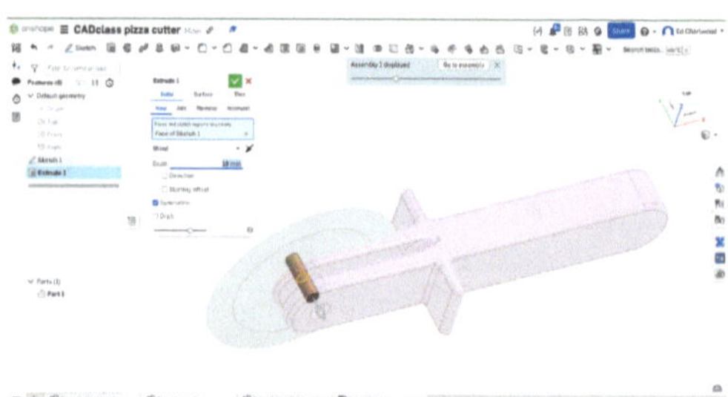

Now you have your Pizza Cutter assembled!

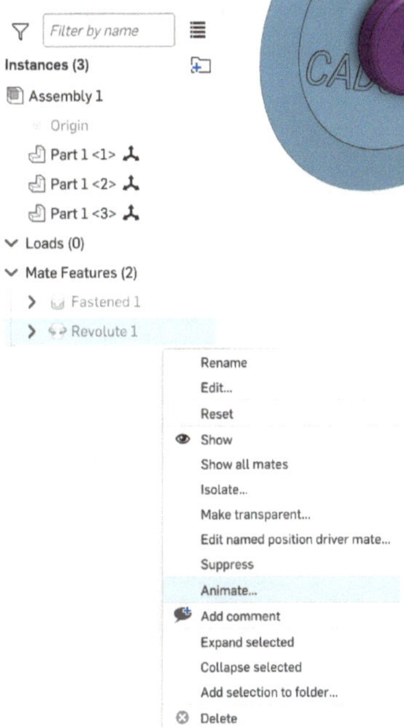

The Pin and the Blade have a Fasten mate so all degrees of freedom are removed. They won't move.

The Pin and the Handle have a Revolute mate so they can turn like a wheel and axle (or to be more technical: it allows rotational movement about the Z axis.

To make it move, right click on Revolute 1 in the Instance list and select Animate.

Experiment with the animation settings to make the blade spin, and press the play button to preview it.

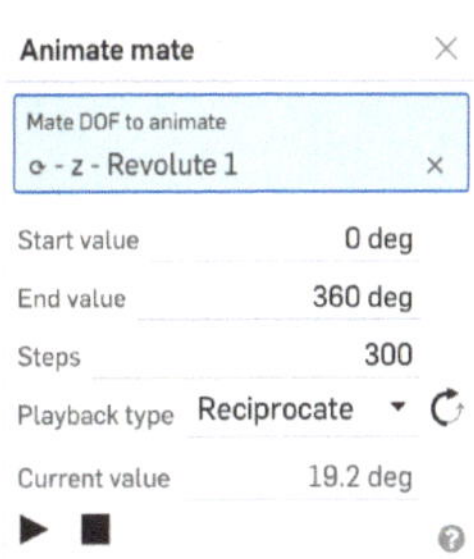

Celebrate the last model in this course with a fresh slice!

Reinforce & Stretch

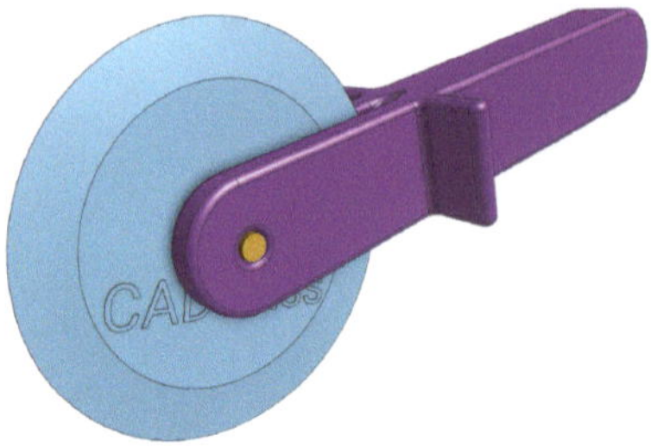

Try to design and assemble a pizza cutter starting with the pin, then the blade, then the handle.

Compare and contrast the approaches, was one "better" than another?

Q? What does the icon for the Fasten Mate look like?

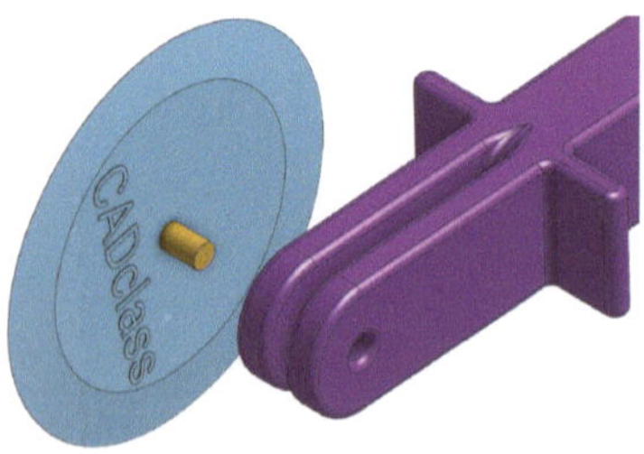

Change the mate type from Revolute to Cylindrical and observe what stays the same and what changes. Both allow rotation, but Cylindrical mates also permit sliding along the axis, how does this extra freedom affect the behavior of your model?

Q? What does holding the Shift key do when applying a Mate?

Right-click on Revolute 1, then select Animate to watch the motion in action.

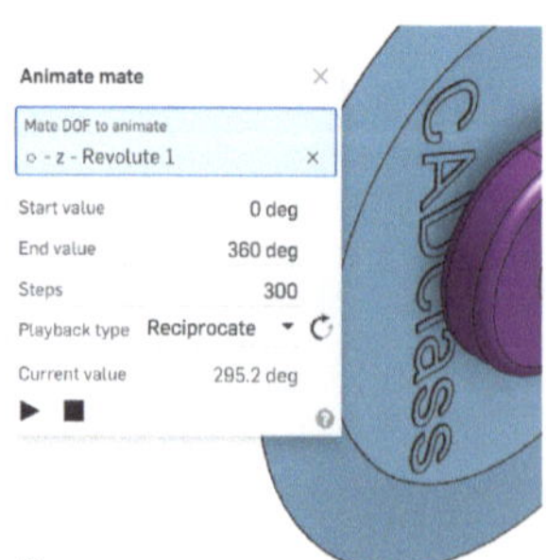

Try increasing the number of steps in the animation settings, this adds more frames to the movement, making the rotation smoother and more detailed.

Q? What happens if you press the Flip Primary Axis button in the Mate Connector dialogue box?

Q? Which new terms can you fill out in the glossary in the back of the book?

Rubric

Criteria	Excellent (4)	Good (3)	Fair (2)	Needs help (1)
Components	Create new components and understand differences from bodied	Can create a new component but struggles with the difference	Can create components with some help	Has difficulty creating and understanding components
Joints	Can connect components using multiple Joint types	Can connect a single component using 1 type of Joint	Understands the concept but has trouble applying it	Has difficulty understanding and applying
Simple Animate	Can add Joints between components and then animate them	Can add 1 type of Joint and animate it	Understands the concept but has trouble animating Joints	Has difficulty animating and understanding
Put it all Together	Can describe design flow from sketch to 3D, to modify, to Joint, to animate	Understands most of the full-arc	Understands some of the full-arc	Has difficulty understanding any of the full-arc
Explore	Can heavily customize pizza cutter and create new designs from scratch	Can substantially customize the pizza cutter	Can make minor modifications	Has difficulty using the tools beyond the steps provided
Problem Solving	Can ask insightful questions and solve issues independently and creatively	Asks for help and tries to solve issues	Tries to solve problems but often gets stuck	Is often stuck and cannot get un-stuck

Tool Review: Assemblies & Mates

Assemblies are the place where you combine the parts you have made together. Parts are joined together with Mates which control how Parts are attached to each other and if they move or not.

When you enter the Assembly tab, you'll notice a new set of tools in the Assembly Toolbar. These tools let you join parts together in specific ways, allowing them to move and interact realistically, just like they would in the real world.

Insert

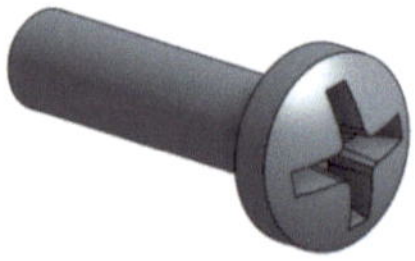

Before assembling, you need to insert parts using the Insert icon. Here you can add Parts (or other assemblies) from the current document, or from other documents.

You can also add "standard parts" like bolts & screws, nuts and washers.

The core of the Assembly is the Mate Connector which you can 'stick' onto different features of parts. Note that it has the same axes and color system as the View Cube.

It acts like a 3D version of the Coincident constraint, you select which parts need to be joined together and where, and one moves to the other to share the same space.

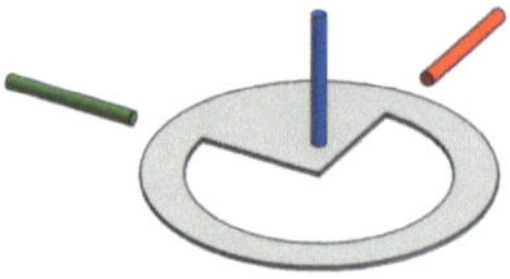

Move your cursor to edges, faces of corners to see a preview of where the Mate Connector will be placed, do this on both Parts to join them into one.

In this example, a Mate Connector was placed in the middle of the underside of a bolt head, and the outer edge of a nut's bore, when confirmed, the nut is threaded up the bolt.

Tool Practice: Assemblies

t.ly/MSnVM

Go to the public library and search for "CADclass Key" or follow the QR code or link and make a copy.

1. Open the "Key Drawing" tab.

2. Use it to modify the "Blank Key" to fit the lock in the "Lock and key assembly" tab.

3. Right click Revolute 1 to animate the joint.

Alternatively, if you want a harder challenge, recreate the key from a new, blank Part Studio and assemble and animate both parts.

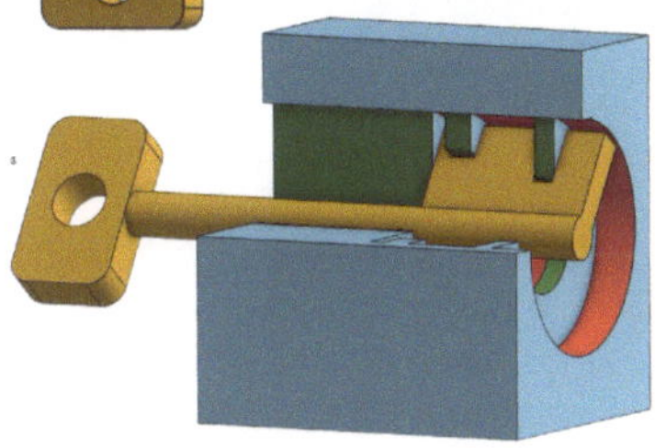

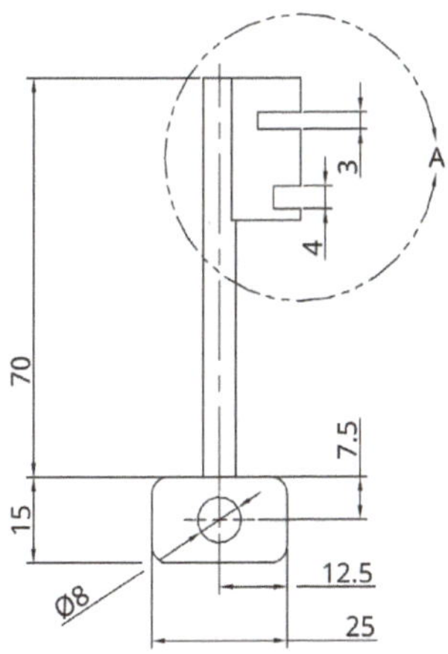

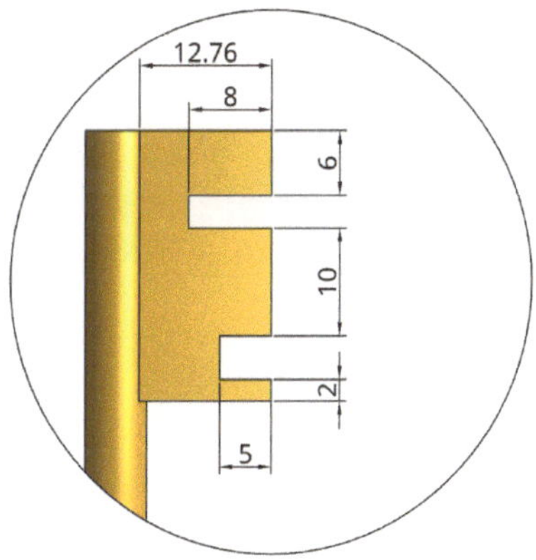

A
2:1

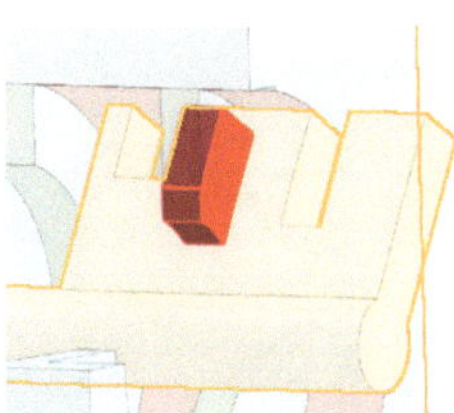

Note: if, when you assemble the parts, you are unsure if they are overlapping/colliding, you can select the protractor icon in the bottom right corner, Interference detection, and select both parts. Interfering parts will show in **RED**

Tool Practice: Mates

Copy the link into your browser or scan the QR code and make a copy. Work your way along the tabs at the bottom to practice the Mates tool.

t.ly/pzN-M

...or go to the Public Library, and search for "CadClass Assembly Dojo " and open the file made by the user ***CADclass***.

Select Make a Copy to Edit.

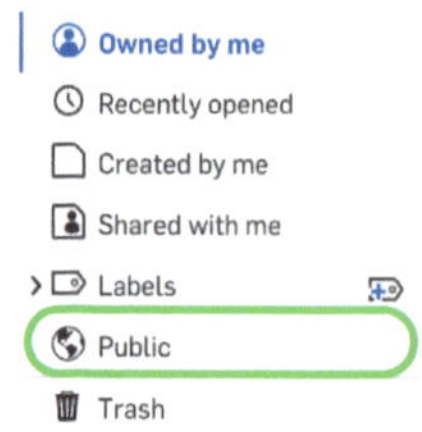

This is a design by Teach Product Design:
www.youtube.com/@teachproductdesign

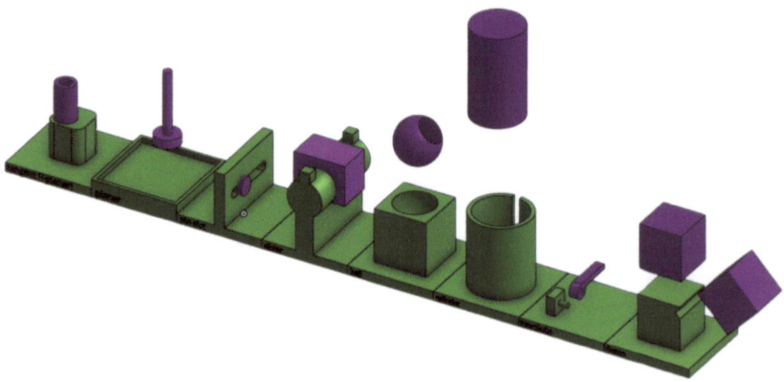

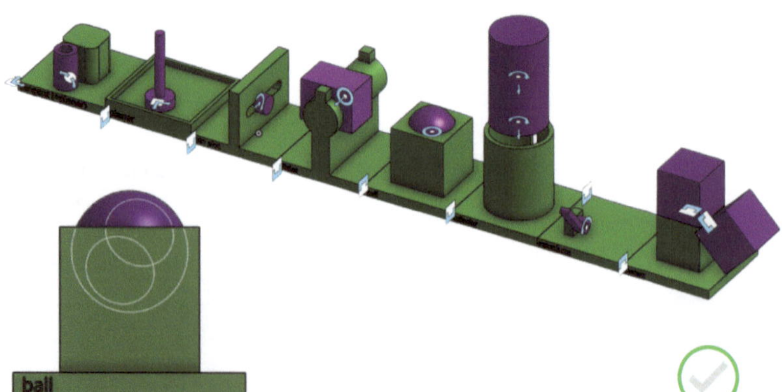

Teacher Notes

Assemblies combine multiple parts into a single product. They define spatial relationships and interactions between parts

Types of Assembly Mates

- **Fastened**: Rigidly connects two parts
- **Revolute**: Allows rotation around an axis
- **Slider**: Permits linear motion along an axis
- **Cylindrical**: Combines rotational and linear motion
- **Pin Slot**: Allows a pin to move in a slot
- **Planar**: Constrains motion to a plane
- **Ball**: Permits rotation around a point
- **Parallel**: Makes faces or edges parallel
- **Perpendicular**: Orients faces or edges at right angles
- **Tangent**: Makes curved surfaces touch at a point or line

There are also a number of "advanced" mates you can explore:

- **Gear**: Simulates gear motion between parts
- **Rack and Pinion**: Converts rotational to linear motion
- **Screw**: Simulates threaded connections
- **Path**: Constrains a part to move along a defined path

Best Practices:

- Start with simple assemblies before progressing to complex ones
- Emphasize the importance of proper part design for easy assembly
- Teach students to plan their assembly strategy before starting
- Demonstrate the use of the assembly feature tree for organization
- Explain the concept of degrees of freedom in assemblies

Common Pitfalls and Solutions:

- Over-constrained assemblies
- Solution: Teach students to use the minimum number of mates necessary

- Incorrect mate selection
- Solution: Demonstrate how to choose the appropriate mate for each situation

Assessment Ideas:

- Create exercises where students must assemble given parts correctly
- Have students identify and fix issues in pre-made assemblies

True or False?

Q: Fastened mates prevent all relative motion between components?

Q: You can only use one mate connector per part?

Q: Cylindrical mates allow both rotation and translation along the same axis?

Q: You can suppress mates temporarily to modify assemblies?

Q: The "Fix" constraint removes all degrees of freedom?

Solutions

Q: Fastened mates prevent all relative motion between components?

A: True. Like toy building bricks snapped together.

Q: You can only use one mate connector per part?

A: False. Use as many as you need!

Q: Cylindrical mates allow both rotation and translation along the same axis?

A: True. Like a pencap.

Q: You can suppress mates temporarily to modify assemblies?

A: True. Just right click it > supress.

Q: The "Fix" constraint removes all degrees of freedom?

A: True. Like covering it all in super strong glue.

Review

Joints are static or dynamic connections between Components.

It is important to note that Joints can only be added between Components, not Bodies.

Match the name to the definition

Name	Definition
Rigid	A Component can rotate in all 3 axes of rotation.
Revolute	Allows a Component to spin about a central Axis, a full 360 degrees or just a part of an arc.
Slider	A linear movement along a single dimension. Example: a piston traveling up and down in a cylinder.
Cylindrical	Locks 2 or more parts together. If one Component is Grounded, neither will move.
Pin Slot	Allows a Component to rotate but is confined to only being able to move in one plane.
Planar	Allows rotational movement about the Z axis and translational movement along the X axis.
Ball	Allows parts to rotate and move linearly at the same time.

Solutions

Joint	Description
Rigid	Locks 2 or more parts together. If one Component is Grounded, neither will move.
Revolute	Allows a Component to spin about a central Axis a full 360 degrees or just a part of an arc.
Slider	A linear movement along a single dimension. Example: a piston traveling up and down in a cylinder.
Cylindrical	Allows parts to rotate and move linearly at the same time along the same axis.
Pin Slot	Allows rotational movement about the Z axis and translational movement along the X axis.
Planar	Allows a Component to rotate but is confined to only being able to move in one plane.
Ball	A Component can rotate in all 3 axes of rotation.

Challenge

Your final challenge in this course is combining the Pizza Cutter project you just made with a celebratory pizza to cut! This will require modeling up your own personal pizza order with as many toppings as you can fit...even pineapple if that's what you're into.

Using the tools you learned in the Pizza Cutter project: making Assemblies, Inserting Parts Studios, and making Mates, you'll model a perfect dinner.

For added incentive, keep a hot pizza near your computer as motivation to complete this challenge and then chow down!

Angle the Handle

- Navigate into the Handle Parts Studio.
- Select the Transform tool.
- Select the Handle.
- Change the Transform Type to Rotate in the pulldown menu.
- Set the Axis as the horizontal line above the hole, and rotate the Handle 30 degrees upward.

Make your Personal Pizza

- Make a new Parts Studio.
- Design a 12-inch Pizza with all your favorite toppings of your own design.
- Extrude Remove a profile that cuts the Pizza into 8 slices but leaves a small sliver at the base so the file remains as 1 Part, not 8 slices.

Second Assembly File

- Rename the Parts Studio tab, not the Part, as My Pizza, and verify it only has 1 Part.
- Create a new Assembly tab and rename it Pizza and Cutter
- Select Insert, select the My Pizza file, and confirm.
- Right click the Pizza model and select Fix so it cant move around.

Insert the Cutter

- Select Insert, change the selection from Parts Studio to Assemblies, and select the Pizza Cutter file. Confirm this operation.

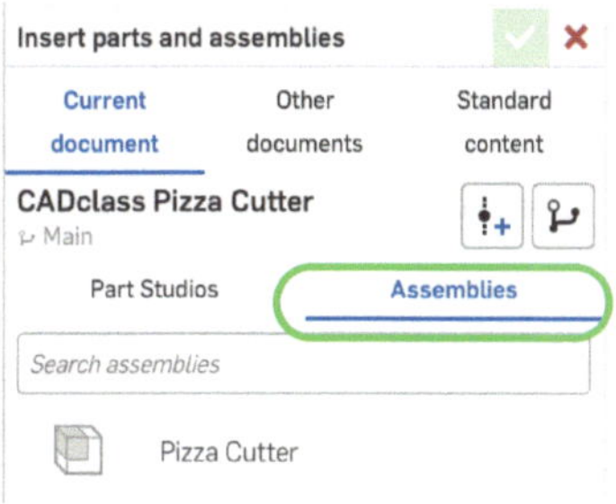

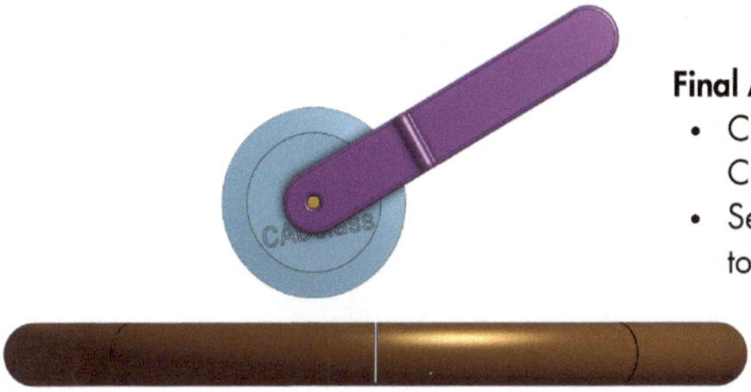

Final Assembly & Mates

- Click and drag the Pizza Cutter above the Pizza.
- Select the Tangent mate tool, the last Mate tool.

- Select the sharp outer edge of the Pizza Blade.
- Select a straight edge of one of the cuts on the Pizza, and your blade will automatically be tangentially attached to the pizza line.
- Click and drag the pizza handle back and forth along the Pizza just like you would in real life.

Congratulations everyone on competing your last challenge!

After the Fundamentals

From Ideas to Prototypes

Now that you've built a strong foundation in Onshape, you're ready to take your ideas further to develop more complex projects, or even products.

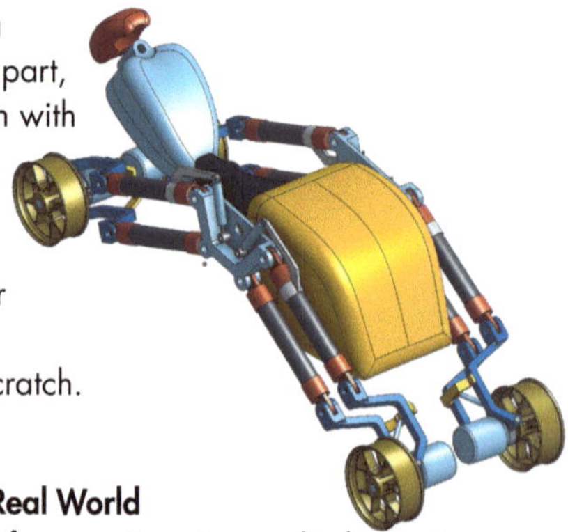

Whether you want to make a phone case, a tabletop organizer, or a custom mechanical part, your CAD skills give you the ability to design with purpose.

Many designers use Onshape to prototype products before 3D printing, laser cutting, or manufacturing. The next step is to dream up something useful, or fun, and build it from scratch.

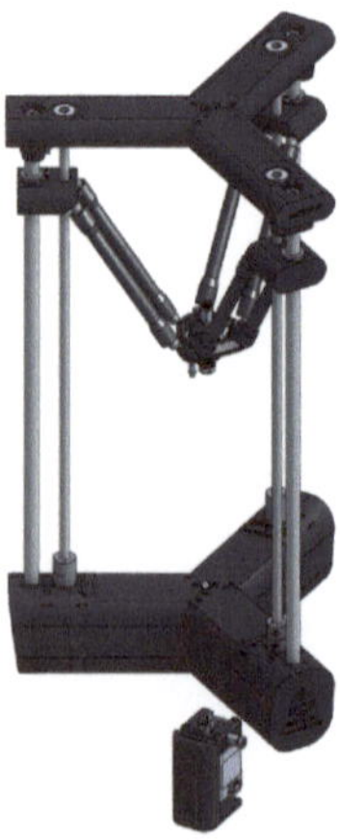

Explore CAD in the Real World

CAD is everywhere, from engineering and robotics to fashion and film. Automotive designers, architects, and even sneaker companies use CAD to bring products to life.

The same tools you've learned here are the ones used by professionals every day.

You can keep growing by remixing existing models, studying real-world parts, or even prepping for certification like the Onshape Associate exam.

Think Like a Designer

Great CAD designers don't just focus on how a part looks, they think about how it functions, how it might change, and how it fits into a larger system. This is called design intent.

For example, if a product needs to be ergonomically designed with multiple materials, then CAD engineers will consider how the parts will be made and how it will be most efficient to be manufactured.

Thinking ahead like this will save time and make your models more adaptable to future changes.

Explore Workspaces

In the following sections, you will explore other Workspaces in Onshape. Our goal is to let you know about the additional possibilities available for more advanced design work.

Since this is a fundamentals guide, we at CADclass want to show you what's available and possible in Onshape if you find you want to graduate and use more of its powerful tools. Most students will be able to make all their projects and creations from the skillsets they learned in this class, but others will be hungry for more!

In the following sections, you will learn about these topics and workspaces:

- **Collaborating**: Ideal for group projects like Robotics
- **Versioning**: Tracking the progress of projects as they evolve
- **Onshape's Mobile App**: How you can make CAD files on your phone
- **FeatureScripts**: How to turn code into CAD
- **Onshape's App Store**: Simulations, Rendering, Animations & more
- **Sheet Metal**: Turn your parts into flat designs for plasma and CNC cutting
- **Surface Modeling**: Create organic curves and ergonomic Parts
- **Engineering Drawings**: Make custom blueprints for manufacturing

Coming Soon ...

If you're feeling inspired after this course, consider taking your skills to the next level with ***Mastering Onshape Edt. 1***, a follow-up full of exciting, hands-on projects for makers who are ready to truly master Onshape.

If you'd like additional step-by-step practice projects, our new book ***Mastering Onshape Edt. 1*** has 21 amazing ones!

Email our team at ***create@CADclass.org*** if you're interested in getting an early copy!

Visit ***CADclass.org/pages/books*** for a free or donation-based copy of this book and other CADclass titles.

Collaboration

Onshape's Share button unlocks a world of collaborative potential that sets this cloud-based CAD platform apart from the others!

This button serves as a gateway to real-time teamwork, allowing engineers and designers to seamlessly share their work and work on the same file simultaneously!

Unlike traditional CAD systems that often require complex file transfers or version control gymnastics, Onshape's share functionality enables instant access to the latest design iterations.

Imagine being apart of a Robotics club, were several members in different places are all working on one robot at the same time. With Onshape, progress can be made faster, more efficiently, and most importantly, with a paper trail!

Collaboration in Onshape just like using Google Docs!

1. It is real-time: Multiple users can work on the same design simultaneously, seeing each other's changes in real-time.
2. Version control is automatic: allows teams to track changes, compare versions, and revert if needed.
3. You can 'branch' and 'merge': Users can create separate branches to explore design alternatives without affecting the main design, then merge changes back when ready.
4. Comments: Team members can leave comments directly on 3D models or 2D drawings, facilitating clear communication.
5. Access control: Granular permissions allow you to control who can view, edit, or administer shared documents.

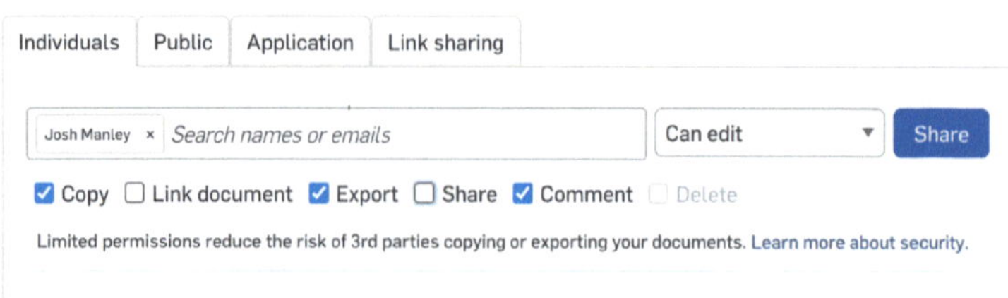

You can also share a link that is viewable to someone who doesn't even have an Onshape account!

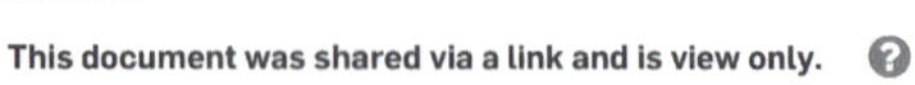

Go to the public library and search for "CADclass Tic-Tac-Toe" or follow the QR code or link and make a copy.

t.ly/1UyWo

Go to the assembly tab then:

- Add Planar mates between the centers of the underside of all the **green** counters and the centers of the blue board.
- Do the same for all the **red** X's.

Press the blue Share button (Share) in the top right and type in the email of someone you'd like to collaborate with. You can set if they can edit, or just view. Have a game!

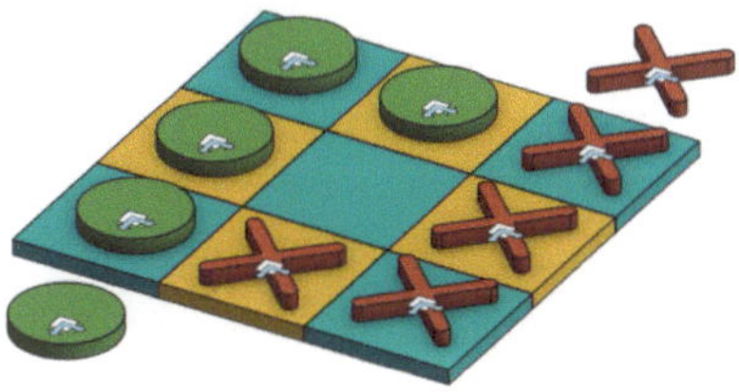

Safety first!

You can always keep control of your document via the Share button. You can choose who can view, edit, and comment and apply different settings to different collaborators

Find the Comments button on the far left-hand side and press it.

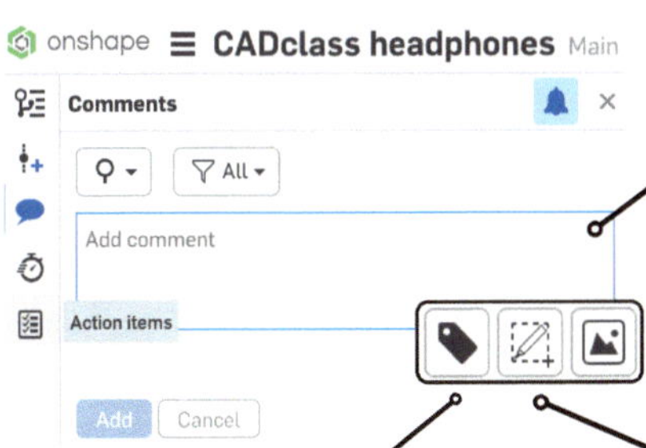

This is where you add typed notes you can @ a collaborator to assign them an action item.

You can add attachments, like PDFs of images.

This is where you can mark-up the image (draw arrows, lines etc).

This is the tool to tag entities (faces, edges etc).

Once you have shared your design and your collaborator opens it, you will notice an initial in a colored box (E) pop up. If you double click, you enter "follow me" mode where you can see everything they are doing. Double click to end it.

Versioning

Think of versions like drafts of a story: Version 1 is your outline, Version 2 adds details, and Version 3 refines the final product. Using Versions is a smart way to track progress, explore new ideas safely, and recover from mistakes. You can compare stages, share snapshots with collaborators, and always return to earlier points if needed.

Onshape tracks all changes, making collaboration safe and transparent. Team members can experiment freely without fear of losing original work. Version comparison tools help you understand what changed and why.

Project leads can monitor progress, review each step of the design process, and reflect on how ideas evolved. In the end, Versioning creates a clear, organized record that's great for reviews and presentations.

The top button takes you to Version History where you can see who did what to your work, and when. You can restore every previous version so nothing is ever lost! Versions are created automatically, and can also be added manually.

Create a version / compare a version.

This button allows you to add comments, tag particular features, tag collaborations with action items.

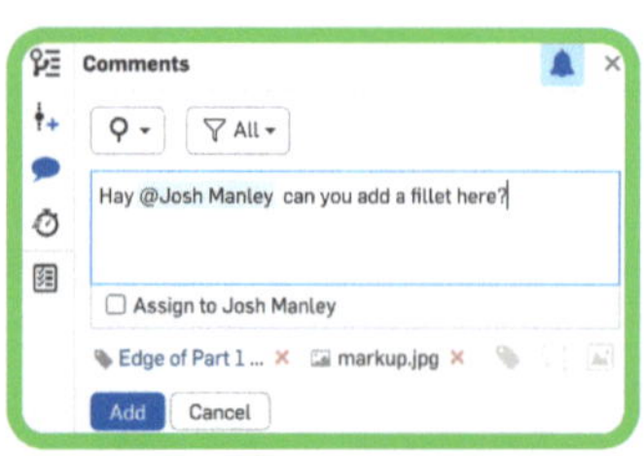

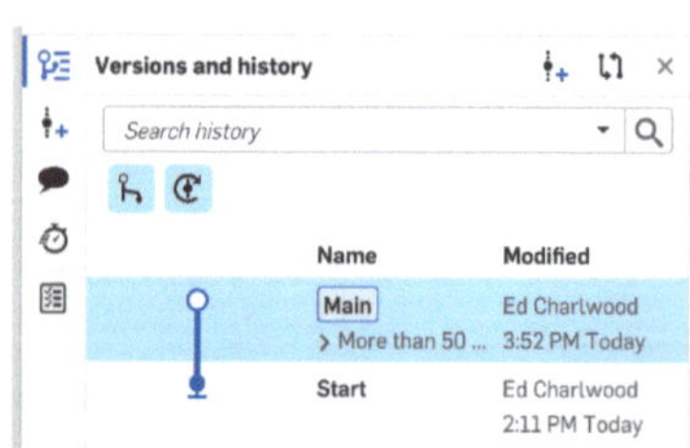

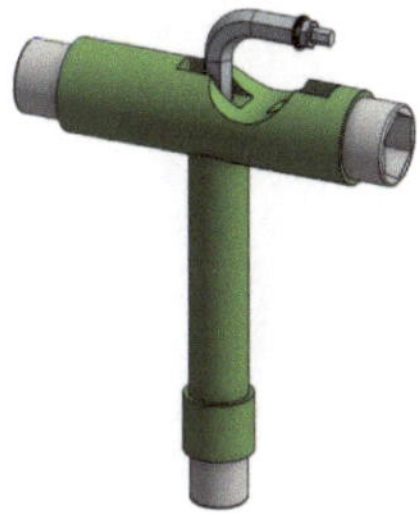

Go to the public library and search for "CADclass skateboard multitool" or follow the QR code or link and make a copy.

Press the Share button and add an email of someone to collaborate with.

t.ly/hM39h

1. Navigate to the **left hand toolbar**.

2. Select Create New Version. Call it "V1 - no fillet"

3. Use the **Tag Entity** tool to identify the junction between the horizontal and vertical features.

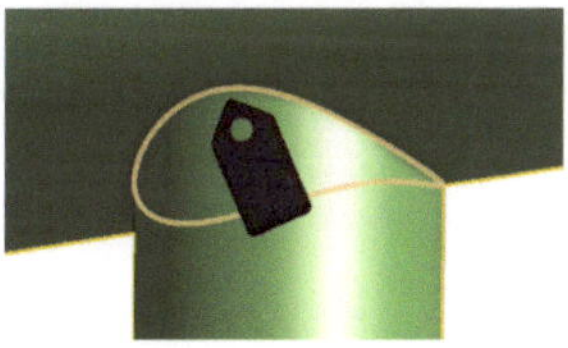

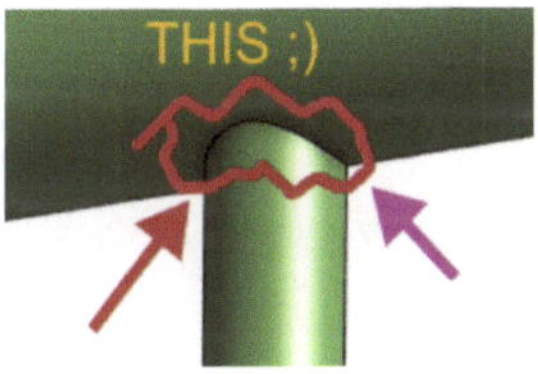

4. Use the **Markup** tool to add arrows, text and scribbles to a screenshot of the feature.

5. Add a comment and tag in your collaborator using @their_email, then **assign /add** them the to task.

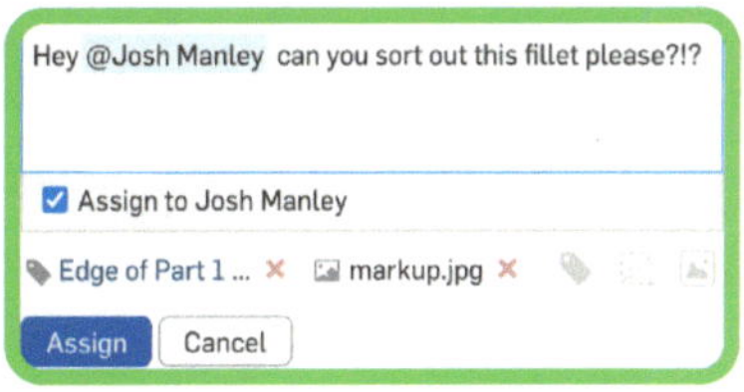

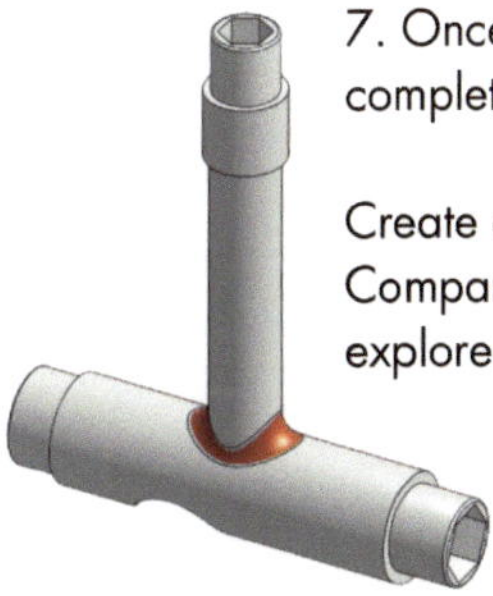

7. Once they have added the Fillet, they can tick the task as complete, and you will be notified.

Create a New Version, then in the Version History, press Compare Versions. Select V1 and V2, then use the tools to explore the changes.

Onshape Mobile

Onshape also has an iOS app, so if you are on a train, or up a mountain you can keep on designing.

It also has an Augmented Reality (AR) function so you can view your design in real-ish life!

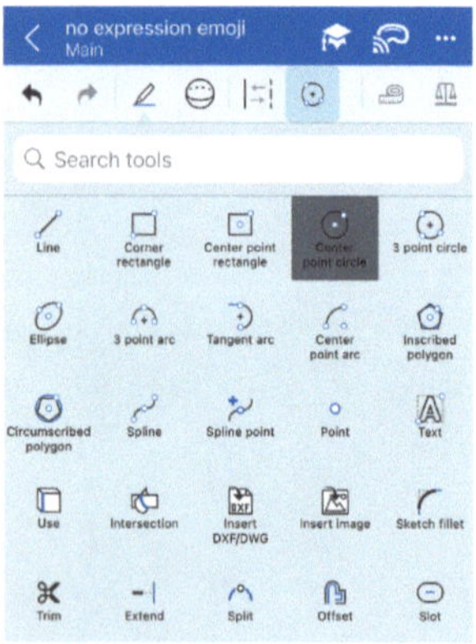

Even a big iPhone has a relatively small screen, so there are a lot of menus, sub-menus, and clicks to navigate to access all the features.

Start by downloading the Onshape iOS app here.

t.ly/plVdz

When you sign in for the first time you will get a tutorial, but here are a few additional tips and tricks:

- If you forget the moves, tap the Help icon in the top right corner of the dashboard page and select Review gesture controls.
- To Rotate; drag a finger across the screen.
- To Pan; drag two fingers and drag in any direction across the screen.
- To Zoom in/out; pinch your fingers in and out.
- Tap a face or edge to select it, and keep tapping to select more. Tap it agin to deselect it.
- To find a hidden context menu tap two fingers in an empty space.
- Many menus are nested, so long press icons to open the full menu.

For more in-detail instructions and a tutorial visit:
learn.onshape.com/courses/onshape-on-an-ios-mobile-device

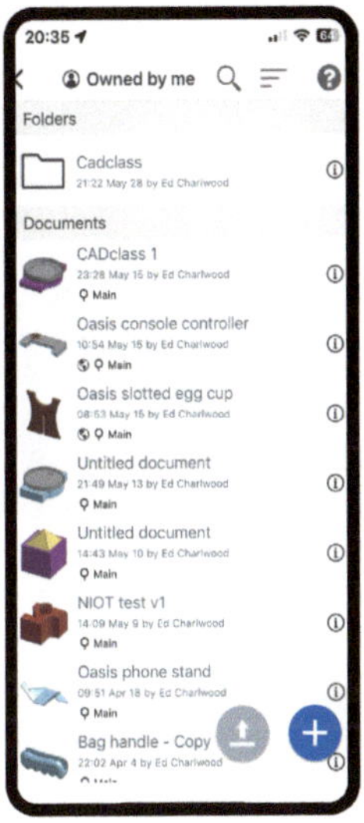

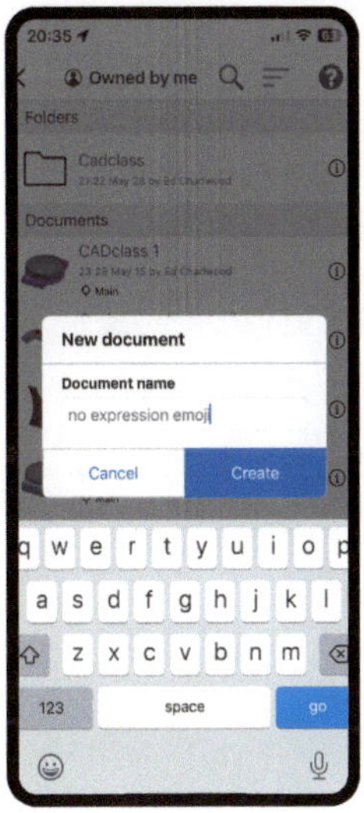

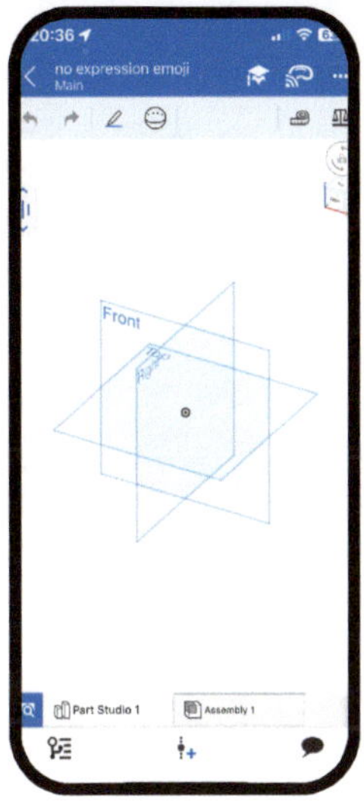

Go to Documents, tap **Owned by me**, and tap the blue plus button to create a new document.

Name it "No Expression Emoji😑" This is the emoji with the simplest design, so it is a perfect one to start with.

Explore the workspace and new UI and try and recreate this Emoji using the same tools available to you on the Browser version!

Designing on a mobile device can feel a bit fiddly due to the smaller screen and limited precision, but Onshape's mobile app is surprisingly capable, especially when you're away from your computer. If your phone or tablet is your only device, it gives you full access to your CAD projects and tools wherever you are. While complex modeling is best done on a desktop, the mobile app is perfect for reviewing designs, making quick edits, adding comments, or showing your work to others on the go.

You can easily scroll through Part Studios, view Assemblies, and even use features like Measure or Section View with simple touch gestures. Whether you're checking a teammate's update on a train or presenting your design to a client on-site, Onshape Mobile keeps you connected to your work—anytime, anywhere.

The Onshape Learning Center offers helpful courses on designing with the iOS app—check it out here:

t.ly/T9mbg

FeatureScripts

FeatureScripts in Onshape are powerful, bespoke tools that allow users to automate repetitive tasks, create custom features, and extend the capabilities of the software. They are essentially code written in a specialized language that can be used to manipulate and modify Onshape models.

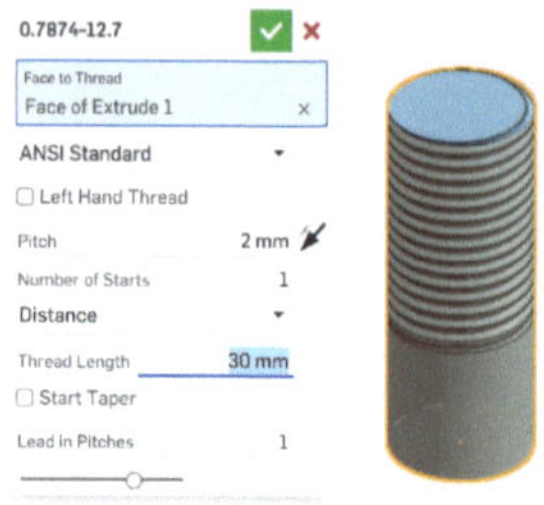

TC Much like how Google Chrome offers specialist extensions, like Grammarly or Ad Blockers, FeatureScripts are often written by the community to help others. You can even make your own.

t.ly/OjVlr

Follow the QR code or link to explore a curated list of FeatureScripts.

When opened, you will see a page that introduces the FeatureScript, has a few examples as Part Studio tabs, and also shows you the source code (.fs). Learn how to install them here: **t.ly/sFBbn**

Some of our favorite FeatureScripts are:

- ThreadCreator (to create internal and external threads)
- Lighten (to create pockets to lighten a solid part)
- Planetary Gears (creates an epicyclic, or planetary, gear transmission using true involute gears)

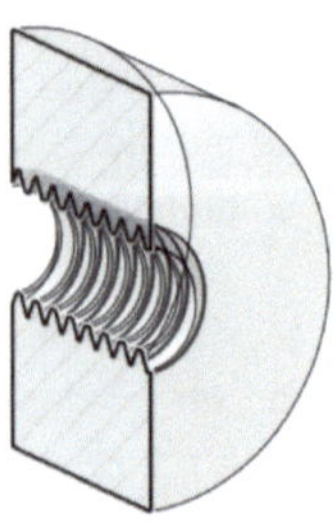

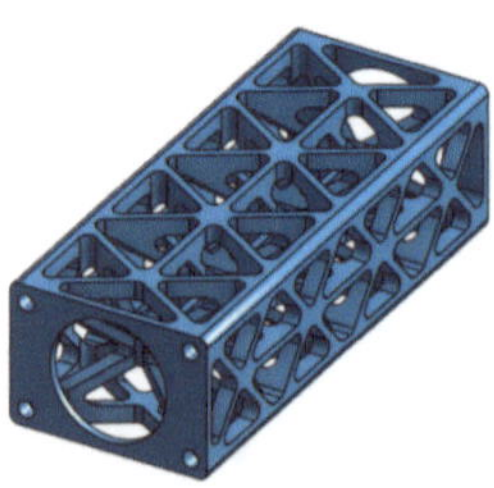

To add these tools to your Toolbar, click on **[+] Custom features** in the top right corner. Select Community Spotlight, search for "Thread", select **Thread Creator,** and select the TC icon TC to add this FeatureScript to your own toolbar.

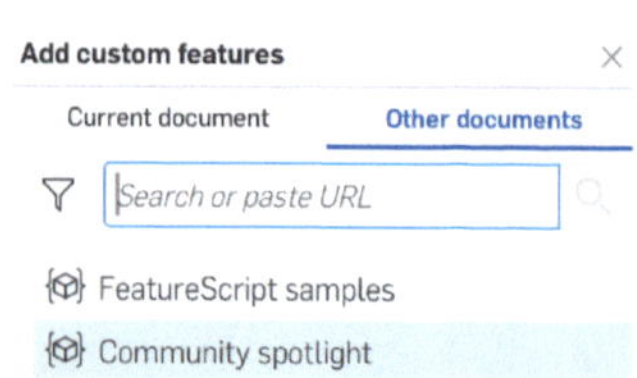

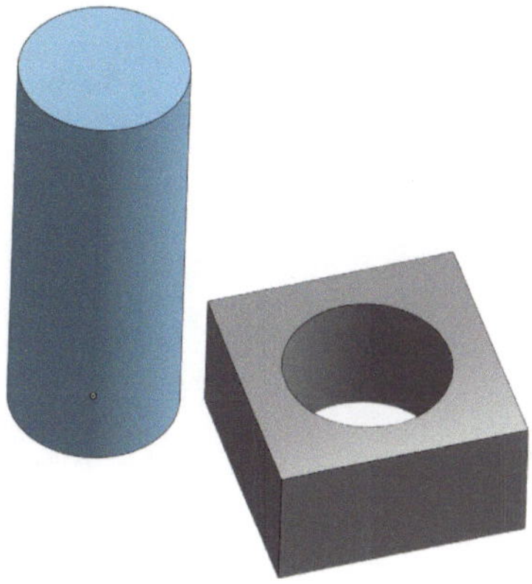

1. In a new Document, create a cylinder 20 mm diameter x 50 mm deep and a 30x30x15 mm cube with a 20 mm diameter hole.

2. Navigate to the FeatureScript button on the top right of the toolbar and select ThreadCreator TC tool.

3. Add an external thread to the cylinder - play with the options in the dialogue box.

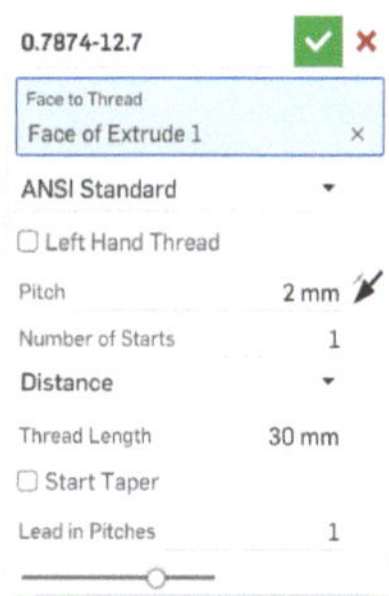

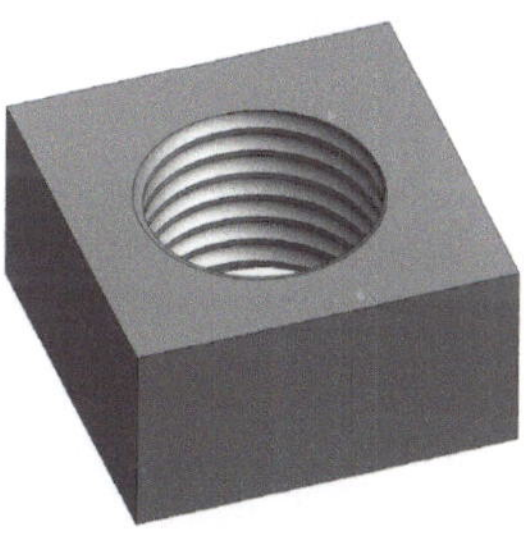

4. And do the same for the internal thread, with the same thread type and pitch so they match.

5. Beneath the View Cube open the dropdown menu and seelct Section View at the bottom.

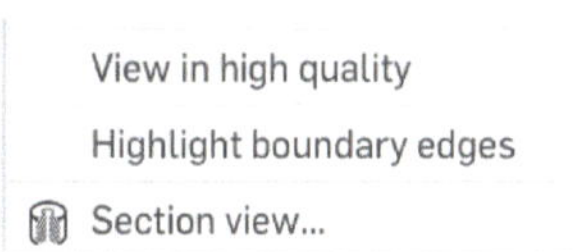

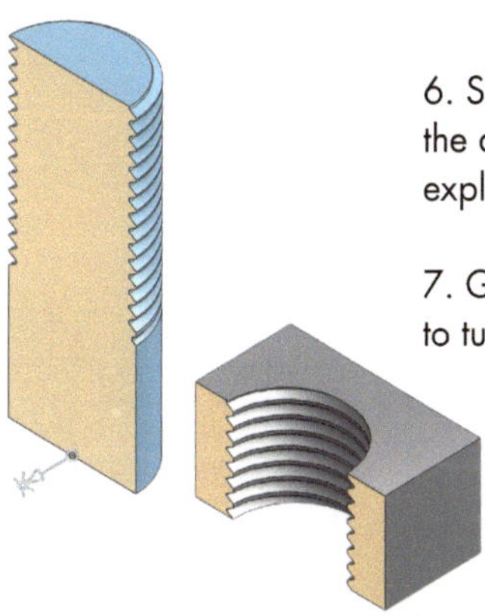

6. Select a face of the cuboid or a Plane and use the arrow to reveal the inside of the object and explore the complex geometry of the threads.

7. Go back to the bottom of the dropdown menu to turn the Section View off again.

Onshape's App Store

The Onshape App Store is a powerful platform where you can discover apps that extend and enhance your CAD experience. Whether you're looking for advanced simulation tools, CAM integration, rendering software, PLM systems, or utilities that improve workflows and productivity, the App Store offers a wide range of solutions.

Many of these apps work directly inside the Onshape environment, allowing for a seamless design process without needing to export files or switch platforms.

You'll find both free and paid tools, along with user ratings and descriptions to help you choose the right app for your needs.

The App Store is located at: *CAD.Onshape.com/appstore*, take a look and see how you can supercharge your projects.

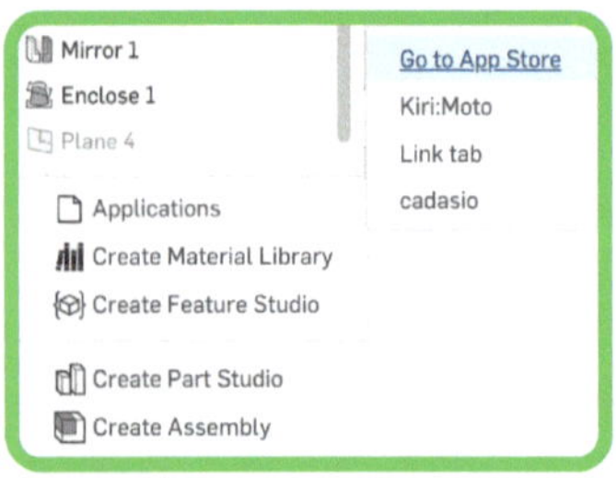

Navigate to the bottom left corner of your screen and click on the [+] symbol, the same button you use when creating a new Part Studio or Assembly.

From the dropdown, select Applications, then click Go to App Store.

This will open a new browser window where you can explore a wide variety of apps designed to expand your CAD capabilities. From simulation and rendering tools to version control and CAM plugins, this is your gateway to unlocking powerful add-ons that integrate directly into your Onshape workflow. Think of it as adding new tools to your digital toolbox!

Many of the apps in the Onshape App Store offer free trials or educational licenses, making it easy to experiment with new tools and see what fits best with your design process.

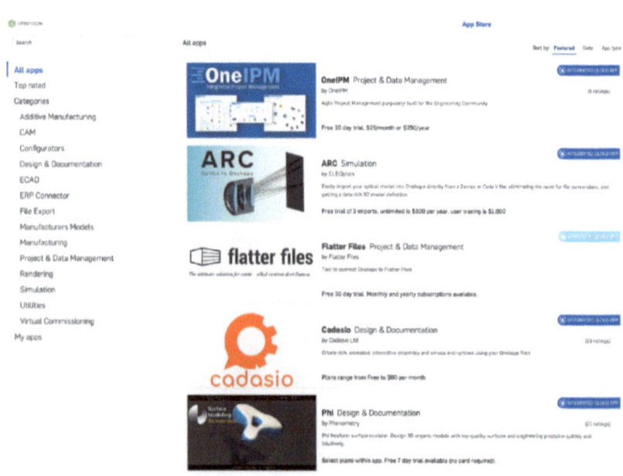

Once subscribed, the apps may appear in a few places:

- In the + menu where apps can be added as document tabs
- In the Context menu of a part, assembly, feature, mate, document tab (Part Studio, Assembly, Drawing, or uploaded file), or a document
- Or on the right side panel on the documents page or inside a document

Here are some of our favorite apps to use: SimScale and MKcad

SimScale is a cloud-based engineering simulation platform that integrates seamlessly with Onshape, enabling users to perform advanced simulations directly from their CAD models.

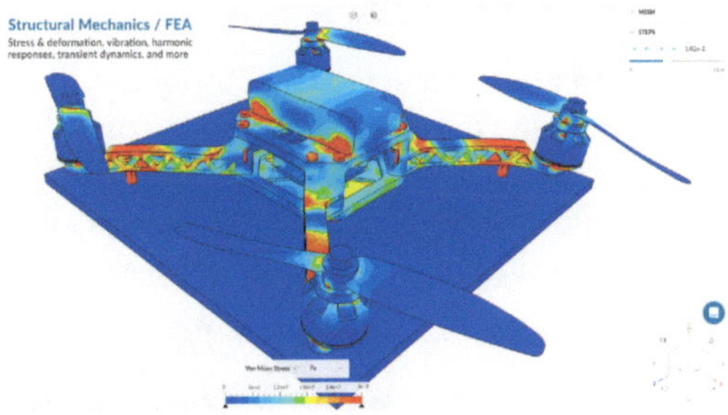

SimScale supports various simulation types, including structural (FEA), fluid dynamics (CFD), and thermal analyses, allowing engineers to test and optimize designs efficiently.

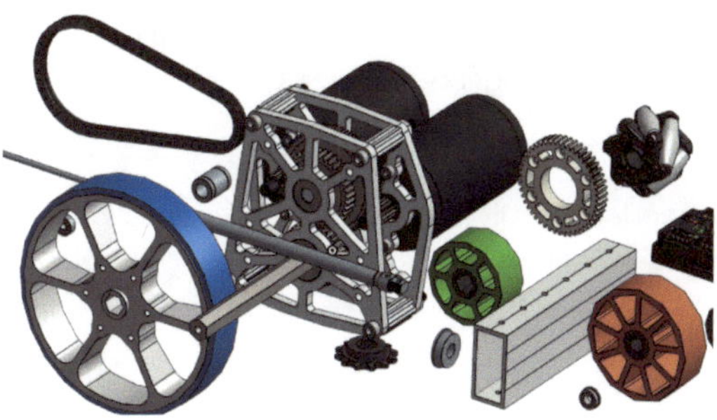

MKCad is an Onshape-integrated app designed primarily for FIRST Robotics teams, offering an extensive library of FRC components such as gears, motors, electronics, and structural parts.

It streamlines the design process by allowing users to search for, filter, and insert components directly into their assemblies without leaving Onshape. Here you can search and insert parts to streamline constructing your robot.

By eliminating the need to import external CAD files, MKCad helps teams work faster and more efficiently, especially during time-sensitive build seasons.

Sheet Metal

Sheet metal is an ideal material choice for design as it combines strength and lightweight properties with cost-effective manufacturing, while its ability to be folded flat for efficient shipping and storage, plus the creative potential of bends and folds, makes it particularly well-suited for creating robust structures like stands and brackets.

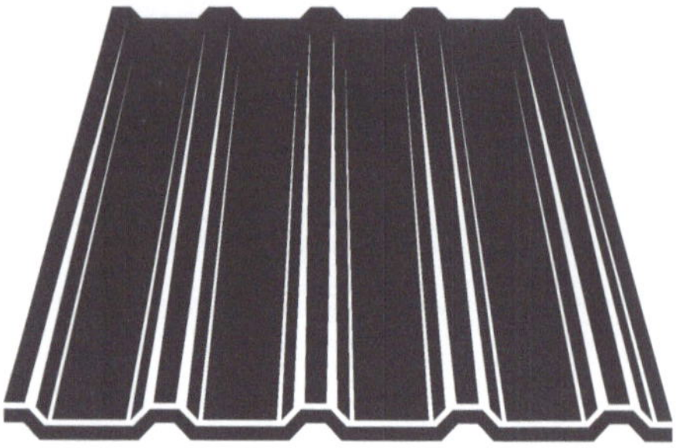

If you don't have access to CNC metal cutting equipment, you can still prototype using hand-cut cardboard or laser-cut sheet materials like acrylic.

Sheet Metal modeling in Onshape is a specialized design environment tailored for creating sheet metal parts - or anything else made from sheet materials for that matter!

One highly useful feature in the Sheet Metal workspace is the ability to "unfold" a 3D sheet metal part into a flat pattern, also known as a net layout, similar to how you may have unfolded geometric shapes in math class.

This flattened view represents exactly how the part will look when cut and bent from a single sheet of material, helping designers visualize and plan fabrication steps more effectively.

The unfolded pattern can be exported directly as a DXF file for laser cutting, CNC routing, or sending to a manufacturer, like SendCutSend.com, ensuring accuracy and saving valuable production time.

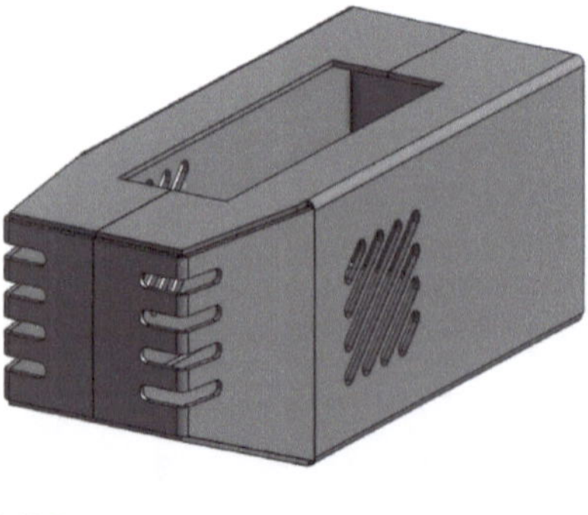

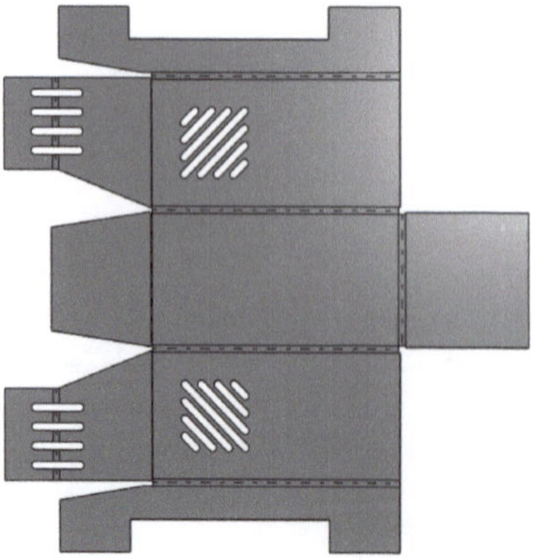

One Sheet Metal project you can make quickly is a headphone holder. In Onshape you can go from a solid Part to a surface with a set material thickness to a final CNC'able flat DXF file.

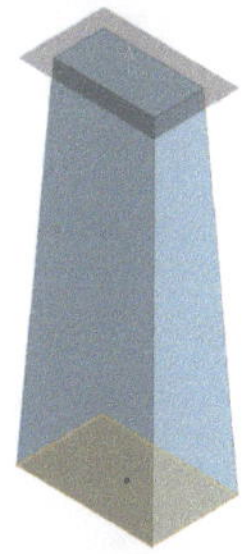

1. Sketch a 50 x 80 mm rectangle, and extrude it 200 mm with a 3 degree draft.

2. Select the Sheet Metal Model tool, select the Part, click Faces to Exclude in the Dialogue Box, and select the front, left, and right faces.

Click Edges or Cylinders to Bend and select the top and bottom back edges where the 3 faces meet. Confirm.

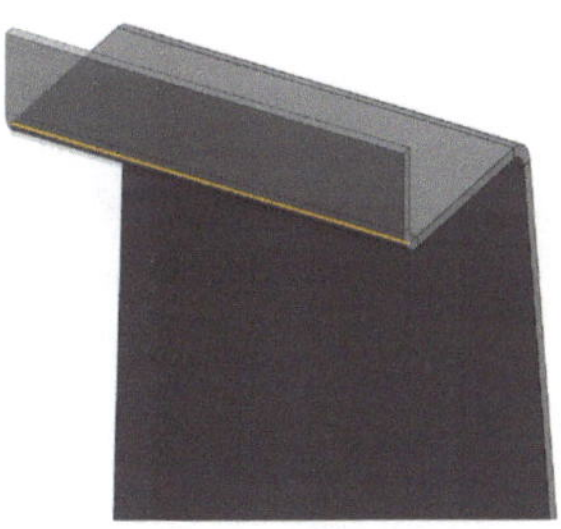

3. Select the Flange tool, and select the top front edge of the Headphone Holder.

This will add a flange to it; reverse the direction and set the distance to 15 mm.

Click the green checkmark to finish the operation.

The sheet metal part can then be treated like a regular solid part, so it can be modified with fillets and chamfers. You can sketch on faces and extrude.

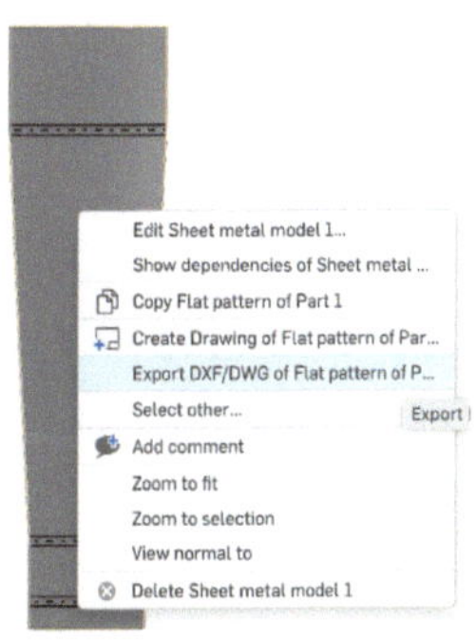

4. Click the Sheet Metal Table and Flat View button on the right, under the Appearance tools, to reveal what the flat view of your design looks like.

Above will be a table showing how the parts needs to bent by the manufacture to make the part. Below is a flat view of the part, right-click it and select Export DXF to get the 2D file.

Surface Modeling

The design work we've done so far has primarily followed a workflow that moves from 2D sketches to 3D solid models, where geometry is defined by faces, edges, and vertices to form watertight, manufacturable parts.

In contrast, Surface Modeling focuses on creating complex, freeform shapes using just the outer skin of an object, without the need for it to be solid or enclosed.

This approach is especially useful in ergonomic products like computer mice, gaming controllers, hand help power tools, and car exteriors, where aesthetic form and smooth curvature are critical.

Surface tools allow you to build intricate geometry with more flexibility than solid features alone, and once the surface is complete, you can thicken or stitch it into a solid model for manufacturing.

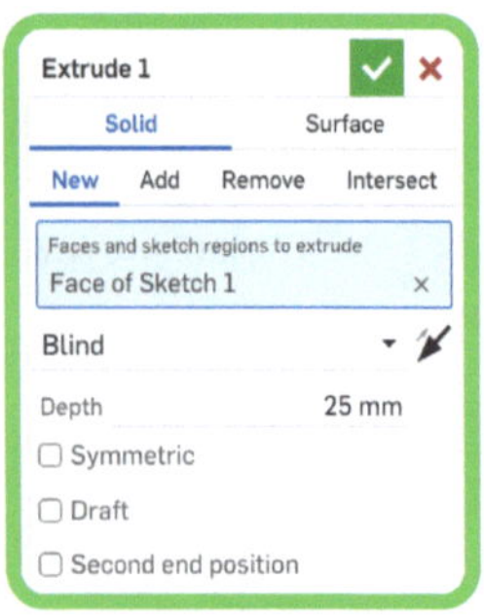

You may have noticed when you moved from 2D Sketch to a 3D Part, using Extrude, Revolve, Sweep, Loft, etc., that there was also an option at the top called Surface.

In the example of Extruding, instead of ending up with a solid volume, you would be left with a 4-walled "room", where the walls had no thickness.

In other CAD software, solid and surface tools are often split into different areas of the software, but in Onshape, they are bundled together, meaning you can easily Solid, Surface, or hybrid Solid-Surface model.

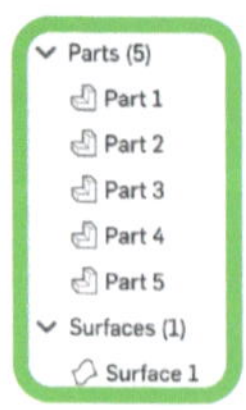

This allows you to model composite 3D Models, parts that have to contain organic curves and exact manufacturable geometries, much faster.

Think about the sculpted curves of a gaming mouse, and then think about all the mounting holes for chip and sensors inside.

Complex right? Well not in Surface Modeling...

Go to the public library and search for "CADclass Skull" or follow the QR code or link and make a copy.

This is a copy of a design in the Public Library by "Daniel Brown" t.ly/ 1pwS

t.ly/e3HNb

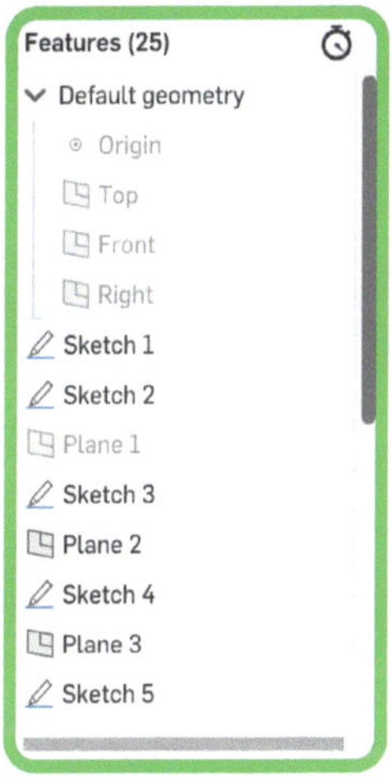

Explore the Feature List using the Rollback bar to discover how the designer created sketches on different planes.

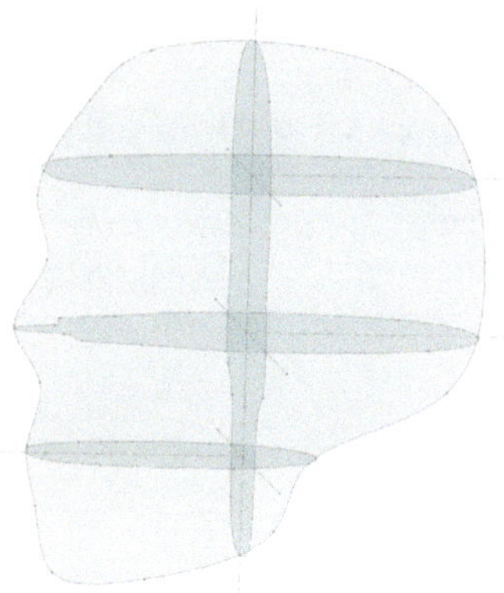

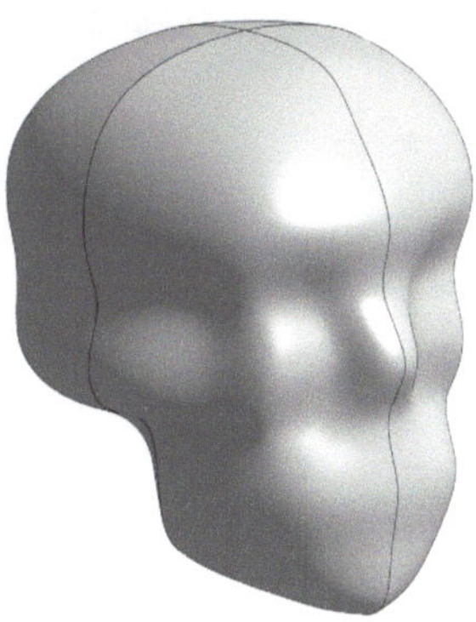

Look at how the designer moved from 2D > 3D using Loft and then how they moved from a Surface to a Soild using Enclose.

And then how they modified the solid using Extrude Remove operations to create facial features like eye sockets and teeth.

Engineering Drawings

Engineering Drawings are a core part of the design process, bridging the gap between a digital 3D model and the real-world object. In Onshape, the Drawings workspace allows you to generate detailed 2D views of your 3D parts or assemblies, complete with dimensions, notes, tolerances, and other manufacturing instructions.

These technical drawings follow industry standards and are used by engineers, machinists, and manufacturers to understand exactly how a part should be made. Learning how to create and interpret engineering drawings is essential for any aspiring designer or engineer, as it reinforces concepts like scale, orthographic projection, and precision.

Onshape makes this process accessible and intuitive—whether you're adding a simple top-front-right layout or creating exploded assembly views with callouts and balloons, the Drawing workspace helps bring your digital designs closer to physical production.

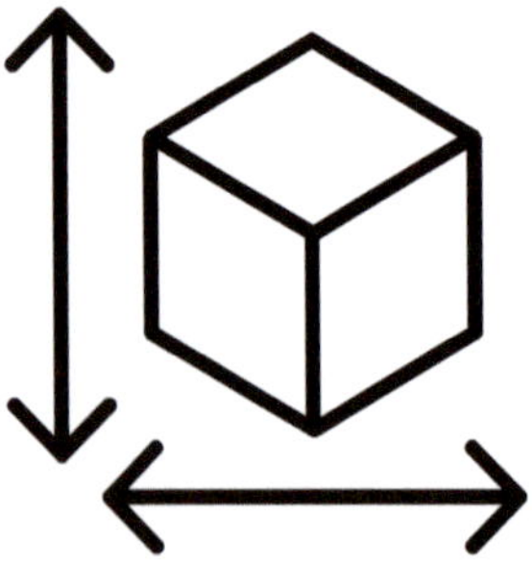

Dimensioning a drawing is crucial for ensuring accuracy and clarity. Here are some fundamental principles to follow:

1. **Clarity**: Dimensions should be easy to read and understand. Avoid crossing dimension lines.
2. **Completeness**: All dimensions should be provided to define the object completely: aim for "just enough."
3. **Consistency**: Use a consistent dimensioning style throughout the drawing, e.g. placed above and to the left.

There are many different Dimensioning standards you might need to learn more about that are beyond the scope of this book e.g. ASME Y14.5, ISO 8015.

The basic workflow is to create an engineering drawing from a 3D Design:

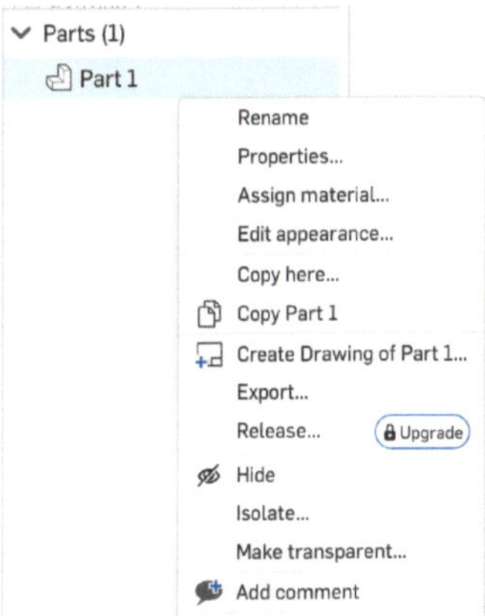

1. Right click on the Part and select Create Drawing of....
2. Select an Existing template, or go to Custom template to set up your own.
3. Select 4 views
4. Start to ddd Dimensions: Select Dimension tool, add critical dimensions, include any necessary notes/tolerances, add title block information,
5. Right click on the drawing tab to Export as a PDF, DWG etc

Hint: work from left to right along the top toolbar

A great way to practice creating an engineering drawing is to choose one of the previous projects you've modeled in this book, like the Brick Ring or the Carabiner, and generate a drawing with dimensions, annotations, and multiple views.

This helps you reinforce how technical drawings communicate key design details clearly and accurately.

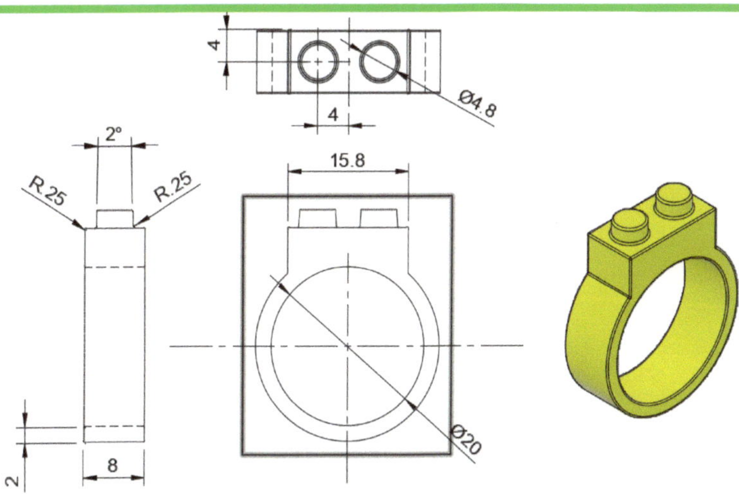

Drawing Pedagogy

Technical drawings are standardized, detailed visual representations of objects, systems, or structures that communicate precise specifications and technical information.

Technical Drawing Fundamentals:

- Shows objects using standardized views (front, top, side) called orthographic projections
- Includes precise measurements and dimensions
- Uses standard symbols and conventions (like line types for hidden edges)
- Can include additional views like sections, details, or isometric views
- Follows standards like ANSI (American) or ISO (International)

As an Input for 3D Design: use a 2D drawing to create a 3D design

- Practice visualizing 3D objects from 2D representations
- Develop mental rotation and spatial thinking skills
- Sketch initial concepts and dimensions
- Create blueprint before starting CAD work
- Identify potential design issues early
- Measure existing objects and create technical drawings
- Drawings can then guide 3D modeling

As an Output of 3D Design: use a 3D design to create a 2D drawing

- Create technical drawings from their 3D models
- Learn to properly dimension and annotate designs
- Practice choosing appropriate views and sections
- Prepare yourself for real-world engineering work
- Include tolerances and specifications
- Understand of how designs translate to physical objects
- Link CAD work to practical fabrication

A great classroom project is having students create an engineering drawing of their own smartphone. It's a simple yet powerful way to practice measurement, sketching, and 3D modeling skills. Students can use inexpensive digital calipers, to take precise measurements of their device. If you don't have calipers, dimensions can also be found online in spec sheets. This project encourages attention to detail, introduces tolerancing concepts, and gives students a real-world object they're already familiar with, making it both accessible and engaging.

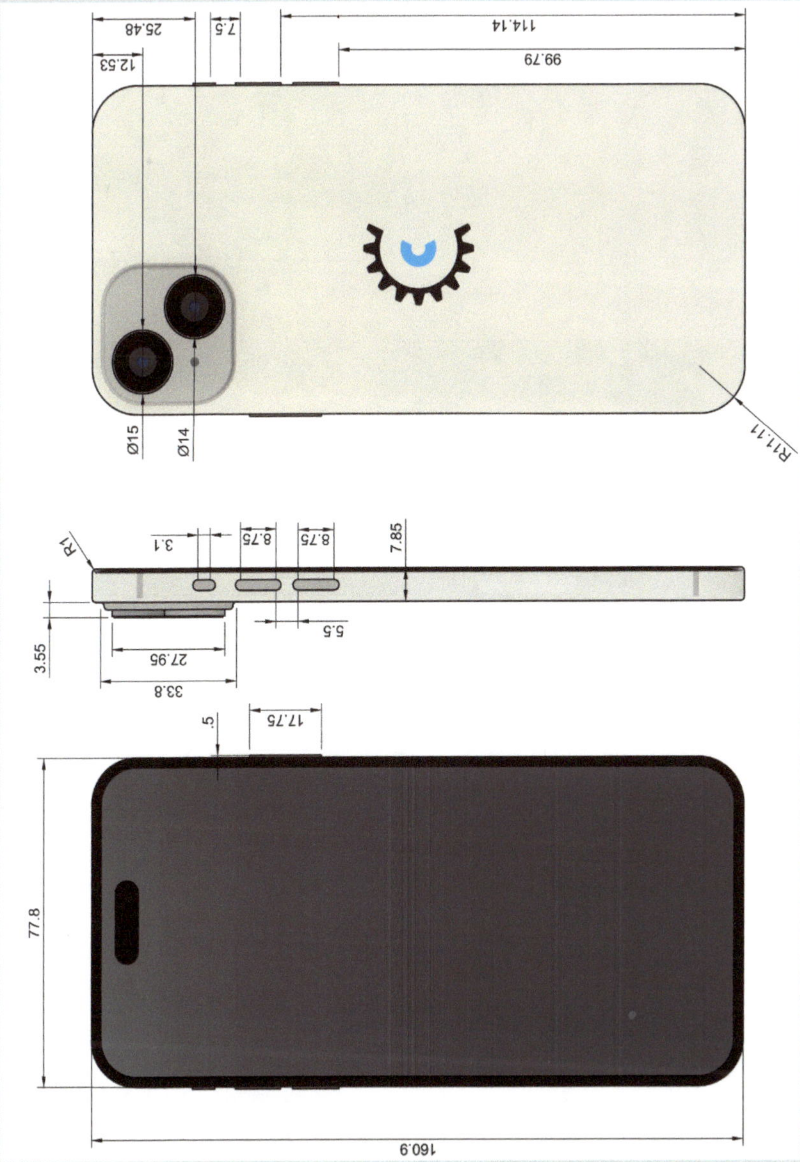

True or False?

Q: You can only add Comments and Arrows to models when collaborating with others?

Q: A drawing is to Engineers like what a recipe is to a chef?

Q: In the Onshape App you can view projects as an AR file without using another app?

Q: In sheet metal CAD work, you don't need to specify material thickness or bend radius?

Q: Surface Modeling is more akin to sculpting than dimensional CAD work?

Solutions

Q: You can only add Comments and Arrows to models when collaborating with others?

A: False. You can also add screenshots and files like PDFs.

Q: A drawing is to Engineers like what a recipe is to a chef?

A: True.

Q: In the Onshape App you can view projects as an AR file without using another app?

A: True. Artificial Reality file viewing is baked into the app.

Q: In sheet metal CAD work, you don't need to specify material thickness or bend radius?

A: False. This is often the first step when designing and defines the project early on.

Q: Surface Modeling is more akin to sculpting than dimensional CAD work?

A: True.

Design Challenges

1

CHALLENGE

Model a wearable product, like a smartwatch or a smartphone.

2

CHALLENGE

Create a set of modular toy blocks with interlocking features.

3

CHALLENGE

Create a headphone stand that mimics design elements from your other tech products.

4

CHALLENGE

Design a product for people with limited mobility with their hands.

5

CHALLENGE

Design a phone stand or charging dock that works with your current device.

6

CHALLENGE

Model a famous sculpture or statue using basic shapes.

Math Challenges

7

CHALLENGE

Design & 3D print a Math tool, for example, a 60-degree triangular ruler.

8

CHALLENGE

Create an Erlenmeyer flask that holds exactly 250 ml.

9

CHALLENGE

Model a fractal object (e.g., Sierpinski triangle or Koch snowflake) in 3D using the Pattern tools.

10

CHALLENGE

Create a model that visually represents the Golden Ratio.

11

CHALLENGE

Model and animate a pendulum to show periodic motion.

12

CHALLENGE

Model polyhedra (e.g., dodecahedron, icosahedron) and explain their properties.

Science Challenges

13

CHALLENGE

O-Chem: Design & 3D print a tool to help with a science experiment (e.g. a test tube rack).

14

CHALLENGE

Physics: Design and test a Rube Goldberg machine.

15

CHALLENGE

Biology: Create and label a cross-section of a cell.

16

CHALLENGE

Chemistry: Recreate a representation of a molecule (e.g. caffeine).

17

CHALLENGE

Microbiology: Design a microscope or telescope with labeled optical paths.

18

CHALLENGE

Astronomy: Recreate Isaac Newton's 1688 Telescope with a spherical ball joint.

Engineering Challenges

19

CHALLENGE

Design and 3D print an egg-drop holder to protect the egg cargo.

20

CHALLENGE

Reverse Engineer and recreate an existing mechanical design (e.g. a workshop vise).

21

CHALLENGE

Design and prototype a tool to help with an engineering project e.g. a multi-tool for a bicycle or robot.

22

CHALLENGE

Research and recreate a Mars Rover from the 20th century.

23

CHALLENGE

Create a robotic arm model with moving joints and simulate its motion.

24

CHALLENGE

Design a wind turbine with rotating blades.

Electronics Challenges

25

CHALLENGE

Design a custom project box/enclosure for an Arduino or a Raspberry Pi Pico.

26

CHALLENGE

Design a light-following robot using LDRs and DC motors.

27

CHALLENGE

Build a 3D model of a breadboard circuit layout which includes the internal copper terminals.

28

CHALLENGE

Design and label a basic electronic component set (e.g. resistors, LEDs, etc.).

29

CHALLENGE

Model a Volt-meter with built in probes.

30

CHALLENGE

Create an RC car chassis and mount locations for motors and batteries.

Art Challenges

31

CHALLENGE

Recreate a historical art piece in 3D and annotate its parts.

32

CHALLENGE

Build a kinetic sculpture that moves based on a motor or gravity.

33

CHALLENGE

Create a 3D printable stencil or stamp with a custom design.

34

CHALLENGE

Make a wearable art piece (like a mask or jewelry set).

35

CHALLENGE

Recreate artwork, like a geometric Mondrian abstract or famous architecture, like Big Ben.

36

CHALLENGE

Create an ambigram tessellation like MC Escher.

End of Book Test

1. What does CAD stand for?
- ◯ Computer-Aided Drawing
- ◯ Computer-Aided Design
- ◯ Computer-Assisted Design
- ◯ Computer-Assisted Drawing

2. Which of the following is NOT a benefit of using CAD software?
- ◯ Faster design iterations
- ◯ Improved design accuracy
- ◯ Increased material waste
- ◯ Enhanced collaboration

3. What is the name of the navigation tool located in the upper-right corner of the Onshape interface?
- ◯ Timeline
- ◯ Browser
- ◯ ViewCube
- ◯ Data Panel

4. In Onshape, what are the three primary axes representing the three dimensions?
- ◯ A, B, C
- ◯ L, W, H
- ◯ X, Y, Z
- ◯ 1, 2, 3

5. Which tool is used to create a 3D object by rotating a 2D profile around an axis?
- ◯ Extrude
- ◯ Sweep
- ◯ Loft
- ◯ Revolve

6. What is the term for a numerical value that defines the size of a design element?
- ◯ Dimension
- ◯ Constraint
- ◯ Parameter
- ◯ Variable

7. Which tool creates multiple instances of a sketch or feature in a structured arrangement?
- ◯ Mirror
- ◯ Offset
- ◯ Pattern
- ◯ Array

8. Which file format is typically used for exporting designs for laser cutting from Onshape?
- ◯ .STL
- ◯ .STEP
- ◯ .DXF
- ◯ .MP4

9. Which tool creates a 3D object by "dragging" a 2D shape along a defined path?
- ◯ Extrude
- ◯ Sweep
- ◯ Loft
- ◯ Revolve

10. Where is the hierarchical structure that organizes parts and sub-assemblies in Onshape?
- ◯ Timeline
- ◯ Feature List
- ◯ Data Panel
- ◯ Feature Tree

Solutions

1. What does CAD stand for? CAD stands for Computer-Aided Design, as it involves using computer software to assist in the design process.

2. Which of the following is NOT a benefit of using CAD software? A: Increased material waste CAD software generally leads to reduced material waste due to improved design accuracy and virtual prototyping.

3. What is the name of the navigation tool located in the upper-right corner of the Onshape interface? The ViewCube provides a visual representation of the model's orientation and allows for quick view changes.

4. In Onshape, what are the three primary axes representing the three dimensions? X, Y, and Z represent the standard three-dimensional axes in CAD software and are used for precise object placement.

5. Which tool is used to create a 3D object by rotating a 2D profile around an axis? The Revolve tool creates rotational objects by sweeping a profile around a defined axis.

6. What is the term for a numerical value that defines the size of a design element? Dimensions are numerical values used to specify measurements like length, width, and diameter.

7. Which tool creates multiple instances of a sketch or feature in a structured arrangement? The Pattern tool enables the efficient creation of multiple copies of features in various arrangements, such as circular or rectangular.

8. Which file format is typically used for exporting designs for laser cutting from Onshape? DXF (Drawing Exchange Format) is a widely compatible format for 2D drawings, commonly used in laser cutting applications.

9. Which tool creates a 3D object by "dragging" a 2D shape along a defined path? The Sweep tool creates 3D objects by moving a 2D profile along a designated path, similar to how a pastry bag Extrudes icing.

10. Where is the hierarchical structure that organizes parts and sub-assemblies in Onshape? The Feature List in Onshape visually represents the design history and hierarchical relationships between components and bodies within an assembly.

End of Book Test

1. Name a specific piece of 'everyday' CAD software (not Onshape).

2. Give a unique advantage of CAD when compared to creating designs using "traditional" hand tools like pencils and paper.

3. Explain the disadvantages of using CAD vs. designing with pencil and paper.

4. Describe 2 ways CAD could contribute to cost or time savings in design and manufacturing.

5. Explain some limitations you came up against when using Onshape.

6. How might Augmented Reality (AR) help consumers understand a product?

7. Name some benefits of designers using CAD that allow for collaboration with other designers.

8. Name the parts of a piece of clothing Onshape is well suited to design in 3D. Why is this?

9. State specific examples of types of products that Onshape is not well suited to designing in 3D. Why is this?

10. Name industries where CAD is commonly used and explain how it benefits these sectors.

11. Describe the relationship between CAD and CAM.

12. Discuss the potential security concerns associated with CAD data.

13. Is copy & paste the same as duplicate? Explain your answer.

14. In what way can keyboard shortcuts help a CAD designer?

15. Think up a question for your teacher/instructor.

Solutions

1. Microsoft Word is a widely used desktop publishing software.

2. CAD allows for precise measurements and easy duplication of design features, which is hard to achieve with traditional hand tools.

3. A disadvantage of CAD is that it requires specialized software and skills, which can take time to acquire, especially for small-scale projects.

4. CAD can contribute to cost savings by reducing the need for physical prototypes and speeding up the design process, leading to faster time-to-market.

5. Some limitations of Onshape include its limited compatibility with other CAD software.

6. AR can help consumers understand a product by providing interactive 3D models and visualizations showing how the product works and can be used.

7. Some benefits of using CAD for collaboration include sharing and editing designs in real-time and communicating more effectively with team members.

8. Onshape is well suited for designing simple 3D shapes and structures, such as buttons and zippers because it has a user-friendly interface and essential modeling tools.

9. Tinkercad is not well suited for designing complex 3D shapes and structures, such as clothing patterns or detailed textures.

10. CAD is commonly used in aerospace, automotive, and manufacturing industries. It benefits these sectors by enabling faster and more accurate design iterations, reducing costs, and improving product quality.

Solutions

11. CAD (Computer-Aided Design) is used to create digital models of products. In contrast, CAM (Computer-Aided Manufacturing) controls machines that produce physical prototypes or final products based on those models.

12. Some potential security concerns associated with CAD data include the risk of unauthorized access, theft, or modification of sensitive design information.

13. Copy and paste and duplicate are similar but different. Copy and paste creates a new copy of an object or text, while duplicate will paste selected objects and perform the previous action.

14. Keyboard shortcuts can help a CAD designer speed up everyday tasks, such as zooming in and out, rotating objects, or switching between different tools.

15 Q: "Can you recommend any resources or tutorials for learning more about CAD software and how to use it effectively?"

A: Yes, go to CADclass.org!

Glossary

Assembly ....

Chamfer ....

Coincident ....

Colinear ....

Constraints ....

Construction ....

Dialog Box ....

Dimension ....

Edge ....

Extrude ....

Face ....

Feature ....

Feature List ....

FeatureScript ....

Fillet ....

Fix ....

Isometric ....

Loft ....

Midpoint ....

Mirror ....

Normal ....

Orbit ....

Origin ....

Pan ....

Part ....

Part Studio ....

Pattern ....

Plane ....

Profile ....

Revolve ....

Rotate ....

Sketches ....

Spline ....

Split ....

Sweep ....

Tangent ....

View Cube ....

Index

Shortcuts

General

- **Shift+?:** Keyboard Shortcuts
- **Ctrl /Cmd+Z:** Undo
- **Ctrl/Cmd+Y:** Redo
- **Delete:** Delete Selection
- **Space Bar:** Clear Selection
- **Shift+N:** Rename Selection
- **Esc:** Cancel Command
- **Enter:** Accept Command
- **Shift+Enter:** Accept Command
- **S:** Shortcut Toolbars
- **Shift+Click:** Open in New Window
- **Ctrl/Cmd+Click:** Open in New Tab
- **Ctrl+U:** Feedback/Report a Bug
- **Alt+T:** Search Tabs

Assembly

- **Shift:** Lock Mate Inference
- **Ctrl/Cmd+C:** Copy
- **Ctrl/Cmd+V:** Paste
- **M:** Mate
- **Ctrl+M:** Mate Connector
- **I:** Insert Dialog
- **Shift+S:** Snap Mode
- **A:** Flip primary Axis
- **Q:** Reorient Secondary Axis
- **J:** Hide/Show Mates
- **K:** Hide/Show Mate Connectors

Part Studio

- **Shift+S:** Sketch
- **Shift+E:** Extrude
- **Shift+F:** Fillet
- **Ctrl+M:** Mate connector
- **Shift:** Lock Mate Inference
- **A:** Flip Primary Axis
- **Q:** Reorient Secondary Axis
- **K:** Hide/Show Mate Connectors

3D View

- **Shift+Z:** Zoom In
- **Z:** Zoom Out
- **F:** Zoom to Fit
- **W:** Zoom to Window
- **←→↑↓:** Rotate
- **Shift +←→↑↓:** Pan
- **Shift+1:** Front View
- **Shift+2:** Back View
- **Shift+3:** Left View
- **Shift+4:** Right View
- **Shift+5:** Top View
- **Shift+6:** Bottom View
- **Shift+7:** Isometric View
- **Shift+8:** Section View
- **N:** View Normal To
- **P:** Hide/Show Planes
- **Y:** Hide Selected Part
- **Shift+Y:** Show Selected Part

Shortcuts

Sketch

- **Shift:** Suppress Inferencing
- **L:** Line
- **G:** Corner Rectangle
- **R:** Center Point Rectangle
- **C:** Center Point Circle
- **A:** 3-Point Arc
- **F:** Fillet
- **M:** Trim
- **X:** Extend
- **O:** Offset
- **U:** Use / Project
- **D:** Dimension
- **I:** Coincident
- **B:** Parallel
- **T:** Tangent
- **H:** Horizontal
- **V:** Vertical
- **E:** Equal
- **Q:** Toggle Construction

Drawings

- **Shift+Z:** Zoom In
- **Z:** Zoom Out
- **F:** Zoom to Fit
- **W:** Zoom to Window
- **P:** Projected View
- **D:** Linear dimension
- **Shift+R:** Radial Dimension
- **Shift+D:** Diameter Dimension
- **Shift+Q:** Quad & Mid Snap Points
- **N:** Note
- **Ctrl+Q:** Update Drawing
- **L:** Line
- **Ctrl+S:** Display Sheet Menu
- **pg dn:** Next Sheet
- **pg up:** Previous Sheet
- **Home:** First Sheet
- **End:** Last Sheet

Scan this QR Code to get a printable list of all of Onshape's shortcuts

Resources at CADclass

Whether you're just starting out or you're well on your way to mastering CAD, CADclass.org is your home base for continued learning. We've built it with makers, students, educators, and aspiring engineers in mind.
Here's what you'll find:

Free & Donation Digital Books

All our CAD books—including this one—are available for free or donation on the CADclass.org/pages/books. Read them online or download a copy for offline learning.

Video Courses with Step-by-Step Classes

Watch step-by-step tutorials that align with every project in this book—ideal if you're a visual learner or just need a bit more guidance.

Teaching Tools for Educators

We offer free curriculum resources for teachers and mentors, including:

- Lesson plans
- Printable worksheets
- Project files and slides
- Assessment templates

Perfect for high school classrooms, after-school programs, and homeschoolers.

Community & Support

Join a growing community of makers, educators, and students learning CAD together. Share your designs, ask questions, and find answers!

Stay in the Loop

Sign up at CADclass.org to get updates on:

- New book releases
- CAD tips & tricks
- Contests & build challenges

Contact Us

We love hearing from students, educators, and makers!
Create@CADclass.org
(415) 941–4114
Discord.gg/5hbt6xDPqf
Youtube.com/@CADclassOfficial

Whether you're designing your first part or your hundredth, CADclass.org is here to help you build cool stuff and learn skills that last a lifetime.

CERTIFICATE

OF COMPLETION

Send an email to
Create@CADclass.org with
"CADclass Onshape Fundamentals
Certificate" in the title to receive a
digital certificate of completion!

Ed, Jake, & Josh

About CADclass

CADclass.org is a 3D modeling education company dedicated to making professional CAD tools approachable and fun for students, teachers, and makers around the world.

We believe anyone, regardless of age, background, or access, should be able to learn 3D design and engineering fundamentals. That's why we build books, courses, and communities that are:

- **Tool-focused:** Teaching practical making skills for hands-on manufacturing
- **Project-based:** Centered on real-world projects that are fun to create
- **Accessible:** Free or donation-based, with open curriculum for classrooms

CADclass materials are already being used in classrooms, after-school programs, maker spaces, and garages across the globe by thousands of students.

Whether you're a teacher helping students get career-ready, or a hobbyist designing your first 3D-printed part, CADclass is here to help you learn by building.

If you like the CADclass style of learning and want to pick up other CAD softwares to see what they have to offer, check out our other fundamentals books and courses!

Our books are available on Amazon and other platforms or for a donation/free:
CADclass.org/pages/books

www.ingramcontent.com/pod-product-compliance
Lightning Source LLC
LaVergne TN
LVHW052148210926
848482LV00018B/13

Articlficial Intelligence

A.I.

Artificiality of life

Versus The Reality of Spiritual Life

I am

Real Intelligence
I exist

Tioliendo

Twinteum

A.I. Artificiality of life Versus The Reality Of Spiritual Life I am
Publisher: Twinteum

Title: A.I. Artificiality of life Versus The Reality Of Spiritual Life I am
ISBN: 9798263703301
Cover: Design Art by Tioliendo

Trade Paperback Edition

Printed in the United States